THIS IS NOT A T-SHIRT

BOBBY HUNDREDS

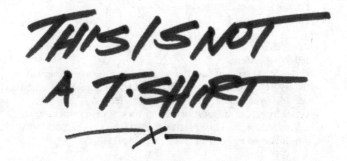

A BRAND, A CULTURE, A COMMUNITY—
A LIFE IN STREETWEAR

MCD

FARRAR, STRAUS AND GIROUX • NEW YORK

MCD
Farrar, Straus and Giroux
120 Broadway, New York 10271

Grateful acknowledgment is made for permission to reprint the
following material:
Lyrics from "Straight Edge," written by Ian MacKaye, James Baker,
Jeffrey Nelson, and Lyle Preslar, © 1981 Minor Threat Music (BMI),
administered by Rough Trade Publishing (BMI).
Lyrics from "Out of Step," written by Ian MacKaye, James Baker,
Jeffrey Nelson, and Lyle Preslar, © 1983 Minor Threat Music (BMI),
administered by Rough Trade Publishing (BMI).

Library of Congress Cataloging-in-Publication Data
Names: Hundreds, Bobby, 1980– author.
Title: This is not a T-shirt / Bobby Hundreds.
Description: First Edition. | New York : MCD/Farrar, Straus and
    Giroux, [2019]
Identifiers: LCCN 2018056437 | ISBN 9780374275792 (hardcover)
Subjects: LCSH: Hundreds, Bobby, 1980– | Businesspeople—
    United States—Biography. | New business enterprises—
    United States. | Branding (Marketing)—United States.
Classification: LCC HC102.5.H85 H86 2019 | DDC 338.7/687092 [B] —dc23
LC record available at https://lccn.loc.gov/2018056437

Designed by Richard Oriolo

Our books may be purchased in bulk for promotional,
educational, or business use. Please contact your local
bookseller or the Macmillan Corporate and Premium Sales
Department at 1-800-221-7945, extension 5442, or by e-mail
at MacmillanSpecialMarkets@macmillan.com.

www.mcdbooks.com • www.fsgbooks.com
Follow us on Twitter, Facebook, and Instagram at @mcdbooks

10 9 8 7 6 5 4 3 2 1

Certain names have been changed whether or not so noted
in the text.

For the music makers. To the dreamers of dreams.

CONTENTS!

THIS IS NOT A T-SHIRT

PROLOGUE...

O N THE MORNING I wrapped my proposal for this book, I
sat in the pews of a Baptist church east of downtown Los
Angeles. I wore my black suit and kept my head above the stag-
nant air. The 10 freeway reverberated overhead, doling out the
yammer of a jittery city. Even on a Saturday morning, L.A. had
no time to pause for young Jimmy Briggs, who lay flat and mo-
tionless in the casket at the pulpit. His dad, the charismatic
preacher Bishop Campbell, stood over him. He called on God to
sort out this misunderstanding. The congregants, although
taken by his heartache, were callous to the circumstances of
Jimmy's death. A couple of Black Panthers stood and called for

vindication. A mother wept. Here lay another young black man, gunned down at twenty-one while running away from the cops.

I watched Jimmy grow up on my shop's doorstep. He was a dark-skinned, handsome kid always wearing baggy pants and a flashy smile. He loved skateboarding, and he loved The Hundreds. So, we put him onto the program: keep skating and we'll keep you dressed. The funeral attendees see this arrangement play out in Jimmy's slideshow. He's wearing our brand across his back in almost every photograph—even on the program's cover. The photocopier's ink coagulates around this portrait of Jimmy crouching down, proudly sporting one of our tees.

For Jimmy, and for so many others around the world like him, our brand has stood for more than T-shirts, stylish caps, and warm jackets. Fashion revolves around art, design, and trends, while clothing is rooted in sales, marketing, and necessity. The Hundreds, however, is powered by culture and community. We like to say, "People over Product." It's like your favorite music artist: you download the album, go to the show, and take home the tour merch to identify yourself with the musician's art and attitude. With us, you visit our shop, you fraternize with our followers, and you wear our logos to profess that you're down with the lifestyle. It's bigger and deeper than a gang. The Hundreds is backed by a global army. That's why we're "The Hundreds," as in strength in numbers.

It used to weird me out that kids would tattoo our logos and designs on their bodies. I felt responsible, pressured to not let them down. Prominent rappers like YG and Travis Scott have the Adam Bomb mascot drilled into their arms. Why? I've never met these people; our lives are worlds apart. But our brand is a reflection of our lifestyle, and our lifestyle is why we've flourished. Our customers feel a sense of ownership with The Hundreds, and if they believe we've sold out or feel we're making off-brand moves, the backlash can be sharp and unforgiving. The Hundreds has come to represent chapters in young people's lives. For some, it's the entire story. Those tattoos signify milestones. Those clothes are war medals.

Jimmy appreciated this. "I'm a good kid," he told me one afternoon after another of his long stints in jail. "I just get caught up sometimes with the wrong crowd." The Hundreds' Los Angeles flagship store on Rosewood Avenue was his haven, a respite from the clamor of life in South Central. Everyone called him RSWD Jimmy, and I like to think he adopted our Rosewood crew, not the other way around. We didn't have a vote in the matter.

I owe this book to Jimmy and to everyone who's loved and lived our brand along the way. As much as it is my story, it is inextricably theirs as well. We're all in this together.

PART ONE

1. WELCOME TO HELL

"**F**UCK YOU AND your weak brand!"

His name is Derek. From what I can see in his profile pic, he's not quite twenty with mangy blond curls and a sharp nose. He looks as if he could be a stony surfer from Topanga, a portly Spicoli. But according to his bio, Derek is landlocked in northern Ohio. I caught him in my Twitter replies, fastening together a chain of insults against my brand. He'd started off tweeting about how The Hundreds "used to be cool" and eventually sank to cheap taunts and lazy expletives.

"Nobody wears this trash. Why don't u just die already?"

By the time I saw Derek's spew bubble up on my feed, I was

sitting in traffic on my commute home from Vernon to Venice. It had been a long day, the sort that mercilessly takes and takes. And here was this snot-nosed teenager burrowing into my scalp. I typically let abuse like this wash over me and dissipate; they're just thoughts, really. Thoughts come and go.

But not today.

I fired back: "Even a small dog can piss on a big building." Then I hit select all, deleted, and rethought my approach.

"Hi Derek. What's wrong, dude?"

It was as if somebody had turned off the faucet. Crickets. I got home, ate dinner, and worked from the couch. Occasionally, I'd check my mentions to see if Derek had rebutted with a goofy meme or let loose a tirade against me. Nothing.

Near midnight, a red notification blipped across my screen, the echo of a star's explosion that took hours traveling from a distant galaxy.

"Didn't think you'd respond. Just having a bad day."

"No problem. Me too."

"Rrrrright. You're rich."

"I mean, we all have our thing. I got a production order of pants back from our factory today, but all the tags were mislabeled. We had to fix them ourselves. Took six of our guys twelve hours, cutting and sewing . . . such a nightmare."

"Yeah? Well, I think I'm gonna fail school and my mom is threatening to kick me out. I can't even find a job that I like in my town. Don't really know where to go."

"That's rough. What would your ideal job be?"

My wife, Misa, walked into the room and plopped down next to me. She teased, "Who are you talking to? Another one of your internet fans?" She'd noticed that I'd stopped paying attention to the TV and was hunched over my phone.

"Some kid in Ohio. He's having a hard one."

"You're so weird," she said, smiling, then retired upstairs for the night as Netflix droned into the background. For the next twenty or thirty minutes, Derek and I volleyed our daily frustrations back and forth. This eventually segued into a discussion about streetwear and fashion.

"So, what's bothering you about The Hundreds?"

"I dunno. I used to feel like it was really special. But now it's sold everywhere, and everybody in my school is wearing it. And it's not just your brand, it's streetwear in general. All these bandwagoners don't even get what it's about and it pisses me off. It was my thing."

I logged on to The Hundreds' Instagram account. We'd been hyping up a big collaboration with adidas, and I watched my comments sizzle with positive emojis and friends tagging each other—the digital equivalent of a high five. Cool, fashionable kids from around the world were checking in. Indonesia, Norway, Mexico City, and—Derek was right—even Ohio. Yet when my partner, Ben, and I first formed the idea of a fun storytelling project, it never occurred to us that The Hundreds would become a globally recognized streetwear label, grow this big, and be sustained for this long.

I empathized with Derek. The Hundreds started back in 2003 with some drawings that I'd put on T-shirts, then blogged about. Ben sold the tees to local stores—a few hundred shirts per delivery. We'd crossed our fingers and prayed for the best, walking blindly into a shrouded future. We didn't even rely on logos or branding back then. We didn't have wide-scale name recognition, but our fan base would eventually become so attuned to what we were doing by following my blog that if I drew a stripe down a shirt, they could spot it from a mile away. It was our own clan, united by a shared love of OG streetwear brands, skateboarding, music, art, and a wide array of other interests like taco trucks, social issues, and cult movies.

Fifteen years later, and I now share my creations with millions of people across the planet. But as the brand grew, so much of that fundamental, personal code was lost. When you bestow your work on the world, you allow others to attach their own meanings to it and draw definitions around it. The Hundreds still means the same thing to me, but it also means millions of different things to millions of other people. I appreciate the money and success, but I also miss the days when The Hundreds was more like a secret-handshake club.

"I get it. It was my thing too," I said, referencing The Hundreds, but more specifically streetwear on the whole. (I'll explain "streetwear" more fully later, but for now imagine young men and women collecting limited-edition clothing like comic books.) In the late 1990s and early 2000s, kids like me wanted streetwear because nobody else wore it. In the span of a generation, that thinking has flipped. Today, young men and women hunt for streetwear precisely *because* everyone else is wearing it. Like all compelling subcultures, the secret was too good to keep to ourselves. Streetwear broke through the underground and went unapologetically mainstream by the early 2010s.*

High fashion is now smitten with street-turned-runway designers, an era ushered in by Kanye West, A$AP Rocky, and their apostles. Indie streetwear labels that sold to obscure boutiques a decade ago now flood malls and department stores. Supreme, once a niche New York skate shop, is now a luxury brand, val-

---

* It's like how rap music went from rebellious counterculture in the eighties to national radio channel fodder in the nineties to mainstream pop culture today. Rap has become so dominant that there's now something for everyone—a hip-hop buffet—with rappers featuring everywhere from SoundCloud streams to Coachella flyers.

ued at more than $1 billion. Meanwhile, every morning, there's a new T-shirt brand, started in a garage by some cool fourteen-year-old, with a pop-up shop opening somewhere with a line around the block. Somehow.

It was well into the early hours of the morning. I sank deeper into my couch and waded back through our conversation. Has The Hundreds changed? Of course it has. Ben and I are older, more experienced, our story has a longer tail. We've made more stuff; we've hired more people. Plus, streetwear is completely different now, powered by resale and celebrity endorsements. The harder questions are, have I changed? And, have we sold out? Amid all the long lines, noisy collaborations, news headlines, and sales reports, were we still true to ourselves and our audience?

2. INSPIRATION.
ASPIRATION.
PERSPIRATION.

I F YOU DRIVE southeast, outside downtown Los Angeles, you'll cross a couple of bridges, duck under an overpass, and eventually enter the hopelessly industrial district of Vernon. A water tower greets you at the city's gates (you might recognize it from the opening credits of *True Detective* season two, which was based on the neighborhood). Next is the Farmer John factory, a remnant of what was once the meatpacking district of L.A., before all the slaughterhouses moved to the Midwest. Then, behind an unassuming facade of pale green walls and razor wire, you'll reach The Hundreds' headquarters, which sits inside a ninety-thousand-square-foot warehouse. The building holds one hundred employees stationed in departments ranging from sales to digital marketing to customer service. There's a break room near the front with vintage arcade machines like *Street Fighter II* and *NBA Jam* and, in the back, "L.A.'s best ramp" (the pro skater Marc Johnson's words). Here, you'll also find our very own screen-printing shop, where we produce shirts and head-wear for ourselves and our competitors: young designers and start-up brands, some of which we even lease office space to. There's also a photo studio, and the rapper Alexander Spit has a recording studio in the basement. Our village is a never-never land of L.A.'s lost boys.

My partner, Ben Hundreds, holds court in the biggest office. I like to tease that we had to find space to fit his ego, but he also makes room for his retro sneaker collection, sports memora-bilia, and a collection of art books. Down the hall is my corner. This is the creative spring that inspires much of our design. The space is adorned with collectible toys, skateboard decks, and vintage clothing harvested from 1980s and 1990s culture—from street to pop. I've re-created the antique store scene from *Back to the Future Part II* in one corner alongside a shelf of rare KAWS and Bounty Hunter figures. Every inch of wall space is dedicated to original art by Mark Gonzales, Mike Giant, Raymond Petti-bon, and James Jean.

The soul of the entire company, however, lies dead center in the fortress. There, you'll find a lone photograph cheaply framed in an IKEA square. It's easy to miss in the corridor next to the Ron English paintings and Aaron Kai mural. It's a picture of our first official studio and clubhouse in L.A.'s Fairfax District that I shot late one night in 2006. I took the photo of our office from across the street, but you can see Ben through the window, lit by the orange glow of a halogen lamp. There's a stack of T-shirts behind him, representing the inventory we had in stock, and makeshift folding desks for our laptops. That's it. That was the entirety of The Hundreds at the time. It barely filled a four-hundred-square-foot room.

We had customers back then, but not much of a following. We printed T-shirts, but didn't exactly have a clothing line. We did, however, have each other. And we had a mission: to design a brand themed around California culture, complemented by an online magazine that painted the backdrop for our lifestyle. Ben and I wanted to put Los Angeles back on the map in terms of streetwear. We wanted to participate in and promote a new wave of street culture. And we wanted to tell our story, in real time, bringing our customers along for the ride. The world of fashion was concerned with making clothes, but we wanted The Hundreds to stand for more than cotton and plastisol.

Over the next fifteen years, we poured our lives into The Hundreds. We evolved from graphic tees and baseball caps to woven shirts, technical jackets, and even novelty food items. Ben and I went from working out of my bedroom to employing our friends out of a massive workshop and warehouse. We traveled the world, sold our line to the best skate and street boutiques in every major city, and opened a few of our own shops in the process. Meanwhile, my blog evolved into a media platform, read and viewed by millions. The Hundreds outlasted most of its peers and then held its own among a new class of competitors.

I can chalk up our success and longevity to the obvious: hard work, brand integrity, discipline. But these aren't the secrets to the success of our brand. We aren't consummate businessmen or trained designers. Ben and I literally made it up as we went along. Today, we still have no idea what we're doing, plugging different numbers into the combination lock until we get it open. Yet our brand is more profitable and notable than ever. Fifteen years is forever in streetwear, so why is The Hundreds still standing strong? My theory is simple. The Hundreds was never just about clothing. In the pure spirit of streetwear, The Hundreds was always about community.

T. S. Eliot once described hell as a place "where nothing connects with nothing." Dissociation has historically been a major source of unhappiness in people's lives. Humans long for connection; we want to feel that our lives have value and significance. Around 2010, many thought social media might be the answer. Facebook, Twitter, and Instagram shrank the earth and granted us a voice—an opportunity to share, to mobilize, to complain about airlines. It seemed as if we'd finally broken down the last of the walls barring communication. We assumed that as long as everyone could express themselves, they'd be received.

We all know how this story ends—with the internet only isolating and polarizing us further. Therefore, as a consumer and purveyor, I believe the future of successful branding lies in genuinely bridging the gaps that divide people. This is something streetwear has always inherently achieved. Because it's youth-driven, streetwear is full of passion, and averse to plastic marketing campaigns. Streetwear is transparent and purposeful by design, not financial incentive. It's brave and invincible. It's foolish and urgent, but that's forever been part of what attracts people to a cause.

When we started this company, I was in my early twenties. I thought I was interested in brand building because I was an enterprising artist and wanted to participate in the cool underground culture of streetwear. But the truth was that I was just seeking a connection with like-minded people. I'd always searched for a home—as a minority, as a skateboarder, as a punk. But I never quite found the right fit until I built my own community. I think our clientele understands the importance of that community and that's why they've stayed loyal to us through trends, recessions, and the distractions of the internet.

There's a ton of bestselling literature out there on how to make a business blow through the tech start-up model—raise capital and exploit influencers. But this is not a book about how to build a billion-dollar business (you'll probably never find your boy on the cover of *Forbes*). There's no worksheet at the end of each chapter or set of universal principles to memorize. This is a story about how a couple of guys created a clothing brand with the intent of fostering a community. It's a story about how, through that relationship with their customers, they have maintained an authentic and successful business that grows as they grow. Our mantra is "People over Product" to remind us that without culture, The Hundreds is just a label. My blog always took precedence over the online shop. We'll sell you a T-shirt, but not before we tell you about the artist behind it and his or her message. Our stores are less about sales and profits, and more about providing a venue to experience our culture. And the more we connect the dots between our people, the stronger the bond they have with our brand, the deeper the roots go.

But like that light in the photograph of our first office, the wildfire of community is sparked by one idea, one voice. Under the right conditions, that flame can spread from one person to the next, until the entire world is ablaze. By the end of this book, I hope you can find that ember within you, just as we did. This is how we kept ours burning bright and leading the way.

3. RIVERCIDE

Then everyone looks at me
They've never seen individuality
—Voodoo Glow Skulls, "You're the Problem"

ORANGES.

Riverside, California, began with round, dimpled oranges. In the late nineteenth century, a gift of three Brazilian navel orange trees took to the ranch town's rich soil and climate. In the following years, a different sort of gold rush occurred here. Spectators flooded the valley with orange groves, setting off the state's citrus industry.

A hundred years later, Riverside County welcomed another influx of residents, the result of white flight from the greater city's escalating crime and housing prices. Riverside's construction boom of the 1980s wooed L.A.'s pale population with affordable tract home developments furnished with matching pools and bleached gables. The opportunities were as infinite as the landscape; virginal neighborhoods snaked through the desert's creases and disappeared into the horizon. Strip malls dressed in Mexican mission architecture merchandised Kmart superstores and Baskin-Robbins ice cream parlors.*

In the summers, the Pacific Ocean breeze would link arms with the hot breath of the Santa Anas and sweep L.A.'s pollution into our recessed armpit. On a 120-degree August afternoon, the opaque smog would bury our town at the foot of the San Bernardino Mountains. I assumed this was typical. (Don't all kids have to stay indoors during smog alerts? Don't they all walk outside after an acid rainstorm and find their basketball corroding into a charcoal briquette?) Most playground days were cut short by the toxic air's spindly fingers closing around our lungs.

Yet when my Korean-immigrant parents moved to Riverside in 1982, they were sold on the suburban American dream of a two-car garage and a laundry room. They bought a house atop a long driveway that my brothers and I would skateboard down on our butts, dragging our Velcro Pro Wings sneakers as brakes. Our home was simple, with a triangle roof and square front windows—straight out of a children's book—but it was our castle. I remember every corner and cavity. The splintered banister I held on to during the big earthquake. The air-conditioning vent in the floor that my brothers and I wrestled over to lie on in the dog days.

I am the middle son of three boys. I was not the prized first-born that my mom and dad could parade around to their friends.

---

* Of course, as the communities diversified over the decades, whites fled again, to the sylvan Northeast and the racially achromatic Midwest, triggering a devastating real estate fallout by the mid-2000s.

Nor was I the overindulged baby brother, loved and adored. Larry and Jimmy were obedient, jock-ish, and academic like my dad. I was different—emotional, angsty, and searching. How come I was the only one to get spanked? Why was I so good at breaking the rules, but so bad at the piano and all those things my Asian-immigrant parents hoped to boast about? Why did I get sent to the principal's office so often?

I was as much of a terror in the classroom as I was at home. I was frequently disciplined for stealing toys, tackling kids by the sandbox, and refusing to stay silent when the teacher was talking (even at that age, I didn't feel invited into the conversation, so I bulldozed my way through). So, on the last day of kindergarten, when the exasperated principal dragged me out to my mom's Volvo station wagon and handed her a white envelope, I anticipated the worst.

I put my head down, crawled into the passenger seat, and watched my mom exchange some final words with Mrs. Woodburn. I couldn't make out their conversation from the inside of the window, but my mom definitely seemed shocked. And confused. She got in but didn't start the car, proceeding instead with the envelope.

My mom ran her finger along the paper's edge, tore the seal, and unfolded a single-page letter. She read it twice—at first mumbling in broken English and again more carefully—then turned to me with a strange expression on her face.

"Do you want to go straight to second grade next year?"

"What happened to first grade?"

"Well, the school is saying that you don't need to do it if you don't want. How do you feel about skipping first grade?"

The September before, on my first day of kindergarten, while the other kids were weaning off naps and coloring outside the lines, I was reading books and completing multiplication worksheets. In my introductory year of grade school, I grew bored of the Lincoln Logs and hopscotch, so the administration figured first grade would be just as dispensable. They suggested moving me directly to second grade in the fall.

I'm not sure how much of that choice was really in my hands, but without hesitation I voted to skip first grade—a decision that continues to impact my relationships today as reflected in my combative approach to work and underdog spirit. For the rest of my schooling, I was at least one year junior to the other kids. As an adult, a twelve-month difference in age is negligible, but the spread between seven and eight years old is an ice age to a population that counts fractions as significant milestones. ("Seven and a half!" "I'm almost ten and three-quarters.")

My age was a strike against me in divvying up baseball teams or riding roller coasters. I was the baby, the butt of the jokes, the kid who was twelve months behind in getting a driver's license or watching R-rated movies. I spent the next fifteen years overcompensating: my girlfriends would always be older, and athletically I would always have to prove that I belonged on the field with the big boys.

To make matters worse, I was one of the only Asian American kids in my school. My hair refused to part like that of the blond kids with Tony Hawk flops, and I hid behind chunky glasses and had rabbit teeth, like a grotesque, stereotypical wartime cartoon. To distract from my age and skin color, I amplified the only thing that would cause me to be showered with positive attention: my artistic skills.

My first memories are of drawing on brown newsprint with crayons. Maybe if I'd been born during the Renaissance, I would have scaled chapel walls painting portraits and landscapes in oil. But this was the 1980s. My childhood was set against the backdrop of Saturday morning cartoons,* breakfast cereal mascots, and newspaper comic strips. I'd fix my pencil in one corner of notebook paper and make my way down the page. Doodles would spool out of my head like ribbon—deformed caricatures, cusswords in 3-D lettering, naked girls with giant circular boobs like the most immature tattoo flash art ever. By bedtime, I'd stack my drawings into neat piles and stash them away behind the heavy encyclopedias in the back of my bookshelf, far removed from my parents' purview.

They weren't exactly pinning my art on the fridge. Even in my early years, my parents watched anxiously as I lost myself to those colored markers and construction paper; they didn't emigrate from postwar Korea so that their son could draw funny faces for a living. They failed to see how drawing *Garfield* comic strips was a valuable asset that would protect me in the merciless Western world (to be fair, neither did I). For Asian immigrants, watching your kid gravitate toward the arts is like when white kids tell their parents they want to drive race cars. I begged my mom and dad to enroll me in art classes, to buy me tutorial books. They denied me this. Time and again, they turned my focus back to my school studies with the end goal of a secure and lucrative degree. They pushed those sparks of creativity down deep, but they only fertilized years later as seeds of rebellion.

---

* The twentieth century was a plentiful farmland for American animation. Studios like Walt Disney, Hanna-Barbera, and Warner Bros. dominated 1950s, '60s, and '70s prime-time television. They erected national treasures out of characters like Mickey Mouse, Fred Flintstone, and Bugs Bunny. But in the 1980s, a syndicated symphony was conducted using these scrambled notes. Networks excavated prime-time cartoons from the past, chopped them into four-hour blocks, and beamed them into suburban households on weekends. An all-American ritual for boys and girls was born: the Saturday morning cartoon. From *The Smurfs* to *The Transformers*, *Looney Tunes* to *Muppet Babies*, Saturday morning cartoons were the iPad and YouTube of my generation. In our foundational years, they acted as an unsanctioned nanny: instructing our social language, teaching us morals, and showing us how (not) to catch a roadrunner.

Unfortunately for my parents, I kinda liked being the art guy. Unlike my race and age, my talents set me apart in a way that was under my control. My classmates would vie over me for group projects, and I almost felt popular. I could draw anything— Ninja Turtles brushing their teeth, Bart Simpson in Mickey Mouse shorts, the Tim Burton Batmobile—and would guarantee that our foam board presentations had the coolest art. In junior high, my skills distinguished me as one of the better graffiti artists and accrued instant credibility. In high school, the football players would pause from picking on me to request illustrated patches for their letterman jackets. I painted murals and campaign posters and got elected for them. I illustrated comic strips for the school newspaper and reveled in a broader audience admiring my work. My art granted me a voice in this world. My drawings set the stage from which I would be heard.

BY MY early twenties, I'd resigned myself to the fact that I didn't have the technical expertise or network to gain acceptance in the art world, but I still believed I had something to offer. If people wouldn't come see my paintings, I'd bring the artwork to them. The world was my gallery. If people across the planet wore my T-shirt designs, I'd be able to affect just as many onlookers, if not more. So, we started The Hundreds with a fall collection of seven graphic T-shirts with designs crudely drawn on Adobe Photoshop and reduced to one-color screen prints to save on costs. A decade and a half later, we've designed at least two thousand unique graphics and have produced over four million individual shirts. And still, T-shirts remain the core competency of our business.

Streetwear, as a medium, is established on the graphic

T-shirt. For one, the profit margins are unbeatable when you're cranking out tees for $5 a pop and flipping them for $35. On a spiritual level, however, the T-shirt is effective because it's about messaging. Young people are not always the best communicators, but they have plenty to get off their chests (pun intended). To this day, that's my primary rule when it comes to designing T-shirts: have something to say. Here at The Hundreds, we begin with an opinion on an issue and then incorporate our signature attitude and personality. The goal is to tell a full narrative with a perspective and a purpose. And even after all these years, we find that we still have much more to speak on.

Everyone has something to say. I believe that's what makes us human and special. Even if you're an apathetic person, that indifference is a chosen way of life. I built my brand and lifestyle around my opinions, and my opinions were rooted in my identity as a Korean American middle child, an underdog, a skateboarding hardcore kid, and a streetwear devotee. My voice was manifested in my art. Those cartoon drawings made their way onto T-shirts, which rolled into denim, and jackets, and furniture. If design isn't your thing, you can use whatever medium you work with to carry your voice, whether it's how you staple together a TPS report, fill the fries at McDonald's, or govern a board meeting. But you have to first home in on who you are. Once you've carved out your little corner, the next move is stepping out and inviting other people in.

4. STEP OUT

A step apart, I don't fit
In with my peers, but I don't give a shit
—Gorilla Biscuits, "Hold Your Ground"

SKATEBOARDING WAS MY first community. At thirteen, I was one of eight misfits in our middle school who found refuge in skate. Eight of us in Etnies and Acme wool caps and XXL T-shirts, piling into the Volkswagen bus of the junior Dan Ballou (the only one who was old enough to drive) after school. Eight of us swarming an abandoned bank parking lot on the wrong side of town, sliding up and down waxed red curbs on the noses of our boards. Thirteen-year-old kids smoking out of Coke can bongs and devouring drugstore porn magazines at dusk in the Death Box (a subterranean drainage ditch off the side of Chicago Avenue). We burned through Plan B skate videos on cassette and scrawled our names across broken windows with Mean Streak paint markers before scrambling home like cockroaches. While our peers were making out at Friday night football games, we were on the couch at C&C Board Shop, grip taping our boards and drawing in our black books.

The skateboard was the key to our clubhouse. And the best part? Anyone could be a member. Skateboarding didn't appraise your skin tone, how much money your parents made, or how you dressed. As a young man, I'd realized that skateboarding didn't reward tough guys, popular kids, or athletes. What mattered more than anything was if you could skate. And because it wasn't a team or competitive sport, nobody cared how skilled you were. It wasn't about talent. It was solely about how hard you tried. How much fun you had. How *down* you were. I was up for all those things.

Yet over the decades, I grew to feel differently about skating as it came to be about point systems and the Olympics; about pop stars in *Thrasher* hoodies and billion-dollar athletic shoe companies like Nike and adidas running the show. I'd romanticized skateboarding as the bastion of the anti: the dark horse. Commercially unviable and built to fail. But by the late nineties, as skate outstripped its subversive layer, I searched for other communities that would accommodate my perspective and became entranced by the sound of hardcore punk. I was most attracted to the hardcore scene's independence and liberty. And the music helped me work out my Korean *han* (a hypothesized, inherited state of emotional frustration) in the mosh pit.

It started with Gorilla Biscuits' 1989 seminal hardcore album. I'd followed my older brother, Larry, to the record store as he loaded up on Fu-Schnickens and Shabba Ranks albums. I'd never owned a CD before outside a Disney soundtrack, so I asked to buy my first, *Start Today* by Gorilla Biscuits, based solely on the funny name and cartoon mascot on the back cover.

When I got home, I cut into my room, slid the disc in, and pressed my ear up against the speakers.

"What do you mean that it's time, time for me to grow up?" the vocalist, Civ, bursts forth in the opening verse. "I don't want any part. It's right to follow my heart."

I had never heard a sound like this—pulverizing guitars, the desperate call-and-response—it felt important. It was certainly more urgent than the sound of John Tesh's magical piano wafting from my parents' radio. Staring down the road to adolescence, I knew exactly what Civ meant. He longed for a past that I had just discovered. I wanted to know everything about hardcore.

The R-star logo on the back of that album was how I came to know it was real. Revelation Records: a Huntington Beach–based label that specialized in New York hardcore of the "youth crew" variety. If Revelation could give me a record as powerful and pure as *Start Today*, what else was waiting for me? I went down the line: Judge. Youth of Today. Chain of Strength. Bold. I collected and shared these bands' albums like baseball cards but took them to heart like religious pamphlets. I gravitated toward friends who understood the music. If somebody didn't get it, I converted them or left them behind.

And I was just scraping the surface. Hardcore—as a music genre and culture—went deeper and wider than the New York scene of the 1980s. In my Southern California backyard, South Bay and Hollywood punk bands like Black Flag, Germs, and X owned the stage. In the mid-1990s, I had a thing for the darker Seattle tone of Botch and Undertow. Hardcore bands wrapped in political manifestos like the Nation of Ulysses and Refused captivated me. Then I learned about Ian MacKaye, the cornerstone of American hardcore. The D.C. icon fronted the Teen Idles and Minor Threat in the early eighties. That's when I was born, so I felt like this made a lot of sense. Minor Threat pioneered the "straight edge" philosophy—the most punk rock lifestyle a punk rocker can adopt: abstaining from drugs, alcohol, and promiscuous sex.

I'm a person just like you
But I've got better things to do
Than sit around and fuck my head
Hang out with the living dead
Snort white shit up my nose
Pass out at the shows
I don't even think about speed
That's something I just don't need

I've got the straight edge

I'm a person just like you
But I've got better things to do
Than sit around and smoke dope
'Cause I know I can cope
Laugh at the thought of eating ludes
Laugh at the thought of sniffing glue
Always gonna keep in touch
Never want to use a crutch

I've got the straight edge
I've got the straight edge
I've got the straight edge
I've got the straight edge.
—Minor Threat, "Straight Edge"

Here's the Cliff's Notes:

I don't smoke
I don't drink
I don't fuck
At least I can fucking think.
—Minor Threat, "Out of Step"

This idea of being the anti to the anti blew my nipples off. I thought being a rebel was enough, but this dude was rebelling *against the rebels*! I was on board with the whole kit. The music, the self-discipline, and the subversive attitude.

Hardcore is just one of those things that you have to experience in person to comprehend. I can tell you all about hardcore. I can play you the songs ("How can you understand what they're saying!" perplexed girlfriends would ask). But until you attend a show, meet the people, and *dive into the community*, none of it makes much sense at all. In that way, I find a lot of parallels with streetwear. If you just see T-shirts and hoodies, the campouts and Reddit discussions don't add up. Only when you tap into the history does it all come together.

I don't remember who was up to bat at my first hardcore show, but I do remember where it was. There were only three venues my friends and I would frequent on Friday and Saturday nights: Koo's Café in Santa Ana, Showcase Theater in Corona, and The Barn on the UC Riverside campus. A lot of popular bands got their start at The Barn, including Rage Against the Machine, Korn, and No Doubt. It was a small venue that fit a few hundred people. The punks in the pit would swing off the low rafters like a set of Barrel of Monkeys. I usually took my place on the side stage, shooting photographs.

My favorite part of hardcore concerts was that it was always hard to tell who was performing. The venues were tight, the stages were small (if there was one at all), and the band and the crowd would charge toward each other like frontline soldiers in a swirling mosh pit. At some shows, the singer would rush into the mob and lend the microphone to the fans for the majority of the songs. The songs were shared and communal, belonging as much to the crowd as they did to the band. It wasn't about who owned what; it was about everyone making it happen as a collective. There was no hierarchy, no distinction between purveyor and consumer. After shows, I'd meet band members in the parking lot to discuss politics and compare ideologies; then we'd go to Denny's for a late-night snack together.

Years later, when we started The Hundreds, I carried over the hardcore philosophy into our brand experience. The goal was to be transparent and accessible with our fans just as my favorite hardcore bands were with me. When it came to my back-to-school clothes, I admired all these cool skate and surf companies, but I really didn't know anything about the founders behind them. What were their beliefs? Could I be friends with them in real life? If I were to advertise these clothing companies on my back like a walking billboard, I wanted to make sure our personalities aligned. What if there was an apparel brand that was so public and honest that you knew everything the people behind it loved and supported, and regardless of whether you agreed with them, you felt as if you could invite them over for dinner?*

The second-best thing about hardcore was that it was self-motivating and entrepreneurial. While the lesser-known bands

---

* We actually did eventually implement this idea. The Hundreds hosts EAT MEETs, restaurant takeovers with our community. The goal is to partake of good food, while also breaking bread with the people behind the clothes. There is no wall between us and our fans.

opened, my crew sat outside on the picnic benches, bullshitted, and bought $5 merch (the traveling acts sold homemade T-shirts for food and gas). Many straight-edge kids took their self-discipline further to veganism and animal rights. Usually, there'd be a couple of skinhead girls hosting a Food Not Bombs bake sale in the front of the house. Before blogs and Instagram, most hardcore kids took their ideas to Kinko's, cut and glued layouts to stapled paper, and published their own photocopied zines. I went to a lot of punk and ska shows, even the occasional backpack rap concert, but the hardcore scene was a different animal. The kids weren't satisfied with a round of casual dancing and a night of live music. And we didn't just mosh to vent about our parents and homework and break each other's faces in half. There was a true entrepreneurial spirit around nineties hardcore life. Much of this came from the do-it-yourself ethos that built the culture. Kids organized out of habit and participated in the exchange of ideas,* breeding a motivated generation of thinkers and doers. Many of us in streetwear have hardcore roots: Benny Gold, Brain Dead, Pleasures, Bodega, and Babylon. So do other successful luminaries who framed their careers on the straight-edge hardcore ethic, including the chef Tal Ronnen of Crossroads, the pro wrestler CM Punk, and the DJ Steve Aoki.

After Minor Threat broke up, Ian MacKaye's follow-up act was a post-hardcore band named Fugazi. To many fans and critics, this was MacKaye's greatest contribution to music and punk rock philosophy. He abandoned the straight edge† and his

---

* For example, one of my favorite live bands, Avail, was from Virginia and by all means its members could be mistaken for southern rednecks. But they'd set up an ARA (Anti-Racist Action, a precursor to Antifa) table next to the stage, distribute activist literature to the kids, and pass out flyers for Black Panther rallies.

† In an interview, Ian blamed much of his disenchantment with straight edge on its militant turn: "The problem with movements is that [they] start to lose sight of humanity . . .

signature tune. Fugazi developed a sophisticated, mature sound that played more to funk and reggae than to D.C. hardcore. Compared with MacKaye's prior punk repertoire, Fugazi songs were easier, more anthemic. The song "Waiting Room" even worked its way up the mainstream rock radio charts.

But Fugazi's influence went way beyond the music. The real distinction: the band's ideology on business and "selling out." Fugazi refused major label deals, preferring to establish their own indie instead (Dischord Records). They insisted on $5 tickets for their shows, which made for affordable yet extremely crowded tours. They subverted the expectations of their audience by banning moshing and merch at their own concerts. Like the Bill Watterson of punk rock, MacKaye denied die-hard concertgoers official tour T-shirts, stickers, and paraphernalia.

"I just don't give a fuck about T-shirts," he once said.

Someone, somewhere, at some point in time, couldn't accept the fact that there were no Fugazi shirts out there. So, that person printed an unlicensed T-shirt that read, "This is not a Fugazi T-shirt," and sold a ton of them, and to this day that shirt has become virtually synonymous with the band's legacy. So much so that Ian MacKaye eventually endorsed the shirt and requested that all proceeds benefit a cause. That this random person printed an illegal T-shirt of a band that didn't believe in T-shirts and that it became one of the most iconic T-shirts in music history is just so perfectly punk. It's like the inception of punk rock negation.

In straight edge, people who really pushed the idea of a movement, especially a militant movement, really lost sight of human beings . . . I don't want people to ever use my words ever to injure anybody. Ever. That is the antithesis of my desire in life . . . It's unfortunate that this minority of people, who've engaged in fundamental and violent behaviors, have gotten so much attention and have put such a stigma on [straight edge] . . . I find it so disturbing when I hear about serious ugliness and it somehow evokes straight edge. It really bothers me . . . Can you imagine how many motherfuckers have asked me if I'm still straight edge? . . . It just drives me crazy."

Skateboarding and hardcore taught me to question everything, repeatedly, to constantly challenge myself. The cover art for Minor Threat's *Out of Step* features a lone black sheep turning away from the white pack. The black sheep is where my eye is immediately drawn. It's in my nature to go against. I know this might sound stupid, but if everyone is moving in the same direction, that's a red flag that I should head the other way. Even if it burns bridges, even if it means less "cool" and less money. This detour from the well-traveled road is part of what distinguished me and The Hundreds from other brands, helped me to see things before everyone else did, and granted me the freedom to wander. I identify with that black sheep.

It was at this point that I had a vision. Black sheep, like me, dotting the rolling hills of skate culture, flocking to the new frontier of streetwear. But we weren't lost, not nearly. We were looking for each other. In step with being out of step—together.

Can't keep up!
Out of step, with the world!

5. OUTSIDE THE BOX

I N THE FALL of 1997, at the age of seventeen, I broke up with my girlfriend, rolled up some band posters from my childhood bedroom, and split from the barren strip malls of Riverside.

I moved into the dorms at the University of California, San Diego, as a freshman. And I would give UCSD four years of my life, immediately gunning for a triple major. Eventually, I'd pick up another field of study, majoring in communications with three minors: psychology, theater, and computing in the arts. But it wasn't enough. I needed more.

I DJ'd a slot on the college radio station, playing early emo and indie from Cap'n Jazz, the Get Up Kids, and Hot Water Music.

I threw jungle parties for the rave club and visited the Hare Krishna temple in Pacific Beach twice a week. I did stand-up comedy, produced one-man shows in the school's black box theater, and published an on-campus zine to promote inter-faith religious dialogue. In my last two years of college, I ran for office and won the AS commissioner of communication position by a landslide.*

I threw *Project X*–style house parties, but I was still afflicted with boredom. By junior year, I had grown impatient with the pace of college life and was eager to find out what I'd be when I grew up. My professor's boyfriend, Kevin Imamura, was an editor at *Warp*, one of the magazines under Transworld Media (*Transworld Skateboarding*, *Snowboarding*, and at the time *Surf*). *Warp* was one of my favorite magazines because it wasn't dedicated to just skateboarding, snowboarding, or music. *Warp* combined all those interests into one journal. I applied for an internship and, with my professor's recommendation, got the job.

In my time with *Warp*, we re-branded as *Stance*, positioned celebrities like Eminem and a sixteen-year-old Mila Kunis on the cover, and formatted the book to cover all relevant youth culture from skateboarding to cars to fashion. It's arguable that *Stance* was a precursor to what *Complex* is today; it was just far too ahead of its time in the early 2000s to survive on grocery store shelves (midwestern kids were more interested in Fred Durst than in Nigo). *Stance* owed a lot to Kevin, who had a knack for picking up early on subculture vibrations. He was the one who had me calling the Supreme store for editorial product in

---

* I was personally responsible for distributing hundreds of thousands of dollars of the school's money for student-run media and handed the majority of it over to the Latino/Chicano publication *Voz Fronteriza*. I believed in the paper's cultural value and was pissed off that UCSD's brown student population was underrepresented. The campus newspaper, *UCSD Guardian*, wrote scathing editorials about my misuse of funds, to which I responded with an open letter eviscerating the editors for their lack of coverage of larger issues.

1999 or flying up to San Francisco to profile ROLO and Recon. Kevin also introduced me to my favorite artists to this day, like Barry McGee and ESPO (in their Street Market era), as well as to the mysterious world of Japanese street fashion.

So, nothing was more shocking than the morning I got to the office and saw Kevin opening a box of Nikes at his desk.

"Nike?" I questioned. Nike was for pigheaded jocks! Plus, the corporation was dogged with child labor scandals. For an anti-authoritarian skate punk, there was nothing cool about Nike. The swoosh had no place in this building, let alone in skate culture.

"These are the Alphanumeric Dunks," he calmly replied. He situated the sneakers on the shelf—right between his Michael Lau Gardener figures—not to be worn but to be displayed as collectible art. The Nike Dunks were low-tops with reflective 3M panels. On the toe, right where a triple-stitched, double-layered ollie pad should go, was a high-density embroidered yellow Alphanumeric logo. I was utterly confused. Why was Alpha—a reputable skate brand—collaborating with a giant athletics company on basketball shoes?

I knew the retro Jordan trend was emerging out of Tokyo and there was a cult of curiosity around rare Japanese streetwear and Medicom Bearbrick toys. What I failed to realize was that all of the coolest skaters of the period like Eric Koston, Scott Johnston, and Keith Hufnagel were avid collectors. Although those guys were sponsored by skate-shoe companies, they were flying back and forth from Japan and hoarding vintage Nike Dunks for a hobby. A few years earlier, when I was in high school, Nike had tried to penetrate the skateboarding market with a team led by Gino Iannucci, playing commercials on ESPN. I even found a pair of the early normcore-style shoes on the Ross sales rack. The backlash against the corporation from the core skate community was swift and pitiless, however, and Nike rip-corded.

But here was a sudden, unexpected break for Beaverton. Prior to this, no amount of compensation could persuade skateboarding's biggest, core idols to back the swoosh. Skaters were averse to framing their pastime as an organized sport, and the traditional athlete sponsorship looked corporate and disingenuous—a total sellout move. Yet if Nike approached skateboarding via culture and community (like Japanese *otaku*—hyper-obsessive collecters), they could tap its biggest stars.*

This collision of worlds was transformative for youth culture and fashion. I want to highlight this point: as much as we can trace modern streetwear back to the surf/hip-hop interchange of the 1980s and Tokyo's obsessiveness in the 1990s, this concept of sneaker culture meets skateboarding, perhaps more than any other factor, catalyzed the early-2000s chapter of street fashion. The lineups and resellers, the collaborations, the hype. Sneaker culture made it okay for straight young men to participate in fashion, it brought money and publicity into the industry, and it unrolled a terrain from which streetwear would sprout. It started from the ground up. These streetwear kids were shopping for something to match their shoes. Ruminating on those Alphanumeric Dunks as a teenager, all I saw was a sports company culture-vulturing off independent skateboarding. What Nike did for streetwear, however, was connect disparate youth communities through underground tunnels.

Eventually, Kevin exited *Stance* and moved to Oregon to help start Nike's skateboarding division, Nike SB. The remainder of the original *Stance* crew dismantled. I stayed at Transworld a bit

---

* In my opinion, like it or not, Nike and skateboarding were destined for each other. But first, Nike had to learn to appreciate skate through a lifestyle lens. And skaters had to feel like it was their idea to go to Nike, like they held the power in that exchange.

longer, but it never felt the same in Oceanside without the architects around. Plus, my interest was piqued by this budding movement of renegade T-shirt designers and sneaker collectors. The more I scraped at the surface, the more I found oceans of information roiling underneath. From skateboarding to hardcore, I forged my identity around subcultural communities. But this underworld of brands spoke to me directly. I was inspired by the art, captivated by the personalities behind the labels, and drawn in by the clandestine culture. Little did I know how much I would end up shaping it and how much it would come to shape me.

I learned a lot in college, but the greatest lesson didn't come from professors or textbooks. I still carry this note I wrote in my journal during my last weeks in San Diego: "The more I know, the more I realize I don't know anything at all." I had no idea.

6. STREETWEAR: A BRIEF HISTORY

To break the rules, you must first know the rules.
—Jav Dolla

NO MATTER WHERE we begin the streetwear story, we start in the middle.

Defining streetwear is like fencing in a mirage. Streetwear's just one of those phenomena—the tighter you crop in, the less focused the picture becomes. Like the way memories slip through your fingers the harder you hold on to them. Most people see T-shirts and ball caps and think streetwear is hip-hop clothes or skater style (that's typically how I explain it to anyone over the age of forty). Streetwear, however, is simply the merchandise associated with an attitude. Teenage rebellion, youth culture, and fashion snobbery have long been parts of

American life. Whether it's called "beach counterculture" or "urban," young people have long adopted T-shirt labels as identifiers and differentiators.

Today, we call it streetwear, but we didn't always.* "Streetwear" came into widespread use in the mid-2000s as a handy media catchall for the start-ups in our class—the designers standing up to department store labels and corporate sportswear. Without cut-and-sew capabilities and capital, we centered on graphic T-shirts and collaborations. Our brands were inspired by designers who sold exclusively through their retail stores like Bape and Supreme, but we wanted to open up wholesale doors on an indie level. We also wanted to open up streetwear via the internet.

So we blogged. Some of the most notable websites included mine (thehundreds.com), Honeyee, Beinghunted, SlamXHype, The Brilliance, Highsnobiety, A Silent Flute, and Hypebeast. The web also gifted us with the online shop, wherein brands could cut the middleman altogether. Despite e-commerce, streetwear boutiques boomed. Suddenly there were more than a handful of stores in the world that catered to our kind. Skaters became disenfranchised by organized action sports and wanted something more grounded, rootsy, and fashionable to wear. The burgeoning retro sneaker culture needed to be dressed from the ankles up. All of these factors converged on an industry, a movement, that required a catchphrase. Moreover, this new customer—young, mostly male, and preoccupied with fashion—sought a flag to brandish. "Streetwear" fit just right.

When we started The Hundreds, brands in our category were classified as independent, underground, or hipster. Stores and trade shows didn't know what to make of our catering to such a

---

* Exceptions: Vision Street Wear and Tribal Streetwear.

diverse demographic. In the mid-2000s, the stores and trade shows compartmentalized young men's fashion in two silos: "skate" and "urban." As brands like LRG and Ice Cream started to outgrow this binary portrait, the industry concocted the embarrassing portmanteau "skurban" to explain the black kids on their skateboarding teams.

I recall standing outside our trade-show booths and getting asked by buyers and journalists, "Are you hip-hop or action sports?" Translation: *"Are you for black kids or white kids?"*

Ben and I would look at each other. He, of Iranian Jewish descent. Me, a Korean American kid who grew up thinking I was Latino. "Neither," we'd respond.

It's as if, subconsciously or by design, we'd created a streetwear brand just so we could exist. There's no contesting the white male majority's contributions to youth fashion through the decades, but as a person of color I felt excluded from the lifestyle. There were few role models who looked like me in clothing, rap, and skateboarding. I pinned *Thrasher* ads of Daewon Song, Gideon Choi, and Spencer Fujimoto to my wall, but the industry itself never called to me as a potential career. If you look up and down the halls of menswear history, you'll see white faces everywhere. The surf industry was founded on board shorts, sewn by the hands of white Aussies and Americans. In the 1950s, the American couple Nancy and Walter Katin cut boat cover canvas to make the first-ever surf shorts. Decades later, in Australia, Gordon Merchant would triple stitch his Billabong shorts. In the seventies, Bob McKnight discovered Quiksilver board shorts down under and introduced them stateside. Today, the surf industry is still dominated by Orange County–based Caucasian men with the exception of Pat Tenore of RVCA. Bob Hurley helms Hurley, Volcom was founded by Richard Woolcott and Tucker Hall, and Vans by the Van Dorens.

The same can be said for skateboarding. Although its participant base has opened up and diversified with time, the majority of the companies remain owned and operated by white men. Meanwhile, the urban clothing sector of the late 1990s—although fronted by black rappers and designers—was also controlled by white men and Jewish garmentos. That's why streetwear was important, necessary, and inevitable for an era of kids who looked unlike any generation prior. Although the men's marketplace lazily spun a tale of two narratives—teenagers tidily divided into white and black culture—the youth broke the levees. What about the black kids who skateboarded and the white kids who listened to rap—not to mention all the shades of brown in between? Finally, it was time to hear from—and speak to—Latinos, Asians, Native Americans, those of mixed backgrounds, the LGBTQ community, and women! All peoples left out of the traditionally binary dialogue. These kids found residence in streetwear, and today's brand founders are more reflective of their multifarious followers.

Did hip-hop music originate in the late 1970s with Kool Herc's playground parties in the Bronx? Or do we follow rap's bread crumbs to Muhammad Ali's ringside insults or to the dozens or to West African griot?

Likewise, does streetwear commence with the Orange County designer Shawn Stussy's namesake T-shirts in the 1980s? He was the first to popularize the hip-hop-meets-surf aesthetic within street chic, pairing luxury logo mash-ups on drop-shouldered tees with baggy trousers. Powered by the surfboard shaper's graffiti-like signature, Stüssy caught on globally and continues to drive streetwear trends to this day.

But if we point to Stussy, then we'd have to rope in his peers and predecessors in surf like Peter Schroff and Jimmy Ganzer of Jimmy'z. Theirs were the wild-styled surfboards and neon-patterned pants that derived from aerosol paint and graffiti art. We can't neglect the Zephyr freestyle skate team of 1970s West Los Angeles and their fusion of Venice gang culture with local surf politics. Craig Stecyk documented this synthesis of shaggy blond hair and cholo style—embodied in radical figures like the late Jay Adams—and broadcast it to global youth. Streetwear can dig deeper still, pulling on inspiration from the street gangs of 1970s New York, with their crews' names and iconography branded across denim vests, to Angeleno pachucos (rioting in billowing zoot suits).

Whatever and however you call it, streetwear is rooted in diversity and an exchange of cultures. Not solely skateboarding. Not just hip-hop or runway fashion or the avant-garde. Streetwear incorporates all of these effects, and the nineties street labels understood this well. This chapter bestowed a new breed of underground T-shirt iconoclasts: Freshjive, X-Large, and Tribal on the West. Triple Five Soul, PNB Nation, and Pervert on the East. L.A. influenced New York, which set off London and Tokyo. Streetwear had already gone global, courtesy of the International Stüssy Tribe's presence in London and the aforementioned cities. But Stüssy's disciples would eventually step out of their shadow. The best example of this was a Japanese DJ and designer named Nigo who appropriated what he admired from American street brands and created A Bathing Ape, otherwise known as Bape. Nigo's $300 sweatshirts and upscale gallery boutiques set the benchmark for how streetwear would come to be considered—as art piece, as obnoxious Bentley driver's uniform, as status symbol. Supreme, James Jebbia's skate company out of New York, also offered its perspective on high-end, exclusive streetwear. Its trademark retail a-hole attitude, cross-grain fleece, and premium collaborations captured the imagination of streetwear connoisseurs from here to Harajuku.

In the early 2000s, I was a big fan of Alife, a four-person New York City design collective that produced small runs of thoughtful streetwear pieces and co-branded sneakers. Their original shop on Orchard Street featured a vast mural for guest artists, a curated selection of product from obscure makers, and, overlooking it all, a second-story studio on a mezzanine. As a customer, you could look up to the office window and see the tops of Jest's and Tony's heads, bowed over their desks, working on something important and cool. I loved how connected the designers were with the product and boutique.* Sure, the T-shirts were woven with the same cotton as those of a mainstream label, but the clothing felt personal and special because of the experience. I appreciated the independent, artistic spirit that drove the Alife name, and I'd leave the shop feeling inspired and even a bit envious. I could design and print T-shirts too. I wanted to play.

I wasn't the only one.

The next streetwear progeny was forged in the shadows of desktop publishing and garage screen printing, far from the spotlight that showered major designers. Streetwear's raw and seditious spirit made a lot of sense during this period when Old Navy commercials governed the fashion landscape. Fashion is funny because as unique as they strive to be, consumers ultimately want to swing in the same direction, but there are always the black sheep running toward the other end of the pendulum's arc, in defiance of the establishment, championing independent thought.

---

* Alife's transparency influenced how I spoke and shared with The Hundreds' customers down the line.

People like me and Ben and The Hundreds, Ray and Denis of Mighty Healthy, Greg and Mike of Mishka—we followed in the steps of the OGs. But we also learned from their mistakes. Like all arrogant youth, we were drunk off ego and believed we knew better, could fix the broken scene, and design cooler clothing. The new era of streetwear was open to wholesaling, anchored by heavy plastisol-ink graphics on Alstyle blank T-shirts, and communicated with the customer through blogs.

The internet brought us together, and we joined forces at trade shows with other American brands in our class like Crooks & Castles, Hellz Bellz, Reason, Married to the Mob, and Huf.

Although streetwear's roots sprouted decades earlier, the mid-2000s apparel companies and retailers gave the genre a name, erected an industry, and transformed a wishful subculture into big business. The sneaker blogs and hip-hop magazines sank their teeth into this hot new trend. Some argue that streetwear as we know it today started here. Taking cues from Nike, Supreme, and Japanese lines that applied a luxury-goods philosophy to casual street clothes, we retooled and remastered streetwear. We honed the art of limited-edition distribution, produced collaborations that were low on profit and high on noise, and refined the science of branding.

Depending on how you slice and dice it, streetwear today is pumping hundreds of billions of dollars into the economy. It's been elevated from niche fashion to mainstream uniform and can be seen on the backs of the coolest and trendiest, whether you're a sixth grader or a sixty-year-old. Streetwear has gotten so big that it's overtaken all other sectors, from high fashion to athleisure. Any designer with a hoodie in their collection is now deemed "streetwear." The term is practically devoid of meaning. Sometimes, it feels like we're the last standing streetwear brand. At other times, it feels like we're not streetwear at all. Streetwear, like hip-hop music, has gone pop. And as with rap, that doesn't mean there isn't an underground. There are just multiple strains now. Nuanced customers. Today, we're faced with a multitude of voices and languages, a veritable streetwear Tower of Babel. We may not sound alike, or even understand one another, but we all share a cool attitude that radiates from our respective cultures and a love of rare product and meticulous design. It's that love that most readily defines what "streetwear" has become.

7. ESCAPE TO LOS ANGELES

All I know is that I don't know
All I know is that I don't know nothing
—Operation Ivy, "Knowledge"

I N THE SUMMER of 2001, with the late afternoon sun in my eyes, I loaded my life and laundry basket into the trunk of my Honda CR-V and merged onto the 5 North. I'd graduated from college after four years in San Diego and was making the big move to Los Angeles, possibly to pursue acting or design or to intern at an ad agency. I wanted the progressive life I'd read about in New York hipster rags like *Paper*, but here on the West Coast. I envisioned myself as an accomplished artist, following in the footsteps of graffiti artists turned gallery painters like Twist and Margaret Kilgallen. Only problem being I wasn't a vetted artist—not a very good one anyway. I was a dilettante at worst, a dabbler at best. I had never taken a formal art class in my life, nor did I know how to use any of the tools of the trade beyond a Krylon can or a Mean Streak paint marker. Even if I could get my technical chops up to par, how would I get my work seen?

To buy time, I fell back on my experience as a freelance magazine writer and photographer. I shot local concerts, reviewed fashion collections and CD advances, and profiled of-the-moment bands for magazines like *Mass Appeal*. Freelancing was a thin and unpredictable path for a college grad, but it was a lot of fun and it paid the rent. I made up my own hours, got paid a buck a word, and took advantage of the opportunities to travel.

I signed the lease on a shoe-box studio apartment off the shoulder of the 10 freeway, strictly because the surrounding complex resembled Daniel Larusso's home in *The Karate Kid*. It was a lonely and overcast season of my life. I was friendless in a new city with no career prospects. I wondered if maybe I should look into PR or marketing, but advertising agencies—boutique to big—denied me at the door. Most of my college buddies were in graduate school or staking their claim in the real world by working their first big desk jobs. They'd visit me after work in their wrinkle-free Banana Republic clothes. They were growing up, and here I was in my Dickies and Converse, hunting for retro Jordans on NikeTalk. I started to burn through freelance assignments, working deep into the night, only to wake sharply to the sound of 18-wheelers barreling past my kitchen. The windows would chatter, and brown dust would cough into my bedroom. The barren art canvases lined the carpeted edges of the walls, fencing me in like a Stonehenge of broken dreams.

On a Monday midnight at summer's end, my visiting friend the photographer Zach Cordner and I headed out into the night. On the other side of town, Slayer was hosting an album release party for *God Hates Us All* at the Hollywood Forever mortuary, and there was no passing up the opportunity to revel with Kerry King and the thrash metal band in a house of death and misery. The night itself was a blur (probably because any residue of an amusing memory was immediately blotted out by the following morning's news). We stepped over gravestones, noted how the party was more industry than evil, greedily held on to our swag bags, and blearily returned home feeling moderately Satanist in the early hours of September 11, 2001.

The family that managed my apartment building had three police officer brothers who all lived on the floor beneath me. Their steel doors clanged behind them as their wives and children called out farewells in the throes of confusion. But they didn't wake us. Neither did our cell phones, which were dead or on silent. Even the freeway behind us, which was more anxious than ever that morning, couldn't rouse us as we slept off the night's soot.

It was my mom's voice on the answering machine that got my attention.

"Bobby, are you awake? Bobby, turn on the news."

It didn't matter which channel, because it was the same thing on every network. A deformed New York skyline. People washing their eyes and mouths of chalky white dust. I was twenty-one and naive in 2001. But 9/11 frames this pivotal point in my life, as it does for much of the rest of the modern world. Everything before that was now frivolous and foundational— sepia toned and warm. Everything after was cutting, dipped in irony, stark, and unforgiving. It's like the moment Biff screws everything up and sets off an alternate reality in *Back to the Future Part II*.

Work-wise, I felt the effects immediately. The economy froze. Major advertisers got cold feet and withdrew from publications, so editors stopped replying, and freelance gigs dried up. I went from stitching together four or five big jobs a month to one, at best. I smudged that border between night and day and was soon finding myself waking up as people were returning home from their workdays. I lost focus, started rationing boxed spaghetti and packaged tofu, and watched a lot of *Maury*.

I was disappearing.

AFTER 9/11, I found myself with a lot of free time. To make the most of it, I built a website. I'd picked up some HTML coding skills in college, and with the aid of the Dreamweaver web design program I created an online portfolio site under the name BobbyKim.com. If I wasn't going to be the next big street artist, perhaps this was where I could make great art—the digital realm. Truthfully, I just needed a way to showcase my work to potential employers. I laid it out like a book, with chapters dedicated to my art, photography, and writing. The most popular page (to my six visitors), however, was the blog.

At the turn of the millennium, the internet was still finding its footing amid primitive Tripod websites, AltaVista search queries, and Napster. But the Blogger publishing platform was a hit, providing a digital dais for outspoken, exhibitionist, attention-seeking middle children like me. Web logs (or "blogs," as they came to be known) were open journals that could be updated with text and images. Until that point, websites were static home pages, displaying a banner here, a rotating GIF there. The only glimmer of fresh material came by way of terse news feeds. There was scant supply to browse on the web, and new content came at a glacial pace.

By contrast, a blog was more like a coursing river. Blogs

twisted and turned with each passing day's circumstances. There was something voyeuristic about wading through a blogger's stream of consciousness as it happened. We take this for granted today given our familiarity with social media, but blogs were the first tool to tear down the invisible wall between storyteller and audience. Back then, the prevailing media (television networks, newspapers, radio programming) controlled the flow of information. Nowadays, *we* are the media, and we can reach each other directly and intimately in a faster, smaller world. But none of us knew this back then.

You know what I saw? A free alternative to zines. After all, punks already knew how to circumnavigate the publishing strongholds and media gatekeepers. Photocopied, independently made zines were the lifeblood of the hardcore scene. Being made by literally cutting and pasting xeroxed layouts between stapled sheets of paper, zines were a cheap and efficient means of disseminating information to the community, whether that be music reviews, an animal rights manifesto, or scanned Polaroids. This was what punk and hardcore adherents meant when they shouted, "DIY!"

Do it yourself.

Like keeping a childhood diary, I would recap my day on my blog—everything from what I ate to whom I hung out with to updates on the unbroken California weather. But I also documented outfits (back before this was—never mind, this was *never* cool), shared lists of sneaker releases, and posted photos of my travels and the work of artists I admired. There wasn't an accurate means of measuring traffic, so I hadn't a clue as to who—if anyone—was reading. I blogged for the sake of blogging, filling the gaps in my work schedule with daily updates. I was eventually writing more for my blog than for magazines and other websites and was perfectly happy with it. One day I wrote a long entry about my Evisu jeans, and a rep from the Japanese denim label emailed to thank me and say he was a fan of what I was doing. That letter sat at the top of my in-box, flagged, for months. I told myself that so long as at least one person was listening, I would be interested in talking.

8. RISING SON

B UT BLOGGING DIDN'T pay the bills.* I was tiring of the free-lance life. Plus, I started to suspect that at least half of these *Maury* episodes were fake. Because I enjoyed writing and reduc-ing anonymous commenters to rubble in meaningless message board arguments, a few friends suggested I apply to law school. I knew this would make my parents happy, but I also figured law could yield a steady, reliable career that would open up my nights and weekends to creative endeavors. Most of all, as a po-

---

* In fact, it never has. Even in the years when we've hosted advertising from the *Complex* network across our website, we've never generated a dollar in profit from having a blog.

litical dissident, I foresaw a subversive approach to breaking up the system. If I could work my way into the power structure through a legitimate path, maybe there was a real opportunity to make change in the world.

I wasn't interested in leaving Los Angeles, so I took the LSAT and applied to law schools in my area. While I waited to hear back from admissions, I joined my girlfriend, Misa, for a year in Japan, where she was teaching English to elementary school students. Her program placed her in the third-largest city of Nagoya, in the yakuza-ridden neighborhood of Imaike. In the middle of the night, I'd hear car doors slamming outside and see bands of Japanese gangsters with peanut-butter-colored hair showing up for secret meetings. While Misa was at work during the day, I bicycled downtown, met up with friends for lunch, and skated in the city center. We lived a simple life in Japan. We traveled around the country on weekends and rented English-subtitled movies from the local video store at night. Our apartment was so small that I could stand in the middle, extend my arms and legs, and touch the kitchen sink, dining room table, and bed at the same time.

Unlike the post-9/11 landscape back home, where I was scraping for gigs, I reaped plenty of work in Japan. American street culture was burgeoning in Asia, and local magazines were hungry for stateside contributors. Alternately, the publications back home were curious about Japan's growing street fashion scene. I reviewed Japanese rap albums by King Giddra and Rip Slyme. I documented underground fight clubs set up by drunk salarymen in the backs of cleared-out bars for *Giant Robot* (a relatively unknown artist at the time named David Choe illustrated my stories for the magazine).

For one of my biggest jobs, I spent three months interviewing rappers and designers in Tokyo for a *Japanzine* cover story on the history of Japanese hip-hop culture. Although I detailed Scha Dara Parr's contributions and the proliferation of Japanese B-boying, a big piece of the puzzle was acknowledging Japan's role in sneaker-collecting culture. The vintage Nike *otaku* enthusiasm was exploding in tandem with the resurgence of Levi's and Americana thrifting. Retro Air Force 1s, Dunks, and Jordans were suddenly sought-after, because the kids who wanted them in the 1980s were now young professionals and had the salaries to fulfill their fantasies. Cluttered sneaker boutiques bloomed throughout Japan's shopping districts and eventually made their way overseas to Foot Patrol in London, Undefeated in Los Angeles, and Alife Rivington Club in New York. Sneaker culture was flourishing, but sneaker aficionados needed something to wear above the ankles—clothing that reflected their rare and expensive tastes.

While limited American transplant labels like Stüssy and Supreme were fashionable in Japan for their exclusivity and collaborations with credible artists, A Bathing Ape was drumming up the most noise out of the Harajuku neighborhood. A Bathing Ape's logo and branding were reminiscent of what Erik Brunetti was doing in Los Angeles with his brand Fuct (namely his infatuation with *Planet of the Apes*), but the T-shirts were near US$90 and sold exclusively in Bape stores. Although I was first put onto Bape in college by Kevin (my editor at *Stance* magazine), there was a difference between seeing Ape T-shirts in eBay photographs and walking into its flagship store in the heart of Harajuku. I'd never seen a T-shirt brand like this, positioning screen-printed hoodies and trucker caps as luxe items in superfuturistic boutiques with million-dollar build-outs. The vinyl toys and tchotchkes were showcased in curved glass, while the graphic tees were framed in plexiglass cases that you'd carousel through like lithographs. The architecture firm Wonderwall had meticulously designed the Bape stores with patent leather sneakers rotating on conveyor belts beneath the floor and mirrors strategically angled to distort space and merchandise.

At all hours, there was a steady line of customers patiently lurking outside Bape's central Busy Works shop, which only heightened the anticipation. To shop A Bathing Ape was a privilege, and people traveled from around the world to experience it. I couldn't help joining the queue and getting swept up in the hysteria. I also couldn't afford anything inside, so I took mental snapshots. Bape wallets, Bape outerwear. A Pepsi collaboration with Bape camouflage cans. Co-branded pieces with Supreme. An artist project with Stash. I never looked at T-shirts and hoodies the same way after that. And as much as I was fascinated by this culture, I'd never have imagined that one day I'd be making a living from it.

A Bathing Ape took my hand and led me further down the corridors of Japanese streetwear. I learned that prior to Ape, Nigo and Jun Takahashi were partners in the seminal NOWHERE boutique. Jun carried on to create one of my favorite lines, Undercover—a predominantly women's fashion label that evolved to make avant-garde men's apparel as well. Then there were the very cool and very sought-after brands WTAPS and Neighborhood, propagating a more westernized, military, and biker aesthetic in Japanese streetwear. I also discovered a tiny clubhouse of a boutique, in the back of the Harajuku neighborhood, called Bounty Hunter. The founder, Hikaru Iwanaga, started off with vinyl collectibles but went from toys to streetwear as his audience clamored for his signature black-and-white punk-style T-shirts. Of all the labels and designers making news out of Tokyo, I was most drawn to Bounty Hunter. It was probably the hardcore punk thing, but Hikaru's simplicity in design, frankness in opinion, and integrity around selling out exemplified everything I wanted in a clothing brand.

One day, I returned home to our Nagoya apartment to a stack of mail. Misa was still at her job at the elementary school, so I picked through the envelopes at the kitchen table. There was a big packet from Loyola Law School—"Congratulations!" I had been admitted for the fall semester of 2002. My time in Japan was drawing to a close, as were my Peter Pan years of freelance writing and designing. It was time to grow up and get a real job.

Back to the United States. Back to reality.

IN THE summer of 2002, I started at Loyola Law School in downtown Los Angeles. With my background in activism, I was curious about public interest or human rights work. I could make enough money to live, help out the underserved and voiceless, then focus on my art in the evenings. Maybe after graduating, I'd go work for the ACLU.

On my first day, I signed up for the National Lawyers Guild, the nation's oldest and largest progressive bar association. Upholding the mantra of "Human rights over property interests," I spent most of my time with the NLG wearing its fluorescent-green cap and documenting police brutality at protests.

Then I learned about the big law firms like O'Melveny & Myers and Manatt, Phelps & Phillips.* For almost all legal students, a big-firm gig is the pot at the end of the rainbow. Students invest three years of their lives, racking up crushing debt, in

---

* I always thought it'd be cool and subversive to name a brand like a big law firm. Kim & Shenassafar LLP?

hope of beginning careers with $125,000-a-year starting salaries and offices with gyms and built-in supermarkets (it wasn't until much later that I realized the law firms did this so you wouldn't escape). The prospect of lawyering for a towering Century City firm was enticing. Partners would descend on our campus and coax recruits with Dodgers tickets, fancy dinners, and sports cars.

I was scared straight for that first semester, throwing elbows against Harvard grads and overachievers, gunning for that blue-ribbon placement in the top 10 percent of the class. The only way to secure job interviews with the better firms after school was by standing atop the other 90 percent of your classmates. Because we were graded on a curve (meaning half the class would be in the bottom 50 percent), friends became rivals, study groups splintered apart, and by finals it was every man and woman for themselves.

FOR THE first time in my life, I actually tried at school, instead of sleeping through my classes and cheating on exams. I'd treated high school and college as recreational, but law school was different. Perhaps it was the fear of failing into nothingness or the peer pressure of intense competition, but I was now warring it out against one hundred other sharks like me. We had all cut corners and conned our way to good grades, but now we were pitted against each other, like a battle royal of swindlers. That first year of law school, I ground myself down to the bone and discovered my parents' work ethic buried inside.

I was trying to become a lawyer so that I could be an artist, and although that sounds as dumb to me now as it did to everyone else back then, I was crestfallen with how my plan was backfiring. Law was clearly not for me; neither was a professional life. I wasn't opposed to the work—it was honorable and challenging, and I was good at it. I just didn't feel as if I fit the mold. Deep down, I longed to rekindle my pursuits in design, photography, and creative writing and connect them with my appreciation of street fashion. I devised an extracurricular summer project to follow my first year of law school where I would take my art, print it on T-shirts to be sold at cool boutiques, and write about it on my blog. If my drawings and paintings weren't getting recognition in galleries or on the internet, then T-shirts would advertise my talents. There were no plans to turn this into a brand or to make money. I called it the Bobby Kim Project (very original) and advertised it on my website's splash page to absolutely no one at all.

PART TWO

9. BURN

"GUYS, WHAT THE hell is going on here?" Tommy Hilfiger's partner, Kenneth, is tapping his pen nervously along the edge of a financial report in front of him. Kenneth, my partner, Ben, and I are wedged in the back corner of Park's BBQ. Grill smoke fills the room, heightening the spirited, drunken energy as we clear small trays of *banchan* and pull in closer around the documents on the table. Enclosed are the last six months of our company's expected projections alongside actual hard earnings. Our hearts sink as we survey the figures.

In the fall of 2013, ten years after Ben and I founded The Hundreds, we started a serious dialogue with the fashion designer

Tommy Hilfiger and his team of attorneys and finance officers. We were looking for a fresh set of eyes on our business. We were looking for a partner with experience and resources that would offer an injection of capital. And we were looking to rebuild our brand with an eye toward the future. We were also looking for a bit of peace of mind to the tune of a few million dollars each. It was time to reward ourselves after a decade of grinding. We felt we deserved it.

In the first few months of that budding partnership between The Hundreds and Tommy Hilfiger, all signs pointed to a happy outcome for both parties. Not only did we respect each other, but our revenue and profits were strong, proving a smart investment for Tommy's group. Tommy offered a deep well of production resources, connections to large factories, and of course decades of invaluable experience in the garment business. Dreams of a successful partnership with Tommy Hilfiger robbed me of countless nights of sleep. Finally, I'd be assured that all my years of hard work building and growing The Hundreds' brand were not in vain. If the company crashed tomorrow, I'd still be all right, at least financially.

"No need for alarm just yet, but this is a little worrisome," Kenneth said.

Here we were, wading through page after page of dream-crushing spreadsheets. Our numbers were trending in the wrong direction. Our decline was slow, almost imperceptible, but for a company that only knew how to climb, everything looked upside down.

Of course, we weren't totally asleep at the wheel. For the past few seasons, we'd done our best to adapt to a volatile market. The streetwear bubble of the late 2000s had popped—indie boutiques were caving, brands were folding—and the big fashion houses were shaping a new paradigm by crossing skate culture with haute couture. Having ridden a decade-long wave, The Hundreds had reached its crest and began to crash. One by one, accounts stopped placing orders. Retail stores weren't just adjusting their buys; with the rise of online shopping, many simply ceased operation. Our European business took a hit as the euro plummeted and distributors evaporated, no longer able to afford the markup on American brands. And in China, a drought devastated the cotton crop, inflating production costs.

All breakups trigger the same series of emotions: at first, discomfort and confusion; later, the coldness of finality. As the email chains between The Hundreds and Tommy Hilfiger got shorter and the conference calls fewer, it became clear that we were breaking up. That night at Park's BBQ marked the last of a string of dinners between the two companies. Months later, a low valuation of our business from Tommy's people would signal the end.

Fashion trends can turn at the drop of a hat. It's a fast and schizophrenic beast on which there appears to be no reliable science. In The Hundreds' first ten years, we rejected this truth, like a dinosaur that can't fathom an earth-cracking meteor. In our eyes, everything was going fine, we were thriving, and our success had no foreseeable end. Yes, fashion is finicky, but we'd convinced ourselves that we were more than just a fad. We were running a lifestyle brand based on our own lifestyle; we were in control of our own destiny.

We were, unfortunately, gravely mistaken.

10. KILL 'EM MALL

I'm not a punk, how can I be?
Show me the way to conformity
—Descendents, "I'm Not a Punk"

BEN AND I have only ever really gotten into one fight. Of course, there have been plenty of disagreements, and there are times when I've wanted to tackle him through a window. Those clashes arise out of the friction between art and commerce. Like, when I want to collaborate with an obscure sculptor who designed album covers for a nineties stoner rock band with a cult following. It's a cool story, but not exactly a fruitful return on investment. Or in our seasonal previews when Ben cuts weaker pieces from our collection without compassion or warning. As a designer, I'm sensitive and exposed; my art leaves me splayed wide open. And Ben can be abrasive. It never feels good to, for example, be told that a piece you've worked on for weeks "sucks ass." Oh my God, he'd be the worst dentist.

Ben gets frustrated by me too: by my volatility and wild trains of thought. Like the time I installed an aquarium in our shop while he was away on vacation. The rare tropical fish died within a weekend after someone poured beer into the filter. I had to haul the tank out of there, dead, bloated fish and all. "What were you thinking?" Ben demanded, irritated that I hadn't run the idea by him. The answer was that I wasn't thinking. I'd woken up that day and just wanted to see fish in the store.

There's a refrain I hear at every one of Ben's backyard barbecues. His childhood friends will pull me aside and half teasingly, half seriously ask, "How are you still putting up with this guy?" My buddies ask Ben the same about me. We are both obstinate and selfish and uncooperative. I imagine this is why we ended up working for ourselves: no one else would take us. I like to think of myself as laid-back, but the reality is that eventually everybody rubs me the wrong way. I'm the most gregarious misanthrope you'll ever meet, like Larry David on Molly. I've never held on to a best friend and can only take people in spurts. Ben, meanwhile, is more my wife than my wife. After fifteen years of growing The Hundreds together—breathing the same office air, sharing at least a meal a day, and seeing the world from the same vantage point—I'd say we're probably composed of nearly identical brain matter.

That one real fight—it didn't involve fists or broken teeth. There were no fingers pointed. It wasn't about jealousy or ego. And we didn't hurl unforgivable insults at each other. In fact, the most haunting part of the fight was its silent end. I'd simply walked out of a meeting with Ben, our sales director, Scotty iLL, our former marketing director, Ashley, and the rest of our executive team. I got into my car and sped off into L.A. rush hour traffic.

The meeting was about selling The Hundreds to the mall. For the first seven years, we had limited our wholesale distribution to premier international boutiques, core skate shops, and purist streetwear retailers. Stores like Union in New York, Wish in Atlanta, and Starcow in Paris. Although there were certain border towns where we sold to independent mall-based accounts—the coolest shops in those area codes—we purposefully abstained from nationwide chains like Tillys, Metropark, and Pacific Sunwear (later known as PacSun). We resisted the call, even after our competitors at the time opened the skate/street chain Zumiez. Beyond any philosophical opposition we might have had to selling our gear in malls, we just never felt ready for the big time.

The first chain store we distributed through was a Southern California–based action sports retailer named Active Ride Shop. Several years into the brand, I was visiting my parents back home in Riverside and went in search of cool stores. We weren't selling our brand in Riverside yet; in fact, we were nowhere close to the county. There were a couple core skate shops, but they weren't interested in streetwear, so I meandered into Active. There were a handful of brands that complemented The Hundreds (like the Seventh Letter and Stüssy) on the tables, so I squinted and tried to imagine our product on the floor.

"Hey, are you Bobby?"

A ginger-haired sales associate with thick black plugs stuck his hand out.*

"I know what you do. It's pretty cool. You're from here, right? So, how come you don't sell The Hundreds in Riverside?"

---

* This kid, Graham, became a prolific streetwear designer and entrepreneur. Not long after we met, he left Active and opened the Us Versus Them boutique in Temecula. His brand went on to sell worldwide, at one point locking in a partnership with Stüssy.

Good point. This was my backyard. Why would I rob my own people of The Hundreds? It didn't seem fair that just because someone was geographically undesirable, they shouldn't be able to buy cool streetwear. How many Bobbys were growing up in this town without access to better brands? Reselling and on-line shopping had yet to take hold in the global streetwear marketplace, so these suburban kids were stuck with second-tier clothing companies. I remember this well, having shopped for back-to-school clothes at the swap meet throughout my youth.

We opened Active Riverside as an official account. Then we went down the line and sold to Active's network of Southern California stores in Valencia, Burbank, Brea, and beyond. That broke our hard-line, restrictive sales doctrine. As much as I admired the exclusivity of prime streetwear, Ben and I and The Hundreds were inclusionary by default. Although we had to fake the funk early to portray a certain elitist image, it's just never been in our nature as humans to be snobs. Our top priority is to design and make quality product, but we also want people to be able to have fair access to our work.

Active Ride Shop was one thing, though. Although widespread, most Actives are freestanding stores, located outside traditional shopping malls. Selling to stores inside the mall—like Zumiez and PacSun—was an entirely different story.

The mall means different things to different people. For midwesterners and the suburban middle class, the mall can be a community grounds—a shelter from unforgiving weather, a haven for bored youth. For senior citizens, the mall concourse is an indoor track for Sunday morning strolls and people watching. In the cities, malls may be classified as tourist destinations.

The mall also means different things to different generations. In the 1970s and '80s, malls birthed their own youth culture (see Jason Lee in *Mallrats* or the zombie flick *Dawn of the*

Dead). The MTV-era American teenager was cast in the foamy mold of Orange Julius and Merry Go Round. This is where Valley Girl–speak originated and big Jersey hair sprouted, where horny adolescent boys stared down girls' B.U.M. tank tops from second-floor banisters (before home video game systems seduced them from the arcades, and even longer before the internet stole their attention). The mall provided many Americans their first job. In the 1990s, there were about three million mall jobs for teens sixteen to nineteen years old. The United States was erecting 140 shopping malls a year. Supermalls, like the Mall of America in Bloomington, Minnesota, pumped hormones into a consumer epidemic. Many Americans planned entire recreational days at the mall, starting with breakfast at the pretzel stand and ending with nighttime desserts at Mrs. Fields.*

In towns like Riverside, which account for the majority of America, the shopping malls host the coolest brick-and-mortar shops in the neighborhood. I confess one of my first jobs was working retail in a rave shop called Limbo Lounge. I peddled choker necklaces made of shower curtain chains, black-light posters, and geek glasses with yellow lenses. I worked with a buff rebel dude named Jason who shaped his eyebrows and wore platform shoes. And by "worked with" him, I mean I covered the floor while he nailed girls in the dressing rooms. My manager was a bottle-blond Colombian woman named Cali whom I'd nicknamed Caliente. I sold visors and UFO cargo pants to teenagers shopping with their parents. They reminded me of myself when I was in the eighth grade, dragging my mom to the mall to hunt for Stüssy and Freshjive. For me, a kid who grew

---

* Today, the North American mall is buckling under the immensity of e-commerce. Its future is predicated on experiential distinctions, like Southern California–style outdoor malls or layouts that mimic mom-and-pop Main Street shopping. But malls as we remember them will soon be history, and retail as a whole will soon be completely renovated.

up ninety minutes outside the city, my comprehension of streetwear was reinforced by the American shopping mall. We didn't have Animal Farm or KITH. In nineties Everytown, U.S.A., the retailers that sold the hot underground "streetwear" were Nordstrom, Beach Access, and Pacific Sunwear—all of them mall accounts. Nordstrom, the upscale department store, was the top-shelf Stüssy depot in the Southland. Beach Access was chiefly a surf and skate shop in the same mall as Limbo Lounge, but it started delving into the stylish beach/urban wear that re-iterated Stüssy's spirit. They carried Drawls and Underworld Element, funky indie brands that printed cartoon character T-shirt graphics. And PacSun was forty minutes out, at the Mont-clair Plaza and Santa Ana Main Place Mall. They stocked Jive and had a strong supporting cast of rave/street companies like 26 Red, Blür, and Sjobeck.

Even though I sourced my streetwear fashion in the mid-1990s from the shopping mall, I was always hesitant to actu-ally shop there. I'd put my head down, make a beeline from my favorite brands to the register, and be back in the car before you could say, "Fall into the Gap." I wanted to be different, to stand apart from the rest of the kids in my school. It's why I rejected pop music* and must-see TV.† Mall clothes, to me, were a by-product of lazy shopping and middling taste. I mean, every-one's mom shopped back-to-school clothing at the mall. Half the kids in my class wore the same Gotcha shorts and Quiksilver flannel hoodies on the first day. As I entered high school, my lifestyle choices had to come from somewhere dark and distant, far away from the uninspired haunts of jocks and cheerleaders.

---

* It wasn't until much, much later in my life that I appreciated the art of radio stars like Tupac and Nirvana. The notion that these artists couldn't be any good because other people listened to them seems ridiculous now.
† To this day, I have yet to watch an episode of *Friends*.

I watched *Faces of Death*, *Dolemite*, and Cheech and Chong, not *My So-Called Life*. And I shopped for my clothes at Rebel skate shop or the California Cheap Skates mail-order catalog, not Marshalls or JCPenney.

THIS WASN'T the first time we'd talked about selling to malls, and it wasn't the last, but it proved to be the tipping point in a discussion that would eventually push The Hundreds into its next chapter.

Ben had initiated the meeting.

After taking a deep breath, he'd said, "We're about to enter a new phase, and I need you to be on board with this next step."

We were sitting in my office in our old downtown L.A. warehouse, right outside the fashion district on a nowhere street. The cops had given up on South Wall Street as two rival gangs shared its jurisdiction. Graffiti wars continued in broad daylight. Metal scrapyards and leather makers repainted their front walls weekly. And there was a homeless encampment that inched closer to our doorstep every day.

Ben had called all the head dudes into my office—a space that barely fit me and a desk. We sat on the carpet, the bookcase, anywhere that was free from vinyl figures and Nikes and would take a sweaty ass. The rest of the guys looked down at the floor while Ben spoke. I wasn't surprised or caught off guard by what my partner was about to propose. There had been whispers of our entering the mall stores for the past year.

"At some point in the near future," Ben had warned me, "we're gonna reach a crossroads. We don't have to open up distribution to the mall, but we have to move more volume somehow."

The Hundreds hadn't yet plateaued, and the brand was far from declining. On the contrary, our rapid growth was outpacing our infrastructure. Without any investors or outside capital backing us, and without the power of e-commerce as it performs today, we needed more money to finance our operation. We were adding product SKUs and had to pay more up front to the factories. Staff had gone from five persons to fifty in a couple of years. Our seventeen-thousand-square-foot headquarters was bursting at the seams—a Noah's ark of salesmen, marketers, and designers. Chairs backed into one another; a private conversation was shared by all. Our warehouse was a Q*bert-styled city of cardboard boxes.

Today, brands like ours have the option of direct-to-consumer distribution, which keeps overhead low. That's because of the shift in attitudes toward buying clothes online. But in 2010, brands still relied heavily on wholesale distribution for sales and marketing. The only way to reach people in most markets was by selling clothes to the right shops in their neighborhoods. This process required more laborers and operations on the brand side. We beefed up our sales team, took on international distributors, and hired more designers to expand our collection, because all the different shops wanted to be blessed with segmented, unique product.

Despite my ignorance, The Hundreds had evolved into a legitimate business. These were the "clubhouse to corporate" years, when much of our original crew couldn't keep up or downright quit.

"Nothing was the same."

Our focus had slowly evolved from being cool to being profitable, and with that came goals and expectations, and that spoiled a lot of longtime friendships. We went from being buddies to being bosses, and not everyone was on board. There was plenty of love lost in the transition, deep beefs that hold to this day with former friends, but the only relationship we cared about investing in—the one that would pay us handsomely back in the end—was between us and The Hundreds and the customer.

Only problem was that in order to sustain this trajectory, we needed to take money (from investors or new partners) or make money. We weren't interested in letting an outside voice speak for—or take a piece of—our brand. So we would have to either open more of our own retail stores (we didn't have the where-withal; after having self-funded and operated four stores in four years, we were panting with exhaustion), intentionally muffle sales to increase demand (which was high-risk at this stage), or open distribution to a greater audience.

We had capped out in sales at the handful of streetwear and sneaker stores worldwide. Next Scotty would conquer skate retailers out of our love for skateboarding and support of the culture. At this time, skate was coming down from a long and dizzying high set off by years of wildly successful shoe sales. DC, DVS, and Osiris had maxed out in core skate shops, so those accounts grew increasingly keen on American streetwear brands that were tangential to retro sneaker culture. As Nike and adidas ate up more share of the skate market, crossover labels like The Hundreds, Huf, and Primitive captured a moment reminiscent of the mid-1990s indie skate brand explosion.

But as the larger skate companies crumbled, skateboarding retailers became saturated with a wave of endemic indie skate/street labels like Dime, Magenta, and Fucking Awesome, and grew resistant to original streetwear. That left brands like ours with little option but to turn up the juice in the malls.

"We're kinda assed out."

"I know, I know," I muttered as Ben broke it all down. "Are we sure there's no other viable option here?"

As much as I couldn't see myself personally shopping in the mall, I was never opposed to selling our brand there . . . some-day. Some of the coolest brands are also the biggest: Nike, Apple, Polo. Did the fact that these names weren't limited, and were found in department stores and shopping centers, make them any less cool? Or, was part of their appeal that they were ubiquitous and adopted by every household?

Plus, consumer patterns had changed, and who knew where streetwear would be in the next decade. As much as I hated when my favorite underground artists made their way into the mainstream, I wondered how long they could survive by play-ing small clubs and fighting change. The hard reality was that as much as I fancied The Hundreds as a small-time creative project, it was a business. And the point of a business is to make money, to sell for a profit, and to keep the ball in the air for as long as possible. That's capitalism, folks!

Furthermore, I wanted to do more creatively. With The Hun-dreds reaching new heights, my scope of possibilities dilated. I wasn't content with graphic T-shirts and baseball caps anymore. I wanted to design footwear, and I wanted to use better materi-als in our garments. Yet as much as we valued the importance of quality and appreciated how our designers were learning and growing more sophisticated in clothing construction, we just couldn't meet the minimums on fabric yardage. Ben and I had our sights set on larger, noisier collaborations with record labels and movie studios, but these were cumbersome licensing deals that demanded minimum guarantees (we were on the line for a specific number, whether or not the collection sold). There's a thin line between avarice and greed, and although I had little need for extra cash to line my pockets, I wanted a better lining for The Hundreds' pockets. Literally.

"No matter where I turn, I end up back at the mall," Ben confessed. "The skate shops are phasing out streetwear. That's most of our wholesale doors. There aren't enough streetwear shops out there, and eventually they'll replace us with a newer, younger brand, because that's what they do. I know Zumiez is in the mall, but they're stocking the right brands for us to sit next to. They're exiting out of the dead surf and skate industry and introducing a whole new generation to streetwear."

Zumiez, one of the two largest mall-based skate/street shops, was excited to take us on. Our friends were already being prominently showcased at Zumiez, and the store's buyers were convinced that The Hundreds would excel in some of the major markets. PacSun, the competitor retailer, had also expressed interest in our label. It had almost a thousand stores across America.

"Then we might as well sell to every store in the mall," I griped. Of course, I didn't actually mean that, but I wanted to make a point. Although Zumiez and PacSun were considered of a different class compared with other mall retailers, I didn't see the difference between their stores and a Hot Topic or a Spencer's. You could smell the grease from the food court combining with the perfumes from Victoria's Secret in these stores. And no matter where you stood in the building, you'd hear the thumping music from Abercrombie and the grating wails of toddlers at Build-a-Bear. The way I saw it—considering everything I knew and hated about the shopping mall experience—if The Hundreds came to be identified as a mall brand, our core customers would surrender their loyalty to us.

Ben answered, "Of course we're gonna lose a big chunk of

our customers, but think about how many new fans we'll be exposed to."

In my head, we were already there. It's a sacrifice that any independent artist faces in transcending their underground appeal. Much of your die-hard fan base, the ones who nurtured your brand from birth, will take your success hard. They don't want to share you with the rest of the world. They feel special, like keepers of the world's best secret. Courting newbie fans will inevitably tarnish that relationship.

From a purely business standpoint, there are always more newbies than there are early adopters. A *lot more*. They're not the ones who keep the brand grounded, and they don't stick around for long, but if you're looking for numbers, that's where you'll find them.* By 2010, our core audience had stuck with us for seven years. But they were starting to graduate from The Hundreds. Most of our young fans started following us somewhere between middle school and high school. Finding themselves among new peers as they entered college, they were beginning to reinvent themselves, creating new identities. And very often, with a new identity comes a new style of dress. Our first devoted fan base was coming of age and saying goodbye to graphic tees and hooded sweatshirts. Some would elevate their style to include trendy, high-fashion labels; some would move into suits and professional attire; and some would start dedicating their hard-earned dollars to sounder investments like property. But every seven years or so, there's a palpable shift in the trends— and the brands—that kids follow, and The Hundreds was about to hit that moment of flux between its first and its second generation of devotees.

---

* Most consumers, of any product, in fact, are newbies. They aren't concerned with setting trends, but they also don't want to be late to the party. This is the bell curve of the "mainstream."

Everything lined up. The mall decision was rational, but I wouldn't budge. And I wasn't just fighting with Ben. At some point, I'd realized that this fight wasn't between me and anyone else in the room at all. It wasn't between me and The Hundreds, either. I was embroiled in a war with Bobby Kim. I was walled in by this fiction I had told myself. I was living a narrative that making money was wrong, that being popular was uncool, and that growing our business would cause us to concede some shred of authenticity.

I was stuck, and the only way I saw to get unstuck was to run away. So, I did just that.

I'D RUN away three times in my young life. The first was when I was a toddler, so I don't remember the specifics. As the story goes, my mom watched me follow my older brother, Larry, out the door; we often played in the schoolyard across the street. An hour or so later, Larry returned with his basketball, but no baby brother.

"Where's Bobby?" my mother asked.

"Huh? I thought he stayed behind?"

A frantic, neighborhood-wide search ensued. Panicked phone calls were made to my dad and family friends. Eventually, my mom would find me in a barren stretch of dirt bordering a nearby baseball field. I'd been drifting through the dry brush like a stray tumbleweed, totally aloof, my jacket flung over my shoulder, my eyes poised on the horizon, marching into the sun and the infinite beyond, like a tiny Korean cowboy.

I was eight the second time I ran away. My mom and I had been snarled in a nasty argument, one of many that would wound and scar me well into adolescence. I'd penned a tragic farewell letter that was two paragraphs short of a suicide note: "I love you all, but I can't stay here anymore." I'd attached the note to my pillow with Scotch tape, stashed my toys and books in a JanSport, and then suddenly realized that I had nowhere to go. In the movies, the runaway folds a PBJ sandwich into a knapsack, hops aboard an empty train car or hitchhikes on the bed of a dusty pickup truck, and wakes up in a magical land. There wasn't a train station within fifty miles, and in my neighborhood those trucks were driven by racist child molesters. I slumped to the floor, stowed away under my bed, curled up as tightly as I could, and held my breath.

What felt like four or five hours was probably only fifteen minutes or so, but my silence barreled through the house and raised my mom's eyebrow. I saw her feet come to the door, her voice genuinely concerned.

"Bobby? Where are you?"

I smiled. I imagined her reading my runaway letter, those barbs of guilt hooking deep inside her heart, the regret and sorrow ravaging her existence. Then I felt an unexpected tug. It started deep down by my toes and crawled slowly up my spine. By the time it reached my throat, it closed my airway and choked me. I pushed it upward into my reddening face and felt the tears burst from my eyes. I was feeling pretty freaking sad . . . and guilty.

My mom's feet shuffled closer to the bed. Could she see me? I heard the rustle of the paper as she unfolded it. She read the letter out loud, and by this time Larry had walked in, confused and curious (and probably smirking).

"Oh no," my mother said in Korean to him. "Bobby has run away! What do we do without him? My heart breaks."

Even then, I knew she was pretending. I'm pretty sure she saw me under the bed as soon as she stood in the doorway. But my imagination had taken creative license with this pitiful scenario. I was already in the final chapter of the saga in my head, with my mother wailing over my limp, lifeless body—a bag of raggedy bones discarded at the bottom of a drainage ditch by a trucker. I was sure that in her final years, with her hair grayed and her skin wrinkled like a peeled chestnut, she would hold on to my ghost, which would follow her to her grave.

"I'm right here!" I reluctantly cried and crawled out from under the bed frame with my head bowed. I sank into my mom's warm embrace. It felt good to be home.

The third time I ran away would be the last time. Six months later, I'd finally leave the house for good. I had just turned seventeen, and my dad and I had butted heads in another one of our epic fights. I was a man and could fight back now, but instead I bolted for the door, jumped into my truck, peeled out of the driveway, and drove to my friend Peter's house. Then to Billy's. Then to Kevin's. I bounced around for a week, occasionally talking to my mom from my friends' home phones. That weekend, I returned home—not because I wanted to, but because I'd worn out my welcome sleeping on other people's floors. I'd run out of rope. My dad and I barely talked for the remainder of that summer before I left for college. I'd hold on to, and channel, the anger that I felt during that episode for years and years to come.

MY TRUCK kicked up a cloud of dust as I sped away from the office. I couldn't think straight and bounced around the freeway feeling angry and defeated. But deep down, I was scared. I flashed back to my childhood memories of running away. Here I was, fleeing again, unsure of where I was headed.

Was I just as lost and aimless as I was at three years old?

Maybe I was trying to prove a point by causing a scene as I did at eight? Or was it simply time for me to move on, like when I left home for college at seventeen? Had I outgrown The Hundreds? If so, I told myself, I should keep driving and never look back.

11. IN GOOD COMPANY

COULDN'T TELL what ethnicity he was. Mexican? Cuban? What I could tell was that this guy was brown, round, and furry. Benjamin Shenassafar and I shared the same class section at Loyola Law School. As it turns out, he was Iranian American (or Persian, as he prefers), like the rest of his woolly entourage.

Yet Ben stood apart from the rest of his Persian clique at Loyola. The first son of a second marriage, Ben grew up with his little brother, Jon, in the Valley. He loved the Rams and hip-hop music and had graduated from Ice Cube's high school. (In fact, if you put him in a Raiders jersey with a pair of sunglasses, he'd resemble an Arab interpretation of the N.W.A. rapper.) And in those first few weeks of law school, there was something else about Ben that caught my attention: he had style. The kid was always planted in a fresh pair of retro sneakers, crispy Diesel denim, and Gucci shades. He'd wear obnoxious lime-green Supreme tees to campus and was the ringleader of his pack. He was the only person to go to law school without ever going to law school. Like in a high school comedy flick, he was the guy who ditched class all year, showed up for the final exam, and would have everyone asking, "You're in this class?" And, of course, he would score high. Don't ask me how (or whom he paid), but he breezed through every semester.

"Nice IVs," I'd remarked. We were standing out front of the lecture hall before class early one morning, and I was admiring Ben's black Nike Air Jordan IVs.* These were my favorite sneakers of all time, and they hadn't been reissued in years, so this guy was either a collector, like me, or about to get robbed.

"Oooh," he sounded, kneeling down to get a better look at my feet. I was wearing custom Louis Vuitton Air Force 1s, a short-lived trend in 2002 that married street culture with high fashion. By replacing the standard Nike swoosh with one patterned with the Louis Vuitton monogram, designers like Raif Adelberg hiked the price tag from $80 to $350–$400 for a pair. Only a select few indie clothing stores like Union on La Brea stocked these black-market mash-ups. Premium sneaker boutiques didn't exist yet in America.

"Where'd you get your Supreme shirt?" I was testing him.

"I just got back from New York."

This was the right answer. In fact, it was pretty much the

---

* Arguably the greatest shoe of all time, the Air Jordan IV is the Nike designer Tinker Hatfield's crowning achievement—a basketball shoe that works well with shorts, pants, or dresses.

only answer in 2002. Before streetwear was prevalent on eBay, before it was stocked at your local mall, and before brands started to open their own direct e-commerce stores, your best shot at owning a Supreme garment was to fly to New York or Tokyo and visit its brick-and-mortar stores. This was true for all streetwear of the period—brands like SSUR, Alife, and Recon. About as many American brands as you could count on two hands sold their product in their own store. Then there were the handful of domestic multi-brand shops and Japanese distributors. In short, if you lived anywhere outside these cities, you were working airfare into your clothing budget.

Ben and I hit it off, in what transpired as a friendly rivalry over retro sneakers. I'd wear maple Dunk Highs on a Tuesday, and Ben would show up in black and blue BWs on a Wednesday. He always had the stronger Air Max game, while I'd win with trainers—the Mitas, the Viotechs, the Bo Jacksons. Outside Nike-Talk, the collectors' message board, there was no online platform that spoke to the sneakerhead. No TV shows, no apps, no official events. About the only thing tying us sneaker enthusiasts together was that unspoken nod over vintage Nikes.

I had my group of friends and Ben had his. Late nights in the library, our circles would meet in the middle, like a Venn diagram. While studying for our first-year final exams, Ben, his best friend, Mak, my homie Drew, and I would take breaks between the bookshelves to dream about the infinite possibilities our futures held. Ben and Mak were always on the money. With summer approaching, they were scheming up ways to make some extra cash. Drew was leaving for Tokyo in a week for a legal internship, and considering the Japanese influence on the sneaker resale market, he suggested sourcing the inventory for us to build a stateside distribution operation. The rare, retro sneaker market was still laying its roots in the United States, so avid American collectors were champing at the bit for the rare Nikes and adidas that Japanese sellers and collectors had been hoarding for a decade. In those days, shoe brands also issued special editions intended for sale strictly in Asian territories, so there was a demand for those too. eBay was a collector's best bet to buy the 3M/snakeskin Air Force 1s or Stüssy Blazers. Or, you could try your luck at back-door sneaker boutiques like Sportie LA on Melrose or Chinaman's in downtown San Diego.* We could charge a premium for importing these treasures, do something we loved and genuinely cared about, and, for a season, forget that we were lawyers.

The morning after final exams, we held our first meeting at Ben and Mak's Mid-City apartment to discuss our looming business empire. The guys lived in squalor like typical postcollege bachelors: dishes piled high in the kitchen, *Scarface* poster in the bedroom, moldy shower curtain in the bathroom. Regardless of the time of day, it always smelled as if someone had just woken up. We sat around the living room coffee table, set aside the *Playboys*, and even removed the bong. This was serious business.

Drew, our "Japanese distributor," cleared his throat and spoke first.

"I'm out, guys. I'm sorry. But I've been thinking about it, and I really won't have the time between school and travels to work on this thing. I still think it's a good idea, and maybe I can find someone while I'm there to connect you with, but . . ."

Ben, Mak, and I broke down and laughed. Our pipe dream had already burst not two minutes into our first business meeting. Drew cut the silence by wishing us all a fruitful summer

---

* Most of these stores were poorly merchandised, flea-market-style shitshows of deadstock inventory that the owners had accumulated over the years. When the retro sneaker boom hit, they'd hatched accidental gold mines. One man's trash became a sneakerhead's treasure.

and making a graceful exit into the balmy June sun and a promising legal career.*

"So, what now?" Mak asked.

Ben started reaching for his bong.

I took a deep breath. "There's this thing I'm trying to do, actually." I explained the Bobby Kim Project. "I want to funnel my art, photography, design, and writing into one outlet. Imagine a company that's half T-shirt brand, half online magazine. The T-shirt graphics all have a substantive story to them, which I'll write about on my blog. That way, you're not just buying a logo or a Che Guevara stencil without knowing the meaning behind it. As far as the magazine, everybody's focused on New York and Japan right now, but we have talented friends here in L.A. who are getting clipped from the conversation. Los Angeles is getting a bad rap with the reality shows, Paris Hilton hijinks, and Von Dutch trucker caps. But I'm a writer; we can flip this. I'll interview graffiti artists, musicians, and designers who are putting our city on the map. I'll use aliases to make it look as if we have an editorial staff. These articles will help build the brand's lifestyle. That's our marketing. It all works together; the T-shirts and the magazine inform each other. The best part about it is the internet is free and it's wide open for the taking. Nobody's doing anything like this. This isn't just a clothing company or an online magazine; it's more than that. It's a 'lifestyle project.'"

Ben and Mak lit up (both figuratively and literally) and latched on immediately. Mak was a slick hustler, a born salesman. Ben had experience peddling garments—cheap downtown neckties out of swap meet booths in high school and Nordstrom

---

* Drew and I are still good friends. He has made a successful career as an attorney and lives in Palos Verdes with his wife, Kathy, and children, Walter and Bea, who are better than you at every board sport you can imagine. And, as of this writing, they only come up to your elbows.

suits in college. But above all, the three of us were big sneaker-heads and fans of the artist-led T-shirt brands coming out of New York and Tokyo. Why couldn't we play too? We didn't have much money, but with the internet who cared? For brand aware-ness, we'd spread the word through message boards that ca-tered to the community like Superfuture and NikeTalk. I would design T-shirts in the spirit of the brands we wore in the nine-ties like X-Large and Freshjive. And our secret weapon, even if we didn't totally appreciate it then, would be my blog. I had a voice and I knew how to use it to connect people. I could mobi-lize a movement around a brand.

I was just happy that I'd be able to draw, take photos, design, and tell stories. I hadn't even contemplated squeezing a profit out of this thing. For me, designing and storytelling were born of necessity. I needed the creative outlet to stay sane after a year of analyzing contracts, dressing like a nimrod, and wrap-ping my head around the rule against perpetuities. I figured the cost of screen printing T-shirts was a fair trade offering, if noth-ing else, the freedom to create. I hardly noticed the two Persians in the room salivating with dollar signs for eyes.

"I know how to make money doing this," Ben said. "Easy."

12.· FANNING THE FLAMES OF CONTENT

WE LIKE TO say "Since 1980" because that is the year in which Ben and I were both born and the brand is a reflection of our lives. But The Hundreds as a business entity officially launched on July 27, 2003. That was the day the website went live. Later that week, once our T-shirts hit Fred Segal in Santa Monica, we'd start directing traffic there. We'd packaged each T-shirt in a clear vinyl bag the way Bape did. I always loved that part of the customer experience, as if each piece held artistic value and needed protection from the elements. On the front, we'd screen printed our web address, thehundreds.com. I wanted the customers to understand that they weren't just buying a T-shirt. Like in a scavenger hunt, the shirt was a clue to a greater treasure buried in the internet. The clothes unlocked a story. There was an entire universe attached to each T-shirt that I was blogging about on the site.

People always ask, what came first, the clothes or the blog? But from its inception, thehundreds.com was bifurcated between "Collection" and the current blog's predecessor, "Chronicles." Under the Collection tab were our latest offerings of graphic T-shirts. Each tee was buttressed with a story behind its graphic, often political in nature or a commentary on society and culture. The Chronicles illustrated the lifestyle around our brand. The section was dedicated to magazine-style profiles on personalities within our community. With the streetwear scene so preoccupied with Japanese and New York designers, we felt like Los Angeles was getting the shaft. L.A. had a burgeoning street culture that was being ignored. The cool crowd in this period of L.A. life congregated around nightlife spots like Nacional or Cinespace, as captured in the Cobrasnake's Polaroids. But we witnessed artistic innovation emanating from local brands like Undefeated and Grn Apple Tree, painters like Craola and Buff Monster, and underground hip-hop artists like pre-Fergie Black Eyed Peas and L.A. Symphony. We also knew that streetwear had started in our backyard and was still thriving in the underground. All we had to do was cut through the reality shows and Christian Audigier's bedazzled noise to excavate it.

The Chronicles section was popular, but heavy and laborious to put together. Between interviewing, transcribing, and editing, I found that each article would eat up a week's time. But there were so many things happening every day that I eventually just started populating the news feed with unedited updates as they rolled in. Eventually, the main page started getting all the attention. Readers came for the news feed and stayed for the Chronicles. Short-form, long-form—thehundreds.com was your one-stop shop for quality street-culture editorial.

At the time, the only people producing content online were larger media outlets and high-profile bloggers like Perez Hilton. Before social media, average people didn't spend their days digging for stories to tell. They weren't interested in starring in their own reality show or sharing their opinions with an audience of strangers. In fact, in the early days of social media, sites like Friendster invited your friends to say something about you instead of granting you the space to talk about yourself. There was a degree of privacy then that would be worth one's weight in gold today. And the few of us who did choose to share our stories did so discriminatingly. As a journalist, I didn't consider thehundreds.com a means to highlight my life as much as a platform on which I might highlight the stories of others. After years of following my blog, my readers learned a whole lot about the culture without finding much of anything about me. Today, social media is all about designing a compelling self-portrait, but back then my writing derived from a belief that real artists make the world look better, not themselves. The more I bigged up my crew, the stronger L.A. came to be, the better for all parties involved. A rising tide lifts all boats.

I interviewed Angeleno designers, artists, and musicians who were putting our neighborhood on the map. To inflate our credibility, I'd assign pen names to different articles. But it was all me behind the screen, writing every line and designing every T-shirt. Ben, meanwhile, was on the operations end, dialing numbers and making sales.

There are a few reasons why the blog worked. For one, it lent transparency to our brand, while our competitors sealed the doors shut. There weren't any other blogs that itemized the steps of making a streetwear line for the thousands of other dreamers out there brainstorming ideas for the next big brand.* Day in and day out, I shared our lessons with our readership. We celebrated the highs with the customers and wallowed in the lows together as well. There's no school for this, but my blog was the closest to it. A generation later, all those kids who were raised on my blog would install the next rung on the streetwear ladder. It's not the most shrewd business strategy—cultivating our own competitors—but it's how we ensure that the culture continues. The purpose of every generation—in streetwear and in life—is to make things better and easier for the next generation. The OGs planted the seeds and tended the soil, and my class watered the sapling, so that the kids today could lounge under the tree's shade and pick the fruits.

The blog unmasked the industry we were diving into. I was simultaneously entrepreneur and investigative journalist, educating readers on starting a clothing company and introducing them to the godfathers and backstage players. Streetwear was a clandestine boys' club, off the grid, hidden from Main Street. Even if you knew this universe existed, it wasn't exactly easy to learn its nuances, its politics, and its unspoken rules. You could knock on the door of Alife Rivington Club all you wanted, but they wouldn't let you in if they didn't like what they saw on their security camera. Even if you made it to the cash wrap, there was no guarantee they'd sell you a sweatshirt. Streetwear's cobweb of coolness was impervious, but on thehundreds.com I'd walk you right up to the window.

The blog offered a fresh stream of compelling content. Years before Twitter and Instagram surfaced, those in the know filled

---

* T-shirts are a cheap and fast gateway into brand building. For any amateur businessperson, T-shirts are an ideal first endeavor. You can stick with the traditional program and catapult into seasonal fashion collections. Or you can make hundreds of millions with a direct-to-consumer printables business as Travis Barker did with Famous or Neek did with Anti Social Social Club.

their free time with the long-format eye candy of blogs. While most bloggers updated two or three times a week, I was broadcasting multiple times a day. No matter where I landed in the world, I was ferreting out the Ethernet cords so I could plug back into WordPress and speak to my followers. I'd upload my photos into Adobe, process them, and sew a storyline around the last few hours from smoke-filled boutique back rooms, hospital beds, airport lounges, and after-hours venues. Trade-show weeks were the worst. We'd stay out all night partying in Vegas, and while everyone else retired in the hotel rooms, I'd stumble through a blog report of the day's developments. The next morning, I wouldn't recall having written any of it. But it was this consistent frequency that allowed us to establish a trust with our readers. They knew that as soon as they woke up (I published every night at 2:00 a.m. PST), I'd have their morning streetwear newspaper ready for them.

The blog era was a moment in time during which content creators spoke their minds with total abandon. Before blogs, Nielsen ratings and advertising dollars drove television, radio, and print media. When social media ousted the blogs as the number one source for online content, the popularity contest ensued. The endless pursuit of followers, likes, and comments husked the culture of originality, auto-tuning everyone's voice to the same dull frequency. Blogs, on the other hand, started off as side hustles and passion projects. Without scores, most bloggers weren't tallying followers or gamifying their storytelling. They didn't cater to anyone or curate their messages to grow their audience or turn profits. With no Explore page to measure themselves against, they furnished their unique personal narratives through their own styles and cadences.

In contrast, today, designers and artists are obsessed with

peer review. They need the validation to continue. We're talking hacking the algorithm, dressing the "influencer," and assuaging the masses. Instead of carving out a niche, the next generation of entrepreneurs is glomming on to the masses. They aren't defining a world for themselves. They are molding themselves to the world.

I had the luxury of crafting my brand identity for years before I met my audience. I attribute much of our longevity to the blogging spirit and this fundamental mantra: DIY and DIFY. Do it *for* yourself.

Even though it's impossible to escape the social media rankings, I rarely check the trade news, mind the industry gossip, or monitor market trends. Of course, it is important to have an awareness of customers and competitors, but I do my best to design for myself, write to myself, and conduct my business how I perform best. I know I could have ten times the Instagram followers (and sales) if I formulaically posted what streetwear kids want to see: expensive jewelry, hot girls, and Drake memes. But that's not me, and I don't want to sound like everyone else. Why would I want my voice lost in the crowd? I'd rather stand onstage with the microphone.

"**PHARRELL KNOWS** about my blog?!" I'm stunned, dumbfounded. I'd been blogging for years and was, of course, aware that *somebody* was on the other side. Family members would occasionally make an awkward remark on something illicit they'd seen (hazards of the trade), and friends would ask to guest star. Google Analytics was beginning to take shape, but I didn't trust it. Frankly, I just didn't care to keep score. We weren't monetizing our traffic against advertising, and I couldn't see how knowing the numbers would affect my course of action. Every time I pounded away at that blog, I was speaking to me—like my eight-year-old self, writing in a lock-and-key diary. I'd log my memories, spill my guts, press "Publish," and shut my laptop. As far as I was concerned, I was singing in the shower.

Imagine my shock when Dominick DeLuca from Brooklyn Projects told me that Pharrell Williams had brought up something I'd published on thehundreds.com. My friends Tofer and Todd Tourso had just printed a new season of T-shirts under their fledgling brand, Plain Gravy. I'd featured one of their tees on the front page: a stark purple font spelling out "Pharrell Can't Skate." Pharrell had taken to skateboarding, even adopting the nickname "Skateboard P" and raising the eyebrows of members of the core skate community. P was one of my favorite music producers, but his skateboarding felt contrived (in retrospect, I was afraid of what the pop spotlight meant for skate's underground nature, and Plain Gravy's T-shirt epitomized this frustration). So I blogged about it.

Dom asked, "What's your problem with him skateboarding?"

"I didn't make the shirt!" I said in my defense. "Does he care? And more importantly, why does he read my blog?!"

I never quite figured out if Pharrell felt rubbed the wrong way about it, but members of his clique certainly were. "Bobby Hundreds is a hater!" Lupe Fiasco declared on the *Weekly Drop* podcast weeks later. And I certainly wondered, if Pharrell was reading my blog—even if he had just heard about it recently—who else might be following what I had to say?

For the first time since I'd started blogging, Ben and I logged in to our analytics and retrieved the stats.

Millions. Millions of unique visitors were poring over my words every month, studying my photography, talking shit, and discussing our brand. There were millions of people waiting for me on the other side of the looking glass.

They had found my diary.

13. GET UP KIDS

THE HUNDREDS WAS growing thanks to my blog and our T-shirts, but word had also spread through good old-fashioned word of mouth.

"How did you get your name out there?"

It's a common question from fresh entrepreneurs, maybe the most common. Where to begin? Most start-ups look down the road, and the open frontier overwhelms them. There's so much ground to cover, especially in the age of social media. You kick the doors open with a bold, brave idea and immediately feel small and insignificant in the ocean of competitors. "How will I convert everyone?" you wonder.

I get it, but you're getting ahead of yourself. It was never our aim to make customers of *everyone*. We just needed *someone*. Never underestimate the power of influence in one-on-one encounters. One person's zeal can arouse a movement and compel a community to action.

Passion begets passion.

If you are madly in love with your cause, that fire will stoke a flame in others. The Hundreds was born of a single idea, a spark that precipitated a wildfire.* Speak to the people, one believer at a time. Think of the way a presidential candidate campaigns. Breakfasts in small-town diners, talks in town halls, and meet and greets in family backyards. There is no shortcut to people's hearts. There is no viral craze that will convince your audience overnight. The routes are long and onerous, but warm handshakes and baby photos win elections.

From the start, we met people on their turf. There were no convenient hashtags to spread the word. There were no trending topics to kick-start fads on social media. There was no social media to begin with! The internet was still in its infancy. Most people lived their lives off-line and off their phones. So, the kids didn't come to us. We had to physically deliver our message to them. We sold T-shirts to our friends and begged them to tell their friends. We seized opportunities to set up folding tables at underground hip-hop shows and fund-raisers. Some of these activations didn't necessarily align with our brand, but we didn't have the luxury of saying no. Beggars can't be choosers, and who were we to be picky? Even if we sold only two T-shirts at an event, that was still two more than we'd have sold if we'd just stayed at home talking about our dreams.

---

* This is the meaning behind our Wildfire flag logo. Through community, a single idea can spread like an inferno.

At that time, we couldn't even afford to meet the print minimums on business cards, die-cut flyers, or stickers. In our first office—my studio apartment located behind an In-N-Out—Ben used to sit in the front room at a rolling side desk where we kept an inkjet printer. My station was in the bedroom, so my morning and evening commutes lasted about three and a half seconds. Many mornings, I'd wake up to the sound of Ben opening the heavy iron gate outside my front door. He'd poke his head into my room, toss a half-eaten bagel on my bed, and rattle off the day's to-do list while I wiped the sleep from my eyes.

After I'd showered, we'd take our corners. We couldn't see each other from our desks, so we yelled back and forth from around the doorway. I was stuck in my artist's head, clicking along vectorizations and writing missives to our blog readers. Ben would be on the phone, hunting stores down, trying to make a sale, or following up on overdue payments or lugging boxes of shirts back and forth from the printers. It might be hard to believe today, but in those first years he was the one packing boxes for stores and shipping out orders to online customers.

During this time, Ben also took to reading our general info email. (That's right. Singular. *Email*. You might be surprised to hear that in 2003, we weren't exactly inundated with them.)

"Some kid just wrote us!" Ben shouted out on that brittle January morning.

This was new. "What does he want?" I was on a deadline and had to get this next round of T-shirts to the screen printer by Friday. It was Thursday and I was three graphics short.

"Um, hold on." I turned down my music and could hear Ben mumbling to himself. "He wants to know if he can be a part of our street team."

"What's a street team?"

"No clue. Maybe it's getting kids together to mob the streets with posters and stuff?"

"Right. Tell him we don't have a street team."

"Okay."

I turned the music back up. Quicksand's album *Slip* was on repeat.

Scared of what you're thinking.

"Bob, he wrote back!"

"Who?"

"That kid! His name is Scotty. Asking about the street team we don't have."

"What does he want now?"

"He wants to know if we can send him stickers. He says he'll post them around the Valley."

"Tell him we don't have any stickers!"

"Okay."

She wonders,
How long, have we been senseless.

"Can we send him any flyers? He's wondering if we have flyers."

I shut my computer and walked over to Ben's desk. I'm not sure who was driving me up the wall more—this kid or Ben.

"We don't. But I guess I can design and xerox some? Where are we supposed to send them?"

"He said to meet him at the Basement show on Friday."

My key piece of advice for bootstrapping brands is to capitalize on any available resources, especially if they're free. Ours was the first generation with widespread access to the internet.

We were the first to take a crack at the web's ability to spread information. It was an equalizer. And it provided free resources in every one of my most cherished fields of interest. But building a brand takes more than just an internet connection. Sometimes it takes a bit of ingenuity: street smarts, if you will.

I wanted to make thousands of flyers without dropping mad loot, but the Kinko's in the nearby strip mall charged a dime a copy, and that added up quick. Back at school, as an editor, I had keys to the *Law Review* offices on the far end of campus. The select few of us on staff found sanctuary there between classes or studying for final exams. To keep us satiated, the school provided the *Law Review* members with free coffee, free highlighters, and most important of all, free photocopies. So, one night, I typed "thehundreds.com" in un-kerned Cooper font on eight-and-a-half-by-eleven-inch paper. Then Ben and I holed up in the library after class. Once everyone had gone home, we took the elevator up to the *Law Review* office and locked ourselves in the photocopier room. Ben stood guard while I churned out thousands of flyers on the law school's tab.

I've made a lot of memories building The Hundreds into the brand it is today. I don't remember much about the strip clubs and the private jets (and there were strip clubs and private jets), but I do remember nights like those. The faint chemical smell of printer ink heating up, the white-hot bulb flashing against the wall, Ben and I chattering into the morning over the clamor of the copy machine, talking about the future of The Hundreds.

I DIDN'T know what to expect of Scotty iLL, but it wasn't hard to find him in the crowd. The Basement (now extinct) was a hip-hop shop in the Valley that was well-known for offering graffiti supplies, art shows, and underground rap performances. Cornerstone rappers from KRS-One to Jeru the Damaja performed on the Basement's narrow stage throughout their careers. But tonight, it was the local collective L.A. Symphony's turn. A bobbing sea of heads in dreadlocks, painter caps, and beanies billowed with the beat as Flynn and Pigeon John rapped back and forth. Off to the side of the stage, a stocky, gnomish white boy in a XXXL T-shirt shook our hand. His wiry Jewfro and scruffy facial hair suggested he was thirty-five, but his enthusiasm and devilish grin betrayed his real age of sixteen. Scotty was one of the most intelligent people I've ever met. He was one of those savants. He'd just landed in sneaker and streetwear culture by accident. Perhaps if he'd grown up in Silicon Valley, he might've developed a game-changing app. If he'd stayed in his native Boston, he'd maybe have gone Ivy League. But Scotty grew up in Valencia at the foot of a Six Flags theme park.* He'd fallen in love with skateboarding and, by proxy, with street culture.

These days, everybody's an expert. You can google it all—who's behind the brands, how they started them, where the designers drew inspiration. Scotty, however, not only had memorized the internet gossip but also had his own IRL sources who'd divulge classified intel. We were technically in the industry, but this precocious teenage outsider had deeper connects in the New York, Hawaii, San Francisco, and San Diego street scenes. He was up-to-date on sneaker releases, inside beefs, and which brands to watch out for. Accordingly, he had been observing us from afar and believed in The Hundreds' culture-driven

---

* Scotty's friend base of degenerate skate rats would transcend Santa Clarita and grow up to dominate the streetwear industry. Diamond, Primitive, Huf, you name the brand and Santa Clarita kids were behind the scenes. We've probably cut paychecks to ten to fifteen people from the original clan; they could star in their own *Dogtown and Z-Boys*–type documentary. Scotty was the first to make it, though, if not the unlikeliest.

ethos. It was what prompted him to reach out to our general info email.

Scotty walked us to his Camry and popped the trunk. Pink Nike SB boxes and broken skateboards toppled out. It looked like a skate shop stockroom during the Christmas season. We cleared a space between a pair of Alife RTFT slip-ons and some Wu-Tang Dunks and transferred the box of flyers to his car. His face lit up. He immediately grabbed a fat stack of paper and walked Ventura Boulevard, littering doorsteps and windshields and diner counters with the endless supply of rectangular sheets. He promised to take them to school the next day and spread the word. And we believed him.

Malcolm Gladwell has written entire books on ambassadors like Scotty iLL. There are the creators, and there are the fans. But it's the Scottys who proselytize on the corners and convert the crowds. They build the bridges between islands and make nations. Today, they're called tastemakers or influencers. Ben and I called our street soldiers the Bomb Squad. They have an infectious spirit and a commanding authority. The best brands recognize this gift in people like Scotty and capitalize on it.

For the next year, Scotty harassed Ben for a job. Ben ignored him. But Scotty kept running out of flyers, and we continued to print them for him. No matter how many times we told him to go away, he'd pop right back up like a prairie dog. His time came, fortuitously, on a cold and soggy morning at the top of Finals Hell Week. By this time, our inventory was stacked to my apartment ceiling. We had begun the business with a scant handful of fresh-pressed T-shirts, which I'd neatly laid out in my towel cabinets. We filled orders as they streamed in—five shirts to Portland here, ten shirts to Houston there. Season after season, the sales mounted exponentially. In a year's time, I'd find myself carving a path through canyons of cardboard boxes full of T-shirts in my living room while Ben packaged deliveries in my bathroom. My girlfriend stopped coming over—mainly because there was no couch to sit on and the TV was blocked by crates of T-shirts. Once Ben and I couldn't get to our desks anymore, we realized it was time to shell out some cash for real storage.

Behind my back alley was a public storage facility that was kinda pricey but convenient. We reluctantly signed up for a ten-by-ten-foot space with a roll-up door. Ben would spend most of his afternoons alone inside our storage container armed with headphones and a tape gun. Nevertheless, once final exams hit he couldn't ship orders out fast enough. He scrolled through his phone and found Scotty's number.

"What are you doing today?" He paused to let Scotty attempt an answer. "Well—not anymore. You gotta get here in thirty minutes. You're up to bat."

Scotty got there in twenty-nine and immediately started running that glossy masking tape across the box flaps. Package after package, day after day, Scotty implanted himself in the operation. Within months, he went from packing and shipping in the storage unit to becoming our intern—running deliveries, picking up print jobs, and rolling blunts for Ben once the dust settled on the workday.

The next fall, Ben came to me and said, "I've been thinking . . . I feel like we should start paying Scotty."

"What! Why? Is he complaining?" I still wasn't comfortable with the idea of paying *ourselves* yet, let alone the intern.

"No, I think he'd work for free forever if we asked him to. But I think we should."

I sat on it. Scotty had done a lot for us, and I couldn't imagine The Hundreds without him. He had become a part of the family.

Ben sensed my hesitation. "But don't worry!" he said to comfort me. "I'm just gonna pay him minimum wage. Peanuts!"

I relented.*

THE GOAL was (and continues to be) to bring people into our community and introduce them to The Hundreds' ongoing story. We believed that if we could know our customers as friends, they'd support our business. It wasn't as crucial to us to pry dollars from their hands or pick data from their hard drives. That was guaranteed to come later.

We used what we could to direct people to thehundreds.com (and then @thehundreds on social media). We threw parties and curated art shows, collaborated with other brands and held restaurant takeovers. Our flyers were showing up all over Los Angeles, and not just by Scotty's doing; I'd made the art free and downloadable on our website. I designed a series of absurd and shocking mock ads that would be stapled onto telephone poles selling weight loss pills (LOSE 500 LBS. IN A WEEK!) and get-rich-quick schemes (MAKE $5 MILLION AN HOUR) with "thehundreds .com" tagged along the border. We announced Nirvana reunion tours and garage sales for used body parts and kids wheatpasted them around the world. The most downloaded flyer was a silhouette of a girl's face with a trucker cap. What Pharrell had ini-

---

* Scotty stayed with us for the next thirteen years. He spent the majority of that time being our sales director, which also made him our highest-paid employee. Almost everybody who interacted with Scotty—his clients and buyers—believed that the brand was his. Not because he peacocked around with that claim, but because he owned The Hundreds' name with pride. He wasn't there from the start, but pretty damn near it, and it was a sad and tearful evening when he told us it was time to say goodbye. We'd watched this kid elevate from bonehead to businessman and felt as if we'd raised him. Ben and I were proud of Scotty and, in a strange way, proud of ourselves for having brought him along.

tiated as a cool headwear trend had rapidly devolved into a Von Dutch punch line. Newly minted *TMZ* stars like Tara Reid rocked truckers hard with their Juicy Couture sweats. The flyers pointed to the hat and shouted, "Take it off, Stupid!" and "Boy, that looks dumb!"

I liked flyers (and stickers, once we could meet the minimums to make them) because they functioned outside the digital space. Paper that could cut your fingers. Ink that could stain your hands. "Getting up"—an old-school graffiti term for writing your name up high for the world to take notice—required jumping out of the car in the middle of a busy freeway or scaling a rusty fence. Alternatively, publicizing The Hundreds on the internet was easy and almost lazy. It felt cheap to me and ephemeral. Plus, there was a disconnect: If it didn't feel meaningful and enduring to me, would the casual observer take it seriously? I'm the kind of guy who prefers to meet people face-to-face as opposed to via conference call. I need to sense a human link. As companies transitioned to online advertising, brands started to take less advantage of the streets. Anyone could slap a rotating web banner on a Google ad, only to be forgotten moments later. I wanted to hit people IRL, off freeway exits. So, we did just that. While everyone was moving left, toward the internet, we cut right, toward the physical, permanent world.

The flyer campaign was clocking a lot of mileage, but the mark was too broad and unspecific. (Remember: Don't aim to make customers of *everyone*. You just need *someone*.) As fun as it was to confuse forty-year-old mothers in minivans with our ads on the 10 freeway, forty-year-old mothers in minivans were not our target. We had to sharpen our focus and zero in on a younger market.

Where could we find a concentration of eighteen- to twenty-two-year-olds—tens of thousands of young people equipped with open minds, seeking independence from their parents' institutions, and searching for their own brands to identify with?

BEN HADN'T set foot on the UCLA campus since he'd graduated.

"Do you see any security guards over here?" he asked no one in particular.

We were still in shock over how effortlessly we were able to roll onto the college campus in the dark of the night. Ben's brother Jon had tagged along, sitting in the backseat with thousands of our flyers, still fuming hot off the press. We'd driven straight from the law school copy machine to Ben's alma mater in Westwood. We'd planned to reupholster the campus with our propaganda while the students slept. We scurried across the quads, courtyards, and lecture halls like frenetic mice, puncturing student organization signage with flyers and annihilating bulletin boards with staple guns, glue, and wheatpaste. We figured, "Hey, at least it isn't graffiti," nestling into the gray area between criminal vandalism and public nuisance. "If they don't like it, they can just pull the flyers down, right?"

By the time we were done, there wasn't an inch of exposed space left at UCLA. You know those stories of farmers waking up to crop circles on their land, clueless as to how a prankster accomplished such a supernatural feat in the dead of night? The next morning, students traversed the dewy grass to a school they hardly knew. There were so many sheets of white paper layered in certain areas that it looked as if it had snowed. The popular advertising adage says you have to see something three times before it sticks. That day, the Bruins witnessed The Hundreds' name fourteen thousand times over.

We had only been asleep a few hours before the first complaint hit our in-box. From the head of UCLA's Veritas Forum:

I am writing you in order to let you know about several signs that were recently ruined at UCLA, and in the place of the missing/destroyed signs is a large number of flyers bearing your company's logo and website stapled to the sign. There are also other flyers bearing your company's information stapled onto the posters of other group's signs at UCLA. We are planning to gather the other affected student groups, contact the university, and file a complaint and/or legal action against your organization. Please contact me ASAP to let me know about any arrangements that could be made.

By lunchtime, a flood of outraged emails from students, professors, and faculty would fill our in-box. They ranged from polite grievances to blinding hate mail. The grand finale closed out the fireworks a couple days later, after the student groups convened with the administration. A formal letter from the Office of the Chancellor, University of California, Los Angeles, declared that Ben and I were not only banned from UCLA but disallowed from entering all UC campuses up and down the West Coast (including my alma mater, UCSD). If we broke this order, we would be subject to arrest and legal consequences.

Two years later, I recounted this story to a lecture hall full of UCLA students not more than five hundred feet from where we'd set off the midnight raid. UCLA's Campus Events Commission had gotten wind of The Hundreds' rising success and invited me to speak to the university students, telling me that I'd be in good company—previous guest lecturers included presidents, tech founders, and celebrated movie stars. Since then, I've been invited to speak at four other University of California schools.

OF COURSE, the internet—even in its prehistoric form—played a pivotal role in getting our name out. And while I've often been asked to speak on the secrets of social media—on amassing followers on Instagram, Twitter, and Snapchat—I don't have a magic touch or some kind of inside track. I simply obey two rules: (1) see the numbers as people; and (2) look at the platforms as mere tools.

Every generation has access to different tools with which they might connect with each other. When I was a teenager, we photocopied zines, writing and editing and collaging material in order to communicate our worldview to strangers. When we started The Hundreds, zines were digitalized into blogs. And since the late 2000s, social media has been the primary tool. The answer isn't the tool itself (VR and AR technology aren't going to miraculously solve your growth problems). The solution lies in facilitating human connection. You must understand that it is our nature to long for relationships. People will always go to lengths to find each other. They'll migrate across continents, cross oceans in ships, and even explore outer space to make contact. As a brand, you should focus on making it easy and convenient for them to do just that. Today, it's a text-messaging platform and tomorrow it'll be *Demolition Man*–style cybersex, but if you center on binding communities, you'll always have a way to foster a large and loyal audience.

CASE IN POINT: NikeTalk.

NikeTalk was a forum, a message board like Reddit, often uncredited as an early leader in connecting the dots for sneaker and streetwear culture enthusiasts. The website was just a black page with red font and blue hyperlinks. But it was the community, the people who used the platform to work together, that made NikeTalk powerful.

I'd first logged on in 1999, while I was still in college. My friend Jesse had introduced me to sneaker collecting, but I wanted to know who was informing him. He pulled niketalk .com up on Internet Explorer and gave me a tour of the different rooms. There were discussions on various retro Nikes, as well as current releases, rumored drop dates, and sneak peeks.

Most of the guys (and the occasional lady) were hunting for Jordans. Nike was beginning to reissue Js to a generation of young adults who had thirsted after the first editions of Michael Jordan's footwear in the 1980s. My favorites were the classic Jordan 1s, the cement IVs, and the black Vs. Back in grade school, Jordans were like iPhones. Every year, there was a new Tinker Hatfield design to love or hate. These weren't straightforward Nikes with laces, a canvas upper, and a rubber midsole. Jordans were designed like military-grade airplanes or Transformers. Like Voltrons for your feet. They made you cooler. They made you jump higher. And they made you more popular.

The majority of us had parents who'd winced at the thought of buying their kids $90 sneakers. But as adults, we were more than happy to make room in our budget for a pair. And Nike fed into the nostalgic demand.* Of course, much of this collectors' obsession was fostered by Japanese *otaku* culture. The Japanese

---

* This has been true for every generation since. Nostalgia explains not only Nike's cyclical retro resurgence but also those of other luxury brands, like A Bathing Ape, which people admired in their youth but couldn't afford until they caught a paycheck.

made the trend exotic and cool but eventually made sneaker collecting even more obscure. There was no centralized source from which you might get your sneaker news—no StockX or Sneaker Shopping—so the real heads plugged into NikeTalk to gossip and share. I don't know the numbers, but I'm sure there couldn't be more than a few thousand of us in the world who were truly dedicated NikeTalk users. Lots of prominent personalities on the message board would go on to be known for their role in street culture, like the celebrity jeweler Ben Baller, John Mayer, Anti Social Social Club's Neek, and the rapper Wale. Ben and I were also big NikeTalkers.

This wasn't a coincidence. At every point in this story, we were on the front lines of progressive street fashion, whether intentional or situational. The media likes to think that cool culture begins with elusive influencers and mysterious socialites, but the sneaker-collecting movement (which segued into streetwear's modern iteration) was led by nerd-ass firebrands trading shoe news behind computer screens. These collectors were feverish, educated on the subject matter, and looking to build together. It's that unbreakable passion that catches on with any trend. It was hard to ignore the fastidious upkeep of the marbled leather on Jesse's Jordan IIIs. It was easy to get swept into the fanaticism running through the message board once a phone pic of Pharrell's Ice Cream sneakers leaked. These guys cared so much, believed in something beyond the walls of their office cubicles and their mundane lives. In my opinion, it wasn't about shoes at all. They're just leather moccasins with air bubbles. It was about the community, the nod of approval, and the respect of your peers.

And then there were sneakerheads like Ben and me for whom consuming and trading weren't enough. We wanted to be on the other side of the frenzy*—the brand side. We couldn't make shoes and didn't work at Nike or adidas, but we did know how to print T-shirts. Who was dressing these guys from the ankles up? Here was a predominantly male audience that not only cared about how they looked but were spending hundreds of dollars at a time on their outward appearance. Yet there was no brand or aesthetic that signified a sneakerhead. NikeTalk members dressed in everything from premium streetwear like Supreme and Bape to Orange County surf labels like Volcom and RVCA. There were the athletes in Nike head to toe, the clean-cut J.Crew types, and the sneaker collectors in the South who paired Air Max's with Southpole and Mecca. Outside a couple sneaker-specific T-shirt labels like Skoold in Korrectnuss and Well Bred, nobody was out there capitalizing on the rest of the puzzle.

The Hundreds' first marketing endeavor was seeded on NikeTalk. Fashion bloggers have built entire careers on Instagramming their ensembles, but in the early 2000s, kids influenced each other's dress in threads like "What Did You Wear Today?" WDYWT, for short. It was NikeTalk's most frequented link, featuring thousands of pages of mostly boys posing in their bathroom mirror with their favorite kicks on (this would come to be known as the selfie). They were trying to stunt on each other—hurt each other's feelings with a fresh pair of Supa Dunks or almond AF1s—but they were also learning how to style their outfits from one another. Instead of a generic T-shirt, Ben and I started injecting our T-shirts into product

---

* For me, this is par for the course. I can't just enjoy a medium as a fan. If I get deep enough into it, I want to do it myself. I can't watch a movie without putting myself in the director's seat. I can't read a book without rearranging paragraphs to my liking. And I couldn't be a passive fashion consumer without figuring out how I could do it better myself. I wasn't the type of kid who opened up the radio just to see how it worked. I was the kid trying to build a better radio.

grids, mimicking the layout of the Things Organized Neatly Tumblr. I paired our chocolate-brown "Love" T-shirt (a photo of Don King and Mike Tyson together with neon-green lettering) with the jungle-themed Safari Atmos AM1s. Pink was trending courtesy of Cam'ron's Range Rover and Pharrell's and Kanye's upturned-collar Polos, so Ben took the bacon-themed DQM Air Max collaboration and juxtaposed it with The Hundreds' burgundy-and-hot-pink "Big Money" tee.

The NikeTalk community loved The Hundreds because it belonged to one of their own. Like any niche fan base, they asked themselves, "Why support an outside corporation if you could big-up someone from the community?" They could now promote their brethren and be on the forefront of the next big thing. Sneakerheads were also dying for bold, colorful apparel to match their loud and splashy shoes. In mainstream urban fashion, the more popular labels emphasized earth tones and muted neutrals. On the other end of the spectrum, NikeTalkers hankered for lemon-yellow hoodies with turquoise designs. Some popular Nikes, like the kaleidoscopic Viotechs, combined every color in the rainbow. They didn't make much sense with a dark navy track jacket, but a shoe like the Union Air Max 180 really popped with our "Make 'Em Scream" multicolored T-shirt.

Today, it's not odd for a young, straight guy to be super into his clothes. And in a strange twist, men's fashion is even dictating women's fashion. Just a mere decade or two back, however, Americans weren't comfortable with boys being as into shopping and style as girls. In a homophobic culture, this behavior was perceived as effeminate or gay. People have forgotten this, but at the time there was even a pejorative term for heterosexual dudes who cared about fashion: "metrosexual." We can thank Kanye for opening up the dialogue on men's fashion enthusiasm, but sneakerheads were the ones who gave straight men the pass to be engrossed with their wardrobes.

As sneaker culture proliferated in the mainstream, the demand for streetwear labels grew. Specialty footwear shops like Undefeated, Atmos, and Foot Soldier weren't the only stores accommodating sneakerheads anymore. Practically every city now featured a sneaker boutique with some variation of an exclusive Nike account. Aside from the shoe wall, those shops had racks and hangers to fill. So, they called on upstart T-shirt brands like The Hundreds, Spoon Fed, and Undrcrwn to round out their orders. There were also those shopkeepers who highlighted the clothing as much as—if not more than—the shoes. Where once stood outlier streetwear boutiques like Behind the Post Office, Supermax, and Mathlab, a new crop of street fashion stores flourished. Ben hung a whiteboard above his desk in my apartment. Together, we wrote down the fifty best boutiques around the world, focusing on those that not only understood our genre of streetwear but stocked the names which we wanted to sit alongside. One by one, we scratched them off, and by the end of the year we were stocked in all fifty stores. In-4mation in Hawaii. UBIQ in Philadelphia. Colette in Paris. The Hundreds was growing and sneakers were booming. Streetwear was taking hold and putting pressure on the giants. All of a sudden we went from having a concealed culture to a full-blown industry on our hands.

THE HUNDREDS got a lot of fast and thirsty press in those days. Although streetwear would need another decade to break aboveground, our brand was on the forefront of this internet-led, brand-centric, renegade entrepreneurialism. The 2008 recession knocked the wind out of stalwart American companies that adhered to classic business models like Blockbuster, Pontiac, and Virgin Megastore. The larger fashion labels that couldn't adapt to internet trends also suffered a direct hit, causing department stores like Mervyn's to shutter. Anchor Blue (a store I had grown up shopping in, under the Miller's Outpost name) closed fifty stores at once and petered out over the years.

Small businesses absorbed the brunt of the recession. On average, the Small Business Administration claims that nearly two-thirds of all small businesses will not survive their first two years. But the recession stretched that margin further. Between 2008 and 2010, the recession caused 170,000 businesses on our level to shutter. Eighty percent of those that survived had no employees and made less than $45,000 a year. Yet while the economy was going down in flames, The Hundreds was not only insulated but accelerating, and the journalists could only wonder how.

In October of that same recession year, *Inc.* magazine awarded me and Ben two individual spots on its annual "30 Under 30" entrepreneurs list, right above the Tumblr and WordPress guys. Most of the other picks were Silicon Valley or finance MVPs. Ben and I were the odd men out, wearing T-shirts and Jordans in the magazine's group photo. My bright green zip-up hoodie was a sharp contrast to all the suit blazers and shiny shoes. While the shutter clicked and the bulbs popped, Ben and I whispered to each other—as we often do when we find ourselves at such inexplicably monumental milestones—"How the hell did we get here?"

Rob Walker was asking himself the same question. In 2006, just a mere thirty-six months into the brand's life, the author and veteran journalist contacted us through our website's email form. He was curious about what we were doing and how we were doing it. For the next twelve months, he'd fly out from New York to observe, poke, and prod us. He followed us to the print shop and asked us questions like who our parents were and what we thought about malls. And he sat behind our booth at the MAGIC trade show in Las Vegas. Rob was most intrigued by The Hundreds' attitudinal principles. He sensed a punk rock ethos in the approach. At the time, a twenty-six-year-old Bobby told him, "It's just the idea of trying to be rebellious, or trying to be a little bit anti, questioning government or your parents. Trying to do something different." Whereas punk culture incorporated style and iconography to augment the music that was the heart of the subculture, Rob wrote that with streetwear "the symbols, products and brands aren't an adjunct to the subculture—they are the subculture."

Rob Walker's *New York Times Magazine* cover story (wherein he also discussed the labels aNYthing and Barking Irons) was titled "The Brand Underground." His seven-page write-up was the first mainstream, long-form piece on not just The Hundreds but contemporary streetwear as a whole. The cover art featured a photograph of a white T-shirt with three questions screened onto the front:

**CAN A HIPSTER T-SHIRT BE AS INCENDIARY
AS A ROCK ANTHEM?**

IS A COOL LOGO SOME KIND OF MANIFESTO?

**DOES SHOPPING FOR WEIRD NEW STUFF
MAKE YOU SUBVERSIVE?**

The article resonated not just with *New York Times* readers but with fans and critics alike from around the world. It was our first mainstream press, and for most people who'd read Rob's story, it was the first time they'd heard of The Hundreds. And they didn't exactly know how to receive this story of two cocky kids with a swank T-shirt brand.

"I think Rob Walker gave today's hipster youth too much credit in his interesting article (July 30). I think what he describes is a new breed of entrepreneur rather than a new artistic or social movement," a reader named Ted argued. "Offering a fashion alternative to kids looking to express their individuality is not art; it's just good business."

Ted's sentiment was meant to be critical but echoed what a lot of business analysts at the time thought about The Hundreds. We had a four-hundred-square-foot store but were selling over $2,500 a day in T-shirts. That was more dollars per square foot than the biggest department stores. Meanwhile, Macy's and Nordstrom had never heard of us. Trend-forecasting companies reported that high school kids were ranking The Hundreds' notoriety next to established lines like Quiksilver and DC. And there were no bells and whistles; we were printing our T-shirts on the same Alstyle Apparel blanks with the same ink as any other garage start-up. No celebrities hawking our goods, no skate dream team to explain our popularity. Most notably, no family capital, investors, or venture capitalists to whom one might attribute our rapid growth and success. We didn't even have the means to produce broader advertising or marketing campaigns. So how were we connecting with the kids?

The answer lies in our dedication to community building. The Hundreds is an utter anomaly in the fashion world, following no previously established business model. So, I can't attribute our success to anything other than community. And the blueprint has, in fact, always been there. Ted was right: our brand was just another run-of-the-mill business. What he didn't appreciate, however, was that at its center were Ben and I—two streetwear and sneakerhead fans, just like the rest of NikeTalk—who were simply sharing what they loved with a supportive audience. People were buying other labels because of the image association, their perceived value, and the clout that came with them. Our customers were moving toward us because they had found kinship.

I tried skateboarding; I dove into hardcore. I adopted sneakerhead culture and even stuck my toe in the legal field. I thought I'd finally found a permanent home in streetwear. Then, in founding The Hundreds, *I found the hundreds.*

14. UPSIDE DOWN AND BACKWARD

T HE OTHER DAY, a friend showed me an app on his phone. You take a photo of anything, upload it onto a T-shirt template, and within two days you get your physical T-shirt in the mail. You can even order a crate of these if you want. There are websites out of China that are doing the same with cut-and-sew apparel. Factories will make you one-off jeans or jackets featuring your logo and design. If you have a Shopify account, you can set up a personalized online shop within minutes, connect it to your bank, and have a full-blown clothing company up and running out of your bedroom by lunchtime. I saw this, closed my eyes tight, ran headfirst into a brick wall, and came back from the dead to tell you this.

This is how we made T-shirts in 2003: first, we'd buy an allotment of blank T-shirts from a gray-market wholesaler downtown. These were slightly defective goods that the manufacturer had dumped on some grumpy Korean garmento in Santee Alley—T-shirts that were too short or too long or off by a shade of purple. Because these were the remnants of much larger orders, they came in assorted and unordered sizes and colors. We couldn't afford to place the minimum order directly with the manufacturer, so we were stuck sourcing boxfuls of weird tan shirts containing twice the number of XXLs as mediums. But we took what we could get and designed around it.

Speaking of which, I didn't know how to design and prepare T-shirt graphics when we started The Hundreds. I knew how to draw. And I knew how to shoot photos. But I didn't have the requisite design programs, let alone the skill set, to convert my art into digitally usable screen prints. I ripped copies of Adobe Photoshop and Illustrator online and have taught myself the programs over the years. That first summer, however, all I could muster were font treatments of "The Hundreds" and stencils of scans of my photographs. Paired with some gimmicky Photoshop effects, this was the extent of our first season's graphic design prowess.

Next was the hardest step: finding a screen printer to transfer our art onto T-shirts. Back then, once a year, someone would drop off a cinder block of telephone numbers and addresses on your doorstep. The Yellow Pages are an encyclopedic directory of businesses and residents in your area. One option was to blindly call screen-printing shops in our city to inquire about minimum orders and pricing. Another option was a referral from a friend. There were no crowdsourced reviews to narrow the search.

Ben, Mak, and I pooled our cash, throwing in roughly $200 to $300 each. We assumed that would cover the blank T-shirts and printing costs. Ben's brother Jon had a friend who had a manual one-color printing press in his backyard. We'd already tried the arts-and-crafts route, buying an eight-by-eleven-inch Speedball kit and trying to screen print our T-shirts individually. It was like watching fourth graders conduct a class project that was just bound to fail. Jon's friend's name was Alan. He would go on to be a well-respected tattoo artist in the Valley. But at the time, he was a struggling artist whose hobbies included homemade screen-printing projects.

"Sure, I can handle that for you," Alan said over the phone. "How many shirts?"

We had about one hundred blanks in that cardboard box and handed our entire inventory—the whole company, really—to Alan later that afternoon.

"I'd say give it about two to three weeks," he added. Ugh. That seemed like a long time to wait for our dreams to come true, but we had to be patient.

Between my courthouse internship, applying to *Law Review*, and filing the business paperwork, I found that the third week came faster than expected. We were eager to hear from Alan.

"Oh hey, guys," he stammered. Alan seemed distracted and not quite as warm and interested as he was before. "Look, I got caught up with some work stuff. I'm gonna need another week, if that's cool."

Another week! We didn't know much about screen printing, but we did know that he wasn't running an actual print shop with other orders in the way. Plus, we only had a hundred shirts. "Any way we can get them sooner than that?"

"No, I'm sorry. I haven't had a chance to start. Just gimme one more week and I got you guys."

Over the years, I've mastered the art of spotting red flags. In this business, the flags fly high with underqualified job interviewees, flaky vendors, and opportunists who mean well but tend to royally screw things up by watching out for themselves more than the people around them. But Alan was a friend of Jon's, and no one had anything bad to say about him. Maybe he was just having a hard month. We could also use that extra week to get our ducks in a row with accounts.

"All right." I capitulated.

The next week, Alan wouldn't pick up his phone. Ben left a polite but stern voice mail noting that our shirts were past due and that a third of the summer had already escaped us. This project was supposed to be churning money by now, yet we were visiting stores without samples or inventory to show for ourselves. Alan didn't call back that day or the next. On the third day, he finally replied that there was an emergency and he had to leave town. He had worked through half of the shirts and would return that weekend to finish them up. Then he asked if we could stop by on Monday.

Sunday night, Alan emailed asking if we could give him until Wednesday.

A month and a half later, our phone calls and voice mails were getting heated. Alan appealed to us asking for patience: "Good work takes time!" Ben and Mak were infuriated, realizing we'd made a costly mistake by going with an amateur. We finally pulled the trigger. "We're coming up there tomorrow. You better have our shirts done, or we're taking all our blanks back."

Alan lived deep in the Valley with his mother in a modest house behind a chain-link fence with an overgrown lawn. On a broiling hundred-degree July afternoon, we pulled up out front and made the anxious walk to his front door.

"What's up, guys?" There was no welcome in Alan's greeting. No handshakes or hugs. "Come on in."

I was happy to get out of the heat. He invited us into the living room and told us he'd be back with the finished shirts. We were surprised to hear that, but his confidence gave us relief. We all loosened up, Alan offered us something to drink, and then he and his friend walked out back.

Five minutes later, Alan was standing in front of us with a big black garbage bag. He turned it upside down and poured out the contents. T-shirts dumped onto the carpet in one wrinkled heap. Where was the box? Why weren't these neatly folded? Before we could get to those questions, Mak reached for the top shirt and examined the print.

"This is off-center," Mak noted. The T-shirt was called "Mic" and featured the silhouette of Slick Rick, traced from a live photo I'd shot of his Boombazzi San Diego concert. "He's supposed to be flush against this edge, but he's crooked."

Alan made a face. "Looks pretty centered to me. You have to leave room for allowance," he said defensively. He picked up the next shirt and said, "See? This one is fine."

That one was not fine. That one was printed on the wrong-colored shirt.

This time, Ben picked out a shirt. "Dude, the front and back graphics are swapped." The T-shirt was literally backward.

"All right, so there's one fuckup. I'll take that back." He threw that shirt over his shoulder and frowned.

"What about this?" I asked. The T-shirt in my hands had the graphic printed on the *inside* of the shirt. I don't even know how that's possible, unless Alan had turned the shirt inside out, printed it, and then flipped it back to normal. Was he *trying* to screw us? I couldn't tell.

"What the fuck!" Ben cried. He was holding two T-shirts in the air. No print at all. We found ten more like that.

Alan had gone from being on the defense to taking a knee. "All right," he admitted. "What do you wanna do?"

We needed a moment to think. "Give us a minute," Mak said. And we marched back out into the hot Valley air. We retreated to Ben's car and kicked the doors open. For the first five minutes after we climbed in, we didn't say a thing. We were all searching for solutions in our head, like rats in a maze.

I cracked. "What're we gonna do with all those dishrags? We can't sell them. And we already burned through all our money buying those blanks, so it's not like we can replace 'em."

Mak said what everyone was thinking: "We're out of business before we began!" Alan had ruined our goods, sending us into a tailspin. But even worse—he had wasted our time. It had been almost two months since we'd started this company, and we still didn't have a T-shirt to show for ourselves. Even by 2003 standards, that was ridiculous. Three capable, intelligent guys and we couldn't get a single T-shirt printed to order in eight weeks.

There've been plenty of crises like this over the years. As The Hundreds grew, the storms became costlier and more devastating, affecting not just the people at the top but the livelihood of everyone on board. There have been errors that cost us hundreds of thousands of dollars. Something as minuscule as a misplaced zero on an Excel sheet would pass undetected by three levels of management, leading to a surplus of a thousand hoodies for which we didn't have a home.

When you find yourself in the midst of such a disastrous miscalculation, it's like having your computer freeze before you've backed up your work. All you can do is take a deep breath, gather your wits, and improvise from what's left. Even if that means starting over. The Japanese have a beautiful saying for this—a maxim that has survived through atomic bombs, economic collapse, and countless tsunamis: *Shikata ga nai.* "There's nothing to be done, so move on." Move forward. It takes a bit of self-deception to mind-wipe the regret and a truckload of moxie to push through the work of regaining control. But sometimes it's necessary.

Fifteen minutes later, we were back in Alan's house, sorting through the casualties. The figures were hard to stomach. Each base shirt represented $5 down the drain. Ten bucks, fifteen, one hundred—there goes rent! By the end, we'd salvaged maybe twenty T-shirts that were decent enough to be worn without being a bad look for the wearer or The Hundreds. We didn't pay Alan a dime—not that we had any money to give.

We flipped those twenty T-shirts to charitable friends and family out of the back of our trunk. We sold them at $20 a pop—or whatever folks were willing to bless us with for what would amount to a new gym tee. Many of those friends have held on to those first-edition The Hundreds shirts. It shocks me when I see how bad the art was. Even if Alan had printed them right, those shirts sucked. He was probably doing us a favor by getting unorthodox with the print placements; at least they looked provocative.

15. UPSET THE SETUP

W E'D MADE ABOUT $400 back from the debacle with Alan,
enough to buy another batch of blanks downtown and get
some printing done. Not as much volume as before, but enough
to get us back on our feet. We asked around to see if anyone
knew of a decent screen-printing shop, one that didn't print designs upside down and on the insides of shirts. Mak's cousin
Goli had used a facility in Van Nuys called STIX for a school project, and she passed on its info.

"They're cool guys," she said. "Easy to work with. They'll get
the job done."

I still remember walking into STIX's front office for the first time. At first, we thought we were in the wrong place. It looked as if we had stumbled into a trucker's man cave, buried under fifteen years of cigarette soot, take-out lunch menus, and *Perfect 10* magazines. The den was carpeted, matted down, and gnarled after years of abuse. There was a pool table in the center of the room that doubled as a spare flat surface on which to lay out print samples, Pantone books, and fabric scraps. Instead of a front desk, there was an L-shaped bar, and instead of a bartender there was Kenny. The guys who ran STIX—Kenny, Rick, and Jason—were blue-collar types who chain-smoked indoors, kept the Angels game on in the background, and screen printed for biker gangs. Kenny was the sales guy, fast and wily—always wiping that bulbous nose of his while shaking you down with a pitch.

"What's up, fellas? What can I do you for?" he said. Kenny was *that* dude.

We were in too deep. Like, literally, too far into the room to back out. So, Mak kicked things off. "We need to get some T-shirts printed. We're starting a clothing company and . . ."

Kenny rolled his eyes harder than a Kit-Cat Klock. "Let me guess. This is your first time printing tees. How about this—how many do you wanna make?"

"Oh, well . . ." Mak looked at us and we all shrugged at each other. After what Alan had put us through, we hadn't discussed numbers yet. We just wanted to see how far we could get. "I dunno, maybe twenty?"

"Twenty? Twenty pallets? Twenty dozen? What do you mean twenty?"

"Like, twenty." Mak filled in the gaps. "Twenty total shirts," he clarified without flinching. Just so you know, print shops can't just spit out a custom T-shirt, or twenty for that matter. The art gets digitized, then printed onto a film that is chemically burned into a silk screen (which is, by the way, not made with silk anymore, but nylon). Multiple colors in the art mean multiple screens, attached to a rotating press. Ink colors get mixed according to the art's Pantones and squeezed into the porous shapes of the screens. The print gets baked into the shirt in the dryer and the shirt is then tagged, bagged, and packaged for delivery. It's a labor-intensive process, which means screen-printing shops require minimums. That is, if you're going to print one T-shirt, you might as well print two hundred, because it takes the same amount of labor and will be charged at the same rate.

And that's why Kenny was so turned off by the idea of printing just twenty T-shirts. "Do you guys know what we do here?" he asked rhetorically. "We make all the shirts for the Lakers. You know when you go to a Staples Center game and they're launching shirts out of a cannon to those thousands of drunk motherfuckers on the Kiss Cam? We print those. We do million-T-shirt orders for the State of California. When you're driving up the 5 and see all those migrant workers hunched over strawberries in the fields, those are our shirts on their backs. So you're asking me to stop everything we're doing, shut down the machines, so that you can make twenty tees for your 'clothing company'?"

Kenny started laughing. He called in Rick, the art guy, to look over my primitive designs. "What'd you draw this in?" Rick wondered aloud, and not in a good way. "Do you know how to use Adobe Illustrator?" I shook my head sheepishly. I was literally tracing my drawings at a super-high resolution on Photoshop. He advised, "Learn the programs. I can do the rest for you—this time—but I'm not always gonna be able to work with this."

"I like you guys," Kenny's partner Jason growled. He looked like a broader, burlier Eddie Munster with a handlebar mustache and two barbell earrings. "I believe in you. We'll give you a shot." And just like that, STIX green-lighted The Hundreds' twenty-T-shirt order. It was charity—performed out of the kindness buried deep in the charcoal of their blackened lungs. But we wouldn't be here today without Jason, Kenny, and Rick. And their print shop wouldn't be here today without us. I'm sure we would have found another shop, eventually. But in hindsight, it seems as if it almost had to work this way. And once we hit that green light, we floored it.

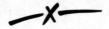

OUR FIRST stop was Fred Segal in Santa Monica, a mainstay of Los Angeles boutique shopping that delved into all points of progressive fashion—from jewelry to maharishi dragon pants to Creative Recreation footwear. It was also one of the first stores stateside to invite men's streetwear into its shop. We had nothing to lose, so we aimed high. In those days, Fred Segal was one of the most reputable clothing retailers in the city, and we knew that if we could slide The Hundreds in there, we could sell anywhere.

Ben, Mak, and I were oblivious to the selling process, so we took a deep breath and marched straight up to the counter of the "Street" department.

"Hi, can we speak with the manager?"

"'Bout what?"

Tony, the buyer, was a husky black dude with cornrows and a heavy handshake. He didn't really seem interested in what we had to say, but it was a slow afternoon, so he humored us.

"We're from The Hundreds," Ben said. "We want to see about getting our T-shirts into Fred Segal."

"First of all, you're looking for the buyer. That's me."

I could feel my ears burning hot but kept my gaze steady.

"Second, The Hundreds? I've never heard of it, guys. Sorry."

"Never heard of it?" I replied. "I thought this was the coolest shop in the city. Don't you always know what's up?"

"Well. Yeah . . ." Tony faltered. "Wait. Who else do you guys sell to?" He was looking for some kind of cosign or credibility.

Ben answered, "We're only looking overseas at this point, but thought that Fred Segal would be a good place to start our domestic business." Before Tony had a moment to mull that over, Ben said, "Here, why don't you take a look at some of our designs."

I placed a wrinkled line sheet on the glass. I'd chopped together a catalog of our first T-shirts in black-and-white, but the JPEGs were pixelated and muddy. It was almost impossible to tell what was going on with each shirt, so we talked louder as Tony's face twisted in confusion.

"What makes you guys different from every other shirt company that comes in here? Do you know how many new brands I see every day?"

"It's not really about the T-shirts as much as it is about our website." I yanked the sheet out from Tony's hands.

"Okay, explain."

"The Hundreds is about the culture and community more than the clothing. Everything we make has a story tied to people. So, if somebody buys a T-shirt, they won't get the full picture until they go to thehundreds.com and read about the story behind the shirt and the person who designed it. The website brings people together. It's like our little club."

Tony stared at me in silence.

"I'll take twelve shirts, but only on consignment. What sizes do you make?"

"We have medium, large, and extra-large. Are you sure you don't want more? You're gonna sell out of them," Mak cautioned.

Tony gave him a look and ignored him. "Four-four-four. Drop them off here by next Thursday."

TWELVE SHIRTS! There was no time to celebrate. While we waited on STIX to screen print our first order of T-shirts, we drove across town to Hollywood and pulled up to Brooklyn Projects on Melrose, L.A.'s skate/street pillar. The founders and co-owners Dominick "Brooklyn Dom" DeLuca and "OG Merf" Osborne (RIP) stocked skate supplies and held a coveted Nike SB account, but their shop was also recognized for supporting smaller, unknown T-shirt labels.

"Can we speak to the . . . *buyer*?" This time, Mak got it right.

"Yo. You're lookin' at him." The domineering former MTV *Headbangers Ball* VJ stepped up. Everything about Dom is big: big voice, big eyes, big hair, big personality.

"Um, hi. This is Bobby and Ben. I'm Mak. We're from The Hundreds. Have you heard of us?"

"No."

"Well, you should have."

I gave him the spiel about my blog, The Hundreds' lifestyle, and why he should be grateful to sell our shirts.

Dom was hooked, but not wholly on board.

"Who else carries you?"

"Fred Segal," Ben said coolly.

"Tony?"

We nodded our heads slowly.

"That's my boy. Okay, I'll take a few tees. *Net thirty*, though."

The Hundreds was now officially stocked in two of L.A.'s prime accounts.

THE MORNING we delivered Tony his shirts, we went to breakfast at Swingers down the street. Then we circled the block and returned right back to the corner of the Fred Segal parking lot. We reclined our seats, stalled for an hour, then called the shop.

"Yeah, hi, is this Fred Segal Street? I'm looking for a company called The Hundreds. Do you carry it?"

One of the clerks answered enthusiastically, "Yes! We just got in a shipment today, actually. You might want to head down here; it's not gonna last."

"Be right there."

Ben called up Jon and then I called my girlfriend to come down to the store. We handed them cash to walk in, buy a The Hundreds shirt, and throw it right back into the bin in our trunk. Then we called more friends and family who would stop by on their way to the beach. A week later, we casually strolled in to Fred Segal on a warm Sunday afternoon and bumped into Tony on his way out.

"Hey! Hundreds guys!" His face lit up. "You were right. Your shirts blew out. Had no idea, man. I need more. What do you got?"

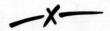

NOT MORE than a week after we'd picked up our first order from our screen printers, STIX, we were back for more.

"We need to make more shirts," Mak told Kenny.

"No way. Look, you guys are cool, but we don't have the time for this."

"We'll take a hundred."

Kenny cocked his head. We were getting closer to the minimum. "Okay, but nothing too complicated."

Deal. I didn't know how to design sophisticated graphics yet anyway.

Days later, Ben's Ford Explorer backed into STIX's loading dock, packed door to trunk with boxes of blank shirts.

Jason came out from the back. "Hey! Hey! What's going on here, guys?"

"Shit's moving!" he called out to Jason. "It's working!"

That afternoon, Jason sat us down and took a serious look at our program. He and Kenny broke down the costs of printing, the scheduling, and all the common mistakes garage T-shirt brands make. I have to really hand it to those guys: I think they saw something in us that resonated differently from all these other kids with start-up labels. I'm not sure what it was, but I know we had heart, we loved T-shirts, and we cared about the science of screen printing—an art in itself. Over the months and years, Rick took me through the artwork setup and preparation: color separations, halftones, spot colors, and the painstaking process of photo prints. Eventually, we'd take up part-time residence in that warehouse. The Valley summers were slow and scalding, but it allowed us to stay on top of the machines, approve strike offs, and ensure our orders were done on time.

And those were the circumstances under which The Hundreds came to be. We were nothing, nobodies, but the work was important and powerful. We had passion and focus. We ate, breathed, and shit The Hundreds. It was our life. We were constantly patching up the holes with duct tape, paddling without direction, sans compass, but there's a freedom and a hopefulness that comes with being stranded at sea. The ocean reached out all around us, the horizon an open-ended question. Life seemed big and infinite, and with The Hundreds we could sail forever.

"**WHAT'RE THEY** doing here?" Ben whispered under his breath as we pulled up to our office. It was seven years later on an unusually warm February morning. The Hundreds' first real headquarters was located at 1729 Wall Street, right outside the fashion district in downtown Los Angeles—a seventeen-thousand-square-foot office and warehouse space that employed about twenty people. In the years since proving ourselves to a couple of commercial screen printers in that smoky parlor room, we had gone from producing a few T-shirts to a full cut-and-sew apparel collection. The Hundreds started out by selling to some local key accounts. Now we were distributed globally, including in our own stores. I had just had my first son, and Ben was about to get married. And we let the interns make the twice-a-day slog through Valley traffic in huge commercial trucks to pick up T-shirt orders from STIX.

From inside Ben's car, we could see a couple Harleys stacked neatly alongside the office curb. Jason and Kenny were standing outside the front door to our building, impatiently leaning on the buzzer. We sat and watched them cave under frustration. Bang! Bang! Bang! Jason hammer fisted the iron security gate and the windows tremored.

"I have no idea," I answered Ben. "Did we forget to pay them or sleep with their girlfriends or something?"

Ben didn't laugh. "No. Let's get out and see what they want."

We slowly stepped out of Ben's car, invited Jason and Kenny

into our showroom, and poured them coffees as we made small talk about usual business stuff. But the STIX fellas hadn't journeyed all the way downtown to talk T-shirt numbers and new printing technologies. There was something heavier weighing on their minds.

"We want you to buy us out," Jason went first. "As far as clients, you guys are the vast majority of our business now." This was bananas. It wasn't long ago that we could barely print twenty shirts with these two, and now they were asking us to take their company?

Kenny naturally wound up for the heavy pitch. "Take out the middleman, guys. Why are you paying us? You should own us. Buy STIX, take the equipment, then we work for you and all you owe is a paycheck. Now you just eliminated all that unnecessary cost."

Ben and I were speechless. We hadn't seen this coming. Kenny and Jason's offer made a lot of sense; we just didn't believe we deserved it. When you first set out on building a brand or company—or any impossible dream, for that matter—you fight like hell to make it happen. You grow accustomed to the lower ground, adopting a habit of overcompensating. You're programmed to prove a point. The thought of owning our print shop had never crossed my mind. In my head, The Hundreds was still a ghetto-rigged, two-bit science project, a couple wires short of a potato battery. But the outside reality was that The Hundreds had become a force to be reckoned with—not just in small-time streetwear or action sports, but in global fashion. We were making good money and employing qualified people. Although it was atypical for the industry, a company of our size and growing at the rate at which we were growing could very well benefit from acquiring its own print shop. We had gotten this far by fighting like the underdog, but now it was time to start throwing hands like a champion. The spotlight was shining brightly on The Hundreds. Here's an important truth that I've learned over the years: When a wave rolls in, you ride it all the way until it coughs you up onto the sand.

So, we bought that print shop. Today, it's called Mixed Media Productions. We run the best facility in the city, and the printing business alone employs fifty people who work in two shifts around the clock. We handle all printable items for not only The Hundreds but also friends and rival brands alike. Some of the best clothing companies in the world, the ones who threaten to make us irrelevant daily, do their printing with Mixed Media. They figure we're artists foremost and care about the product in a way that commercial printers can't empathize with. A clean shop. An art department that prides itself on fine-tuned separations. Ink that doesn't cake and crack, and back-breaking techniques that are maddening to anyone who doesn't celebrate the creativity. As for us, we figure hey, if you can't beat 'em, at least take a portion of their sales. This way, the better our competitors do, the more money we make!

But this wasn't a story about a print shop. It was a story about the importance of thinking outside the box in regard to design, marketing, sales, and all other aspects of business. Most important, think outside the box of your own passions. We never envisioned a print shop under our umbrella, just as I never thought I'd own a fresh fish restaurant, or direct a movie, or write a book. The lesson here? Always draw outside the lines of your dreams.

16. THE HARDEST PART

"**H**OW DO YOU feel about Mak?" Ben asked me a year into the business. We're driving around downtown L.A. in his beat-down Ford Explorer, our first utility vehicle.* "I know this is a weird thing to ask you, but I'm going a little crazy and want to know if I'm alone here."

There's something you have to understand about Ben. He's a Persian Jew, which means friends are family and family comes

---

* We ran that poor truck into the ground with deliveries back and forth from the screen printers and shops. Once the back window was lopped off and the transmission popped, Ben retired it and left it for two years in the corner of our parking lot, where it was converted into a makeshift home for pigeons, the way a shipwreck becomes a coral playground.

first, especially if there's a profitable opportunity afoot. My parents raised me with the mind-set that you never do business with loved ones. They themselves were self-made, never borrowed a quarter from their parents in building their American dream, and kept their familial relationships intact by proving they could stand on their own feet. Even asking my parents for a cosign on an apartment lease was a formidable dinner conversation. Ben, on the other hand, invited his dad to be our accountant, Jon to run our print shop, and his friends to do everything for The Hundreds from IT to flooring. And Mak was not only his best friend but a virtual cousin. Not to mention they were roommates.

"I love Mak," I answered in short. We were only a year into knowing each other, and I had to tread lightly here. What if I drove a wedge into their friendship? What if what I said was perceived as talking shit, and would circle around on me down the road?

"Yeah, but do you think he's holding up his share of the work?"

There it was. The elephant in the room. "I mean . . ." The reality was that in our second year of law school, Mak dove deeper into his schooling. Which is *exactly what law students are supposed to do*. Heavier course loads, internships, *Law Journal*. But by this time, there was an even larger pachyderm to address: Deep down, Ben and I were falling head over heels in love with The Hundreds. Unbeknownst to each other, we were both hedging our bets that The Hundreds was going to be our future, not law. We slowly receded from our studies. I would split screen in class, taking notes in a Word document on one side while designing T-shirt graphics with Adobe Photoshop on the other. The last thing I would tell people was that I was a law student. "I run a clothing company" or "I'm a designer" always came first. Any spare hours were spent visiting stores, or browsing Japanese fashion magazines in the Little Tokyo bookshop, or going out to local streetwear parties like Grey One's anniversary. I slumped from the top of the class to the 50 percent marker in a single semester. I was fervent and dumb, as if I were engrossed in a steamy affair. I even failed a class. The other law students stopped looking at me as a threat and instead started thinking of me as a nuisance. Just in the way, taking up space.

And as uncomfortable as it was to broach, that's how Mak started to feel to us. He was procrastinating on duties or shirking them altogether. "I'll pick up the shirts next Tuesday!" On Tuesday, "Wednesday." Mak was the consummate sales guy, but Ben had to start picking up the dialogue with store buyers. When we'd sit down for design meetings, Mak was on another plane—wrong colors, divergent styling. He hadn't read those same Japanese magazines, he hadn't seen how the kids were wearing their jeans at the parties. "I can't go out tonight," he'd say, "and you shouldn't either."

It wasn't his fault. "I've never lied to you guys," he said in his defense when we first brought our frustration to his attention. "My goal has always been to be an attorney. I'm in law school to become a lawyer. I love The Hundreds. It is just as much my company, and it always will be. This is a fun side project to make some money, and I plan on keeping up with both." But this didn't suffice for me and Ben. The Hundreds wasn't a side project—I was almost offended by that comment—it was our everything now. Law was not an option. How could we share a third of this company with someone with divided interests?

Days later, the next conversation we worked through at their apartment was a painful one. Like a divorce. Ben and I treaded lightly into the discussion around dinner, while Mak climbed the stages of grief. Mak is irreplaceable. Mak is critical to the equation. But Mak isn't here. Mak doesn't share our interests. Mak doesn't care as much. Denial. Anger. Defensiveness. Then long bouts of silent interludes and reflection. "Sounds like you two already made up your mind," he muttered. Anger, again. Nastiness. Then a vow to be better.

That promise was never shipped. Two weeks later, we were embroiled in the same battle. Six hours in Ben and Mak's living room, pointing fingers and yelling. There was also a lot of fear. I saw the worry in Ben's eyes: What irreversible damage was he carving into this lifelong relationship? Mak was injured and disgusted. "No matter what happens, I'm always gonna be mad. If The Hundreds succeeds, I'll wish I was a part of it. If it fails, I'll know I could've saved it." By 2:00 a.m., he was clawing at any solution, trying all the keys. The negotiator had been out-negotiated. No more runway. A brief and spiteful buyout agreement was discussed. I told Mak, "Thank you," which fell on deaf ears, put my head down, and left the apartment.

"Bob! Wait!" Ben called out to me as I turned down the sidewalk. We walked in silence as we got to my Honda CR-V. The streetlight cast an amber triangle on us as we sat on the curb. "I want you to know that I am committed to this company," he declared. "I don't know where your head is at, but all I see is The Hundreds now. There's nothing else for me."

I stared at my shoes. Then his. Then mine. "Are you and Mak gonna be okay?"

"We'll be fine. It might take years and maybe it'll never be quite the same again, but we'll be okay. That's my brother in there. Nothing can break that."

"Okay, because this isn't worth it for me if you've lost that relationship. Nothing is worth that. I feel horrible right now," I said. "But if you want to know where I stand, yes, I'm with you. I love doing this and I'm in. I don't have another choice either."

We shook hands that night in a way that grown-ups do, like those sepia photographs of founders cutting a ribbon in front of their first business. I still admire Ben—and am eternally indebted to him—for putting The Hundreds first that night. All these years later, it's still just he and I. No matter how many people come and go, how big we grow or how small we shrink. I still think of the business as just us two hungry kids with ridiculous ideas and gall. The only person I care about when it comes to The Hundreds is Ben. I work my darnedest to impress him, and I do whatever I can to make sure he's performing his best every day.

And as a happy epilogue to this chapter, Mak and Ben are better and closer than ever. Today, Mak is one of the most powerful and successful civil attorneys in the city, just as he'd predicted he'd be. Earnings alone, he makes Ben and me look like we're running a lemonade stand. He's been a good sport over the years as we've softly written him out of our history, but here's the facts: There once was a Mak Hundreds and there always will be. Long live the triple OG, Mak Hundreds.

17. THE BLACK TARP STRATEGY

HEARD YOU *guys were assholes.*"

It's the summer of 2005, and we're exhibiting at the MAGIC trade show, a principal industry convention that takes place twice a year in Las Vegas. Women's shoes, urban apparel, licensing—all fashion comes to a head for three days in the desert. Brands sell their upcoming collections to stores, bikini models walk the carpet, and rappers parade through the show grounds with entourages. But nights are when the real business goes down. Deals are planted over extravagant dinners, germinated around club bottle service, and blossom in strip clubs. By morning, the sun rises on a new crop of brands and designers.

MAGIC is about discovering and being discovered, and Ben and I were crossing our fingers.

We'd rented a narrow corner of carpet that barely fit a folding table, a couple chairs for Ben and me, and a rolling rack for us to display ten T-shirts. We're about to wrap it up for the third and final day when we look up and see this bald man and his crew standing by our table, making snide remarks.

Assholes?

He finishes: "So I had to see what the commotion was all about." I look down at the plastic badge hanging by a lanyard around the man's neck. His name is Mike Brown, the owner of a famous San Francisco streetwear boutique named True.

We're not assholes, although people assume this all the time. I'll meet someone, and after conversing, they'll literally shake my hand and say, "You know, I thought you were gonna be a total dick, so thanks for being cool." I'm never sure who's more surprised in these encounters—them or me. Then again, my friend Abram did tell me once, "You know why you're an asshole? Because you're opinionated. And not only do you have a strong opinion on everything, you share it." Guilty as charged.

What I really think it is? Streetwear in general is filled with assholes. It's like an asshole Coachella up in here. The Dicks are playing the mainstage and the Jerks are opening. If you've ever been to a streetwear party, you know what I'm talking about. No females in the vicinity, just clothing-conscious dudes skulking under purple clouds, posturing, and praying for male validation. It's an air of insecurity that seemingly stems from daddy issues. It's that tension that turns otherwise cool dudes into *cool guys*.

Streetwear is also low-key luxury. It's elitist and established on a holier-than-thou mind-set, which makes for good branding but emits bad vibes. We know this well, which is why Mike

Brown and all the other buyers at this trade show are starting to hum, "Those Hundreds guys are assholes!"

Apparel trade shows play a big part in streetwear history. For decades, shopkeepers and buyers have traveled from around the world to visit brands in convention halls, shop their sample collections, and place an order that will take half a year to produce and deliver.* In the nineties, the big show for popular skateboarding, snowboarding, and surf brands was ASR (Action Sports Retailer), while Las Vegas showcased urban labels like FUBU and Apple Bottoms at the MAGIC trade show. MAGIC would eventually spin off into Pool and Project. Then there are Capsule and Liberty for women's contemporary and traditional menswear. Europe has the Bread & Butter show for high fashion, as well as Bright for skate. Back in the day, there were even fringe shows like 432F in San Diego for the underground street brands that couldn't get into ASR (Freshjive, Pervert, Tribal, and an airbrush artist named Marc Echo all converged at the short-lived trade show).

We were invited to participate in our first trade show the year prior in 2004: Agenda.† Back then, Agenda—like The Hun-

---

* In recent years, retail has transcended the wholesale model and moved more online directly between brand and consumer, threatening the necessity of trade shows altogether. Consumer-facing expos like Shanghai's Yo'Hood and Long Beach's ComplexCon are rethinking the model by eliminating the middleman and providing a Comic Con–esque experience for the customer. But trade shows cemented a networking foundation for the industry. As a brand, we've built many of our friendships over the years with fellow designers, sales teams, and media on the show floor (and especially the official after-parties). After all, how else would these dudes get their work done without industry hookups and champagne-room business deals? Trade shows are like summer camp for grown-ups who never grew up.

† These were the early days of Aaron Levant's scrappy Agenda, the premier platform for surf, skate, and street brands. Like our streetwear class that rebelled against the greater men's apparel industry, Aaron was going toe-to-toe with the trade-show goliaths ASR and MAGIC. I've never met someone as dogged and indefatigable as Aaron. He once told me a story of how his parents shipped him off to a boarding school in the mountains and he hiked all the way home. It took a week. Sometimes I think he started Agenda just to prove that the dark horse could win the race. It's a multibillion-dollar industry with but a handful of players. A ragtag, graffiti kid like Aaron Levant was a long shot. He'd been written off and scoffed at in

dreds, like our entire invisible scene—was of no consequence. Aaron Levant hosted his second Agenda show in downtown Los Angeles's LA Mart, a trade building that comprised generic showrooms. He commandeered a couple adjoining spaces at the end of the hall for a week, circulated postcards and blind emails to the retailers, and invited local buyers to shop rising-star brands for their stores. Then he curated the labels, and somehow, someway, he landed on us. His email dropped in our in-box sometime the week before and we were gassed. The Agenda show? The Coliseum of street fashion? Ben and I marked yes on Aaron's invitation. We just had to figure out the trade show's mechanics and what we were supposed to do.

We photocopied our T-shirt designs onto line sheets and headed to the show early on a Monday morning. We spent more time deciding which sneakers to wear than we spent formulating any business plan or strategy (some things never change). Aaron had said something over the phone about being responsible for hanging our sample T-shirts ourselves, so along the way we stopped at a Walgreens to pick up a sleeve of plastic white hangers. We arrived in the downtown showroom with a cardboard box of randomly sized T-shirts, too lazy and ignorant to steam and press them. Aaron asked us where our rack was. We looked at each other blankly, and he asked, "You guys didn't bring a rolling rack? How are you gonna show your samples? You don't have your own chairs? What did you bring?" Ben pointed at the box. I held up the hangers.

Those were three of the longest days of my life. No smartphones to escape the ennui. No Wi-Fi to distract from the drone

---

meetings. Eventually, some of the bigger shows tired of his presence—the cooler brands were fleeing the corporate arena to be associated with his trendier indie show—and tried to absorb him. Their offers insulted Aaron. In turn, it wasn't long before he devoured them. A few years back, Aaron did sell Agenda to the highest bidder. I think his company's valuation clocked in at $50 million (but you didn't hear it from me).

of self-doubt. As the temperature climbed on those summer afternoons, so did the melancholy among the young brand founders. There we were, a roomful of hopeless brand romantics, all believing we had something unique to offer. We'd perk up anytime a new face carrying a tote bag would round the corner, thinking it was a potential buyer. Most of the time, they'd stop at Uppercut (an up-and-coming label that produced *actual cut-and-sew!*) before leaving the show. We were envious. We coveted Uppercut's wide range of button-ups, custom headwear, and selvage denim. We were more a graphic design company than an apparel brand, and the lack of interest from buyers made the fact painfully obvious.

Ben and I sat and stared off into the distance, trying to ignore our neighbors' feigned busyness. We had two substantive conversations with store buyers that week and zero sales to show for it. The Hundreds stuck out like a sore thumb in that space. Although most exhibitors were start-ups, they had a faint idea as to the process of making and selling clothing. Buyers passed our starved rack of bright crispy tees with cartoony graphics for more established brands using ring-spun shirts and water-based applications. At the time, pure New York– and Japan-inspired streetwear like ours was an alien idea, so most designers were emulating potato-sack, backpack hip-hop attire like LRG or line-drawing illustrations on extra-medium hipster tees. Ben and I silently judged the grown men in Kangol hats and double-collared Polos. It only solidified that we weren't like anyone else in the industry. They were focused on selling clothing. We were more interested in telling a story, broadcasting a lifestyle, and participating in a culture. Our T-shirts were distinct—a few pointed parodies, bold graphics on starchy, open-end cotton shirts—but they weren't the main attraction. We were. And in the long run, we were right. Of the forty vendors showing at that year's Agenda, The Hundreds is one of the few brands that survived.*

Agenda was a warm-up for the main event, MAGIC, which was peaking along with the urban market in the mid-2000s. Brands like Phat Farm were erecting $2 million booths and doing hundreds of millions of dollars in sales every year. MAGIC was a larger-than-life spectacle. The aisles were clogged with mixtape artists, skate rug rats who'd snuck into the arena to snatch free stickers, and bloodsucking garmentos champing at the bit for a slice of that hip-hop pie. The year we hopped on board, the Vegas show curated a small section for indie brands like ours called the High 5 Campground. Again, our version of streetwear wasn't a visible component in the larger urban context, so we were lost in an abyss of halfhearted garage T-shirt labels. We sat alongside a girl selling brown shirts emblazoned with Biggie lyrics and Che Guevara stencils and a couple of white dudes with fauxhawks customizing trucker caps.†

We looked pretty pathetic, sandwiched between a music merch table and a couple from Nebraska who had found a modicum of success writing funny sayings on tees—the kind of novelty company you find advertised in the sidebar of a clickbait site. Meanwhile, our entire section was obscured in the

---

* Ben and I met two people that week with whom we remain close friends and business confidants today: Andres Izquieta and Dee Murthy of Five Four. The USC grads had a year on us in the industry but were already charging ahead with some impressive cut-and-sew. That season, Five Four was attempting to be one of those LRG-ish brands that targeted the Creative Recreation–wearing, polished hip-hop set. After a few failed turns and changes of partners, Dee and Andres reinvented Five Four as a respectable menswear line. Today, their brand is heralded as a legitimate L.A. fashion success story, dominating the men's subscription game, pulling in hundreds of millions a year. Oh yeah, and Andres was the guy wearing two Polo shirts at the same time. What a lame.

† The crown jewel of High 5 was a promising brand named Mato NYC—two Chinese kids from New York who had a background in apparel design and production. Like Uppercut, they had a couple pairs of denim and some wovens on their hangers and attracted loving attention from buyers and media hunting for the next big thing. Mato folded soon after that year's MAGIC show.

shadow of supersized booths like Lot 29 and Southpole. The licensed *Looney Tunes* artwork on their walls loomed over us like Thanksgiving Day floats. Between spinning on our thumbs and trash-talking the kooks around us, Ben and I would amble down the halls of the convention center, peeking into these prefab forts. Pretty models in gold heels beckoned buyers and scheduled appointments at the door. Men in do-rags and denim shorts caroused in the lounge, sifting through swag bags of flyers and tchotchkes. Gray-haired downtown Jews in flashy suits were compartmentalized in rooms, waving track jackets in the air and selling like street preachers. Seated like students in a schoolroom, the buyers feverishly took notes, whispered to each other, smiled, frowned, and fantasized about a gangbusters Christmas season. Track jackets were the new snake oil.

It felt like Agenda all over again, except this time we were trying to stand out among thousands of competitors, corporate behemoths, and American Apparel models strutting the grounds in cotton underwear. There was so much noise, so much T&A under that roof, that The Hundreds was swallowed up in the pandemonium. We were on our feet for ten hours straight, shouting over Twista and Paul Wall lyrics from the overhead speakers, forcing stickers and flyers onto anyone who made eye contact. We chased bottom-feeding stores around the corner, asking them if they'd like to browse our line. Nobody bit. "I'm sorry, man," the buyer of a popular Portland-based boutique told me, "but no one's heard of your company before."* As much as I wanted to clothesline him, as painful as it was to hear it, he was right. Why would you buy The Hundreds with no cachet, following, or cosign? Shops have limited shelf space, and every name they stock is an endorsement. Their credibility and brand

---

* This store would close its doors a year later.

value are on the line, not to mention their revenue. Maybe I wouldn't have bought me either.

So, Ben and I devised a plan. Like any situation where we have the lower hand, we reframed the circumstances to reverse the power. In our minds, true streetwear meant "limited edition" and "exclusivity," not peddling our art to the masses.* Streetwear seethed with attitude and particularity. We knew our T-shirts were the smartest, our brand was the coolest, so why give it away? Stores should be honored to buy The Hundreds gear from us. It was a privilege to even see our offerings. (Right? Right.)

That night, self-deception recharged, confidence renewed, we left the convention center and bought a black plastic tarp at the local Kmart. The next morning, we draped it over our rack, hiding our samples. For 99 percent of the buyers at the show, The Hundreds was now closed for public viewing. While our peers groveled and hounded shop owners, we kicked our Dunks back and yawned. Occasionally, the tarp drew the curiosity of an onlooker, who asked what was lurking underneath. We'd consider their badge, give them the once-over, and tell them we weren't conducting business that day. It didn't matter if they were shopping on behalf of Macy's or Up Against the Wall. If their store wasn't on our list of authentic streetwear boutiques from around the world (there were only maybe fifty of them, maybe three of which would even attend a show like MAGIC), then they couldn't see the line. We weren't even interested in a business card.

---

* You know what? Trade shows in general were the antithesis of streetwear in the early 2000s. Most of the brands that we looked up to sold exclusively through their own stores or international distributors. Real streetwear brands didn't wholesale in America. Yeah, we bucked that too.

It was no surprise that this scheme bummed store buyers out.

"Who the fuck do you think you are?" they'd shout.

Many vowed to never return. But of course they came back bright and early the next day. And the next show. Season after season, the same accounts pestered us, knocking louder on our door until we'd acquiesce and open up distribution to them. And when we did? They cherished The Hundreds and protected our brand, evangelizing our message to their communities.

The Hundreds felt special. The T-shirts felt special.

They felt special.

That first MAGIC, while our friends with the ironic tees and the cut-and-sew denim were racking up the numbers, we didn't write a single order yet returned home victorious. One man's failure is another man's success. We hadn't satiated the market's appetite. Instead, we were sculpting our brand, chiseling away the fat, and investing in the long haul. Ben and I were confident; more important than making a quick buck off cheap accounts, we were strengthening our image and brand integrity by defining who we were—and, more important, *who we were not*.

The black tarp philosophy took us far in this business. I know it was arrogant, but it forced us to focus on a future, stay disciplined with our sales strategy, and control the quality of the retail partners with whom we would align The Hundreds' name. Most of the brands on the floor at that MAGIC trade show lost their way, eventually taking that convenient $10,000 order from a shallow run-of-the-mill store and diluting their image in the process. They were all about making money—which is, obviously, incredibly important—but they forsook the importance of branding. Fashion rewards brands that can endure through the peaks and valleys of relevance. When you boil it down, it's all about how many times you can say no. It's a discipline. You have to train yourself to be comfortable with this word. If you're greedy and profit-driven, that means saying no to an easy and available check. If you're a people pleaser, prepare yourself to hurt feelings, be the asshole, and defend your brand against the interests of others.

Of course, I didn't have this all mapped out in my head at the time. I thought a brand was something you sear into a cow's ass; I never imagined I'd be giving brand-building lectures to crowded amphitheaters one day. We became accidental experts by simply playing the cards we were dealt. Ben and I were compensating for our lack of experience, money, and product offerings. Truthfully, deep down, underneath the rare Japanese sweatshirts and limited-edition New Eras, beneath that simmering bravado and snobbery, we knew we sucked donkey balls. I didn't know how to design; we didn't know the right people. The haters were right. We didn't have enough money to afford a rolling rack to show our wrinkled T-shirts, let alone a full collection.

But we flipped the script and championed our weaknesses as strengths:

1. Because we were new, we offered a fresh take. The Hundreds was sexy and different, not imprisoned by routine. We broke the rules and made our own, and that attracted a lot of attention.

2. Because there wasn't much product, The Hundreds was limited and rare. Nobody could get it because we couldn't make it! That built a demand and energy around our clothing that can't be bought or fabricated.

3. Without any money behind us, we did what we wanted. We were accountable to no one. We said no to everyone.

And we maintained total creative control. The Hundreds came first then and continues to come first now. Our financial well-being, let alone someone else's investment, doesn't matter as much as the brand's integrity. And we certainly don't care about anyone else's opinion.

What a couple of assholes.

18. FIGHT BACK

Your dreams are in danger, and "We Must Rise"
Our time has come we are under the gun "It's Do or Die"
—Dropkick Murphys, "Do or Die"

DIDN'T KNOW you did a collaboration with American Eagle?" the tweet read. I was ambling through my mentions in 2009, right when the social media platforms had started picking up steam. This kid, one of my followers, attached a grainy cell phone shot of a freestanding display inside a mall store. There were rows of boxers on the rack, designed in collections of fun patterns like polka dots and anchors. "Look at the second row," he noted. I zoomed in.

There was a set of white shorts printed all over with cartoon bombs making different facial expressions. The characters, however, looked strikingly familiar. I wasn't the first to draw a spherical bomb with features, but the cartoon's gaping mouth, spark, and black-white-red-yellow combination were an unmistakable lift of our mascot, Adam Bomb. But this wasn't a The Hundreds account or one of our flagships. It was American Eagle Outfitters, a nationwide chain with thousands of stores. It looked as if the designer had literally traced over our cartoon and repeated it across the fabric. If our fans saw this, they could be misled into thinking this was an official collaboration between the brands.

Collaborations make up a considerable part of our sales, but they're even more important for image and marketing, so we choose our partners carefully and strategically. Of course we hadn't collaborated with American Eagle Outfitters and never would. Nothing wrong with the colossal retailer, but theirs was a well-oiled clothing company, while ours was an indie label. Plus, American Eagle's style and aesthetic—washed cargo shorts and polos—didn't sync with ours. American Eagle advertised shiny campaigns with frat boys wearing hemp necklaces. I designed what I knew: boxy T-shirts and hoodies to skate in. We needed to position ourselves as far away from American Eagle as possible.

Over the next couple days, our general in-box was flooded with more reconnaissance from the field. Tweets from fans, emails from customers, and texts from friends pinged in from around the country. These bootleg boxers were everywhere, and so was the ire of our followers. If something like this had happened today, we would have said it "went viral." We wrote AEO a letter.

Surprise. They denied any wrongdoing, claiming their bomb character was original art. Then they asked how we could protect such a generic illustration.

This wasn't the first time we'd been ripped off. Larger

companies had stolen from us before; it's not unusual in the fashion industry. Because fashion design can't be copyrighted, the basis of the process is in pulling "inspiration" from peers and predecessors. Sometimes, the designer incorporates enough of a spin on an existing idea to create something relatively original. More often than not, however, the gray area between reference and rip-off is foggy. This is especially pronounced when the big dogs, staffed with bands of designers, ransack younger, smaller artists for fresh concepts.

The pattern on these American Eagle boxers wasn't a trivial T-shirt graphic, though. Not some random design we had used for a season and left by the wayside. Adam Bomb was synonymous with our brand. More than a logo, he was our identity (imagine if they had printed Nike swooshes as a pattern), and now millions of people would associate my drawing with American Eagle Outfitters. Literally overnight, our icon had gone mainstream and, completely unintentionally, so had our brand.

Our lawyers (Ben and I) got involved. Their lawyers (a squad of eight or nine pit bulls in Brooks Brothers suits) got in the ring. And thus ensued a long, expensive, and arduous legal process. We tugged and tore for months, issuing hollow threats, puffing out our chests, and growling through negotiations. At first, AEO told us they'd cough up a flat fee for the art. As if we had freelanced the design and offered it to them. As if we were their gun for hire. As if they were doing us a favor! Like, are you effing serious, dude?

We dug our heels in and rallied the troops. When American Eagle informed us that they'd recalled the product from their shelves, I took to my blog and asked our nationwide Bomb Squad to visit their local mall and confirm that they were gone. This time, the evidence poured in. The boxers were not only still for sale; they were moving like hotcakes, taking up even more real estate in the shops. One by one, we forwarded the testimonies to American Eagle's counsel, until they relented to discussing an ultimatum.

We never thought it would go so far. I didn't think we had a chance of going toe-to-toe with this Goliath. We were up against a publicly traded company that raked in $3 billion a year. And here we were, in our ghetto-ass office on the outskirts of town, eating roach-coach tacos at our IKEA desks. I'd written off the boxers as a disappointing and plaguing loss, one of those lowlights that would stain our history. "Remember the time American Eagle got one over on us?" Their legal team could kidnap our Adam Bomb and crush us under their thumb, slowly siphoning us of time and funds. We couldn't even afford a lawyer, so we manned up. We pooled whatever chops we'd doggybagged home from law school, did some quick push-ups, and answered the conference call.

"Hey, Bobby, hi, Ben, so we think we've come to a compromise."

We bristled. Compromise? These culture vultures hijacked our brand identity and were trying to meet us halfway? Shouldn't they walk their asses right back to where they were keeping our stolen shit and hand over our property?

"We will license your artwork"—I loved how they weren't asking, they were telling!—"whereby you get a percentage of the boxers' sales. The more we sell of your design, the more money you make. We both win here."

Ben punched the mute button. We were upset, hopeless, and cast in silence. I watched our logo swirl down the drain, all the energy we'd packed into Adam Bomb—our first legitimate mainstream hit. The sticker campaigns, the baseball cap embroidery, the watermarks on all our blog photography—all wasted on twenty thousand pairs of lousy underwear. Our hands were tied.

On the other end of the line, I visualized a ring of big-firm attorneys inside a palatial boardroom high atop a city skyscraper. Like a scene out of *The Wolf of Wall Street*. These jocks were probably high-fiving each other and cracking beers at our expense. This wasn't a negotiation; it was a hostile takeover. It was robbery. Somehow, they were calling the shots.

Yet they weren't the ones in power. The fact that a big corporation like this was billing attorney fees to placate two streetwear kids with a T-shirt line showed that they were worried. Maybe they wanted to exterminate the nuisance, or maybe they were nervous about the PR fallout. Or maybe we had more clout than we gave ourselves credit for. Instead of looking at this like American Eagle was too big to fail, we reminded ourselves that we were so small, we had nothing to lose.

Ben cracked a smile. I started laughing. There is nothing more powerful and frightening than someone who is hungry and desperate. Somebody who has everything to prove and the world to gain. This is why teenagers drive culture, even without realizing it. They are reckless in the way they dream and fight for their futures. Childlike in wonder, romantic in revolt. The Hundreds' greatest asset was a community who believed in us. We reached back and pitched as hard as we could with that.

"Hey, everyone, it's Bobby and Ben. We had a chance to mull it over, and we're rejecting the licensing deal. In fact, American Eagle is going to stop selling the boxers immediately."

"I'm sorry. We don't understand. There is a perfectly fair deal on the table. Listen, fellas, you'll get more money than you could have ever imagined for this design. You can take a couple days to think about it."

"Right. No. We thought about it," I said, interrupting him. "And if you don't stop selling the boxers, I am going to go on my blog and tell everyone about what happened here. We may be small, but you do know who reads my blog, right? Everyone from around the world who is monitoring the culture of street fashion, from the industry to the customers. The most influential tastemakers in the marketplace. Think of how this will make you look and how far that trickles down," I threatened.

A female attorney jumped in from their side. "You're not allowed to do that," she said. "Or else we'll sue."

"Sue us? For what? You want a couple T-shirts off our backs? You can have 'em. Or perhaps you'll take them without my permission anyway." I let them sit on that. "Actually, I can do whatever I want, and I've already written up my exposé and am prepared to publish. Just say when."

There was a deafening pause. A third lawyer jumped on the line. "Ahem, we're gonna have to call you back." And then a click.

Ben and I rolled our eyes. I rose up and started making my way out of his office. We figured it was going to take the afternoon, if not a few days, to hear back from the thieves. But as I was opening the door, Ben's line rang.

"Hello?"

"American Eagle is willing to forfeit the boxers without admission of wrongdoing. We will round up all the boxer shorts with the design at issue and donate them to a charity we work with in Africa. Are you okay with this resolution?"

This time, we were happy to concede to their demands. "Yes. Very much so. Thank you."

American Eagle was right. We would have made a lot of money by signing a licensing agreement on those boxers. At twenty thousand pairs, sold for roughly $10 a pop and a 12 percent cut, Ben and I were fit to take home roughly $25,000. This was a lot of money to us at the time (it still is!) and could have solved so many headaches we were wrestling with: our looming rent, a shipment of new sweatpants that had arrived earlier that week, or even our own personal bills like car payments and salaries. Times were tough, but we were perfectly happy having nothing. Ben and I were rich off the hope and promise of what was to come. That's all we needed to survive. But American Eagle had tried stealing that from us. Take our work, take our time, but you can't take our legacy. Fuck that.

It didn't feel great saying goodbye to those twenty-five racks, but we knew we'd see them again. Over the years, Adam Bomb–driven product has been responsible for millions and millions of dollars in sales, making it one of the most iconic logos in streetwear history. It still cracks me up to think that somewhere a kid in Africa is wearing that rare set of The Hundreds X American Eagle Outfitters boxers, skidmarking all over a piece of streetwear history.

19. OUTSIDE THE LINES

The world is my fuse

—Rites of Spring, "Deeper Than Inside"

CLICK-CLACK. I'M SEVEN years old and en route to Seoul, South Korea. It's the summer of 1987. *Click-clack*. The armrest's ashtray opens wide like Hungry Hungry Hippos. I swing the cold metallic flap shut with my finger. Cigarette ashes line the mouth of the tray, like margarita salt, left over from the rolled paper stub belonging to the businessman seated next to me. My hands probably shouldn't be in here, poking around the darkness for buried treasure, but this is my in-flight entertainment for the next twelve hours.

If you're reading this on a plane, this is going to sound crazy. Even if you're old enough to remember, I'm sure you've forgotten.

But until a couple decades ago, adult passengers could wantonly smoke cigarettes in that seat you're sitting in now. The nicotine headaches were real and pounding and the cabin was suffocating. There were no touch screens with movies on demand, no gluten-free southwestern chicken wraps at your beck and call, which is especially bizarre when I think back on traveling for twelve hours straight as a kid. When I was a child, my parents would walk me right up to the gate and hand me off to a random stewardess to cross the Pacific Ocean armed with nothing more than a bright yellow placard and a special pin from the pilot.

I won't even let my children go into the front yard without me. Yet when we were kids, my older brother, Larry, and I would take this international flight in the summers to stay with aunts and uncles and grandparents who spoke in a strange tongue, would squeeze our cheeks as if there were American honey in there, and drowned us with cartons of banana-flavored soy milk. Some of my favorite childhood memories come from those humid summer months spent in the postwar South Korean capital. We walked to school in the mornings, our shirts sticking to our backs under the dank air. Our book bags over our shoulders, we'd cross through street markets and hear local farmers in slippers selling round pears, nuts, and dried fish. We'd often get interrogated at the cash register. "Are you Korean? What a disgrace. Why don't you speak Korean?" Larry and I would shrug, grab our snacks, and run.

Upon returning to the States at summer's end, I'd kiss the carpet in my air-conditioned bedroom. I was so happy to be home under the red, white, and blue. We had so much space, so much freedom and diversity. I loved going to a school where everyone had different-colored hair and ate various things for lunch: sandwiches and burritos and corkscrew pasta. Nothing made me appreciate home more than leaving it. But I always felt like a new person in the fall, as if I'd wrapped my mind a little further around the world over the summer in ways my classmates didn't see and couldn't understand.

My dad worked himself into the ground. The only time he came up for air was for vacations. So, he used those brief windows of family time to pluck us from the California basin and show us the world. There were road trips up north to national parks and south of the border to Mexican beach towns. One summer, we stood on a blue glacier in Alaska. Next, we were whitewater rafting down the rivers of Costa Rica. I was a kid; of course I wanted to stay home with my friends over spring break and Dorito my brains out on Sega Genesis. But my dad was slowly curating our worldview. The more people we met, the more places we visited, the more we saw outside our suburban existence—and ourselves. The world is a big and limitless place. And those trips helped me understand how small and humble we truly are.

When young people come to me seeking direction, whether in life or career, my first suggestion is to travel. Even if it's getting on a bus and going three towns up the highway. The fastest way to grow is by leaving your comfort zone. You gotta stay uncomfortable, constantly adjusting to new contexts, shuffling life's Rubik's Cube around in your hands and studying it from all angles. If you're at ease, if the answers are on your dinner plate every night, you'll get lazy. You'll stop listening to yourself, which can be fatal, and you'll stop learning, which is even worse. If you're being challenged, you'll exercise your brain in creative ways. You have to persist and adapt. Traveling does that for you. Waking up in new beds, tasting exotic foods, deciphering directions when you can't read the language. Traveling puts you in other people's shoes. It teaches you compassion and empathy and, greatest of all, humility. It's impossible to visit a country, encounter new people, and not imagine yourself as one of those people. The goal is to uncork yourself from the center of the universe.

When people ask me what my favorite part of The Hundreds is, I say, "All the people I get to meet around the world." The Hundreds has provided Ben and me (and our staff—from designers to salespeople) with an awesome gift: an excuse to exercise the privilege of worldwide travel. At least once a month, we fly somewhere. São Paulo, Brazil, to check in with our licensing partner. Stockholm, Sweden, to throw a party around a collaboration. Seoul, South Korea, for shopping and design inspiration. But one city in particular stands out as a second home for myself and The Hundreds, and it's maybe not one you'd expect: the Hong Kong Special Administrative Region of the People's Republic of China, or for short, Hong Muthafuckin' Kong.

"DUDE, THAT'S Alyasha."

"Go up to him and say something!"

"Like what? 'Dude, you're Alyasha'? I think he's aware of that."

We're standing outside Agenda's exhibition in downtown San Diego, and I'm gathering my nerve. Aaron Levant has gotten a few of these trade shows under his belt. Now he's taking on the massive, corporate Action Sports Retailer show at the San Diego Convention Center. He's unapologetically parked Agenda in an open warehouse right out front of the larger conference. It looks like a flea market inside with rolling racks gridlocked in a veritable mosh pit of start-up T-shirt brands, indie skate companies, and Etsy-ish women's labels. Lots of fashion mullets, hot pink, and splatter paint. *Relax*, it's 2005.

The cooler kids have congregated on the sidewalk out front

after the show. Ben and I are linking up with old friends and making new ones. San Diego had a vibrant design scene in the early 2000s, an answer to the fashion bubble of Rainbow flip-flops and jarhead fades that have historically demarcated sunny, sleepy S.D. There was Green Lady, who was responsible for HunterGatherer. Shepard Fairey had his Blk/Mrkt agency in Hillcrest with Dave Kinsey (Shep's OBEY wheatpaste propaganda was still in its Andre the Giant Has a Posse infancy). San Diego was also home to the mainstream skate and surf industry. But the more radical designers were looking outside the space for inspiration—everything from designer denim like Diesel, to Japanese street fashion, to experimental hip-hop by the likes of Kid Koala and Deltron 3030. A collective of firebrand artists and brand visionaries was also coalescing downtown—Irons, selfdiscovery.prj, Human Resources—many of them refugees of Alphanumeric—a technical skate brand that was far ahead of its time.

Alpha was founded and commandeered by Alyasha Owerka-Moore, a New York wunderkind in the urban and skate fashion arena who played a dominant role in Russell Simmons's Phat Farm, Shut Skateboards, and American Dream Inc. Aly is lanky; like a Christmas tree that's too big for its room, he curls over at the top. His father is black and Native American, his mother a blond Russian. In the nineties, when mainstream skateboarding was first finding its footing, Aly moved out west to launch Droors and Dub, the apparel component to DC Shoes. He then introduced Alphanumeric to the world, a culturally innovative skate brand known for its diverse team, technical apparel, and tie-ins with car culture. Now he was standing ten feet from me and Ben, wearing Fiberops, his latest project, an upscale Japanese street brand in partnership with Tabo Kagaya (RIP).

"Excuse me, Alyasha," I said. "My name is Bobby. My friend Ben and I started a new brand. It's called The Hundreds and—"

"I've heard of you," he said, cutting me short.

"You have?"

"Yeah! Good to meet you. What are you guys doing for dinner?"

It was that fast and Aly was that chill. He walked us a few hundred yards over to his studio in the Gaslamp Quarter. We shot some pool and went through his custom action figure collection. There were rare vintage Nikes clumped in heaps upstairs, foreign movie posters, punk rock patches, and pinup art. Aly's studio is well-known—the ultimate cool guy's man cave. Knives and pinup babes and timeless records. Later that night, we walked down the street with a larger crew for dinner at a local haunt. I was beside myself. Alyasha was one of my legitimate heroes. I had studied his every move from logo design to the bias of a plaid on a button-up. Why was he being so cool to us?

"Just ride with it," Ben said with a shrug.

"Do you guys do any cut-and-sew?" Aly asked us later that evening, once we were properly stuffed and glazed.

We sheepishly shook our heads. "No, just T-shirts for now."

"What are you doing next week?" he asked me.

"Um, I . . . uh, nothing?" Absolutely freaking nothing. Damn, this was embarrassing.

"You're coming with me to Hong Kong. I want you to meet my agent out there, Ben Cheung. You guys need to be making cut-and-sew. He'll get you situated."

It's Friday night. "Like, *next week*, next week?"

"My flight leaves Tuesday afternoon."

I'm going to Hong Kong.

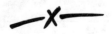

HONG KONG is unlike any other place in the world. But I guess you can say the same for New York City, or Dubrovnik, or your local Cracker Barrel. Every place is unlike any other place in the world, really. Hong Kong, however, is its own reality. It's simultaneously sci-fi and old world. It's hi-tech yet primitive, like a pinball machine. It's the incessant hum of pink powdered gas sputtering through neon signs. It's the cacophony of varied languages colliding with cab horns. It's the smell of churning AC exhaust intermingling with the air of a tropical storm. It's roughly fourteen hours between LAX and HKG. Another half-hour train ride into the city. I remember the first time I emerged from the subway station and set foot into the Atlantic City–meets–*Blade Runner* bustle of Causeway Bay. I stood still for a moment, duffel bag in tow, but it felt like I was moving a hundred miles per hour. I stayed in a friend's tenth-floor warehouse space, a glorified inventory closet, sleeping on a cot behind a fort of brown boxes. In my next visits, I'd lodge in hostels with communal bathrooms. I traveled alone on those first trips, exploring the island in solitude, listening to its rhythms. I ate greasy, delicious foods in unclean restaurants and paid dearly with paralyzing MSG poisoning or worse, dysentery.

Many clothing companies produce their goods farther east in mainland China (in smoggy factory towns like Guangzhou and Shenzhen), but Hong Kong is China's foyer. The nation's waiting room.* The international portal that is Hong Kong retains enough Western flavor to ease the cultural transition for tourists and people there on business. Typically, travelers hang their hats on the island for a few days before forging deeper into

---

* A city where hands are shaken and dollars are made. You don't just have lunch to catch up with friends here. In this city, if there's no business to be made over a meal, no clear path to profits cut by the time the check arrives, it's considered time wasted. Time is currency in Hong Kong. Efficiency is a style of business valued as highly as parsimony.

naked Chinese territory. But this is usually my first and final stop. It's where I was trained and mentored as a young designer. Here, in the Blue Nail office, high in the Kowloon skyline, home to Ben Cheung, lies ground zero for The Hundreds apparel.

If you were walking along one of Hong Kong's busy streets in the middle of the day, you might not notice Ben Cheung scurrying along. He's salt-and-peppery now but maintains a boyish grin and zeal. Sometimes he'll pair funky prescription glasses with a puffy mesh cap, but then so do a lot of H.K. locals. Even if you're sharing an office with Ben, you might miss him. And I often did. He'll camouflage into the fabric swatch books surrounding his desk. Ben Cheung is an unassuming guy, but he's punk rock, and his design speaks for him. As a founding member of the legendary Purple Pin one-stop shop that introduced nineties urban labels like Mecca, he broke off fifteen years ago to start his own venture, Blue Nail. Ben Cheung is our secret weapon—a Hong Kong production agent who is also one of the best designers in the game. You won't find him discussed in any Hypebeast comments thread, but industry veterans know him. And they know he's with us.

I think there's a misconception that because I work in clothing, I'm into fashion. I'm not. I enjoy the imaginative design that high fashion offers. I do appreciate the theater of it all—the extravagant photo shoots, the fashion week paparazzi, and the limited-edition exclusivity of special product. I just don't get the politics and the snobbery that come with fashion—the pretense of it all. There's an ugly classism that lingers in the garments like stale cigar smoke.

That's why I champion streetwear, because it's less to do with the pomp and circumstance and more about the storytelling. I'm a black T-shirt, Chucks, and Dickies guy because (a) it's pragmatic and no-nonsense attire, and (b) it says everything about what's mattered most to me in my life: California, skateboarding, and punk. When it comes to design, I don't look high and I don't look to my side. I prefer to look behind me.

Ben Cheung recognized this appeal to practicality. He appreciated that I'd rather dress everyday people in functional gear than outfit an emperor in new clothes. He wanted me to bear down on the essence of L.A. street style while expanding from within. I could use staple garments and silhouettes as a base while applying a deeper understanding of the materials to make the clothes exceptional. Ben explained the properties of twill, loop back, and ripstop nylon, opening my mind to a language of apparel design beyond T-shirt blanks and swap meet clothing. Men's fashion might not be as flamboyant and complex as women's, but I welcomed this challenge of designing within limited means. As Ben showed me, a half-inch adjustment in sleeve width could make a significant difference in a garment, as did 240 g/m^2 cotton over 320 for a fleece pullover, or a tackle twill for a sewn-on patch versus self-fabric.

Alyasha's influence was also present in my work. I was a fan, then a student, then an unworthy reproduction. In my early Hong Kong trips, he would patiently teach me how to use the Adobe Illustrator pen tool to draw CADs. We'd sit in the shadows of my damp hostel, and he'd explain tech packs to me (technical drawings of the garment, blueprints for the factories to follow). Aly taught me there's not only one way to open a pocket, that screen printing isn't just for T-shirts, and he'd take me research shopping at luxury boutiques and secondhand stores to prove it. Aly's the reason I fell in love with Hysteric Glamour. His gift was in extracting and highlighting the details in garments and allowing his designs to flow from there. From the luster of pearl buttons to the coarse grain of raw denim, there is always a purpose and appropriate application for each design element.

Alyasha is always buried in the minutiae of his designs, like a hacker poring over code. His degree of care is outweighed only by his enthusiasm for narrative.*

I HAVE terrible sleep habits, and jet lag just makes things worse. During my regular Hong Kong visits, I'd overcome the first forty-eight hours of sleeplessness by pounding the pavement in the fabric district. Here, in the bustling Kowloon neighborhood of Sham Shui Po, Ben Cheung and Alyasha Owerka-Moore would guide me through the fabric market, educating me on the feel, stretch, and wearability of different materials. For blocks, these tiny shops hung waterfall racks of fabric swatches. Small squares of tartan, yarn-dyed stripes, and allover-print polka dots stapled onto cards. If you liked what you saw, you'd call the mill's number on the card to order a certain yardage—if there was any left. A lot of this stuff was overage, leftover reams of fabric from major-designer production runs. Occasionally, a Bape camo print might pop up, or a knockoff Burberry plaid, but

---

* Aly has fathered generations of brands in streetwear's young history, from the mass and American urban to the niche and Japanese. Every step was birthed with a story and purpose. Alphanumeric looked at late-nineties skateboarding attire from a technical standpoint—lots of performance fabrics and bungee cords—weaving in Asian car culture and backpack hip-hop. His latest, Thee Teen-Aged, was a denim brand rich with mid-century American nostalgia, rock and roll, and post-skate. There is a reason for everything in Aly's choices. The greatest streetwear designers, to me, stand for the same principles. They all paint a cohesive story with their work, substantiated by experience and credibility. To me, it's never mattered how financially viable an idea might be, how popular a brand gets in the mainstream, or whom the blogs are shouting out. After the hype dies (and it always does), it's the emotional repercussions that bestow a legacy. It's like that Maya Angelou quotation: "I've learned that people will forget what you said, people will forget what you did, but people will never forget how you made them feel." I couldn't tell you the most popular sneaker to drop last week, but I do remember every Undercover piece I've worn and loved, the inside of the original SSUR store in New York, and my first X-Large OG Gorilla hoodie, because of how much culture and narrative were attached to the brands and their offerings. Nowadays, it's all about the celebrity associations and price tag, but timeless design is all about the narratives, the historical and emotional value.

there were also superior Japanese fabrics and premium denim made to order.

Wading through the dense humidity, we traversed the district with tote bags teeming with swatches over our shoulders, the loose fibers clinging to our hair and sweat-stained backs. We'd step over stray dogs and naked beggars, pass sidewalk butchers selling soiled poultry in the sun, and duck out of freak thunderstorms. All to scour for ingredients to cook up in the next The Hundreds collection. There were entire stores just for fluorescent synthetics and zippers. One of my favorite haunts sold every kind of camouflage you can imagine, from tiger stripe to purple-brown French brushstrokes. Checkered flannels, corduroy, lenticular plastics, and speckled slub knits. It's like a music producer finding an entire city of beats to thumb through.

The more time I spent in Hong Kong, the harder it was for me to know myself apart from it. In my earlier travels, I didn't know where to eat outside the mall's California Pizza Kitchen. Now I'd zigzag fluidly through the neighborhoods and MTR subways, stopping momentarily at corner vendors for a swig of bitter black tea or fatty dim sum. I'd bathed in the chaos of typhoons and night markets and let the oily bedlam wash over me. Even at home in Los Angeles, I'd feel most at ease near busy streets and crowded restaurants. Suddenly American sidewalks felt sparse and the rooms deafeningly quiet, and I was strangely lonely. At work, I also noticed Hong Kong's hand guiding mine in the design process. I went from dressing in solids to designing with clashing patterns, the unlikely marriage of colors that reminded me of the dissonant open-market fabrics. While other designers used palettes of primary reds and blues, mine were now montages of kaleidoscopic confetti. I mixed yellow houndstooth with overdyed indigo. Army fatigues with a buttery chambray.

I was already averse to conformity, but Hong Kong persuaded me to color further outside the lines. By its biology, the nation itself exists between rules: Hong Kong is a melting pot of cultures—ethnic, social, and underground. It's the gateway to Asia, but only recently free from British dominion, making for a unique English accent. Because of its geography, there's heavy Australian crossover, and due to its trading ports Hong Kong attracts Americans on business. The fashion manifestation is, unsurprisingly then, characteristically indecisive. In Hong Kong, it's normal to eat dinner at an Irish pub with a French Chinese girl from Melbourne. Just as it's okay to match bright red basketball shoes with a camouflage backpack and a parasol. The people dress more confidently because they're liberated from order and tradition. It's an open-minded fashion that supports experimental design. It was this philosophy that enabled me to see L.A. style anew. I'd learned a lesson that could only be gleaned in the bowels of southern Kowloon, seven thousand miles from home.

At the time, I don't think our customers understood the design direction of The Hundreds apparel. I'm sure it was confusing. We had established our name on colorful parody T-shirts that sourced nostalgic 1980s and '90s culture. So, I'm assuming they wanted something more straight and narrow from us once it got to outer layers. Maybe a basic zip-up sweatshirt? Skinny jeans? No—our first cut-and-sew offerings were made up of $300 raw selvage Japanese denim, wet micronylon jackets, and cardigans. I designed multicolored JAGS-patterned leather belts, zebra-stripe cargo shorts, and a reversible pink-and-brown scarf hoody (a scarf that also acts as a hood). It wasn't a scalable model—nothing that could be packaged and marketed to a broader customer base—but I was throwing everything at the wall to see what would stick. I was experimenting. Actually, I was learning.

Over the years, we've whittled down the collection to a unified The Hundreds aesthetic, merchandised sellable seasons around it, and cemented a "look" that is entirely ours—classic, core California streetwear. But when you get down to the granular details—the warp and weft of the jeans, the railroad tracks of a flat-lock stitch—you'll find tailored into the ribbed cuffs the noise and aroma of Hong Kong, Ben Cheung and Alyasha Owerka-Moore and their invaluable lessons, and a twenty-five-year-old me, splashing paint onto the sidewalks and jumping into rainbow puddles.

20. ALLOVER

T HE EASIEST WAY to chronicle streetwear is by trend. Nobody keeps track of the straightforward stuff—the yarn-dye
striped shirts, and coach's jackets, and knit beanies. That's all
white noise. Streetwear's timeline is punctuated with boister-
ous, and often regrettable, trends that draw store lineups and
fetch fat resale prices. It's on the brands to get a little weird and
design outside the box. But that's not what sets off market
trends. It's rappers and other celebrities who popularize fads.
Like what Tyler, the Creator did with tie-dye and Supreme box
caps. Or how Kanye moved on Rob Garcia's En Noir and made
leather jogging pants popular enough to garner a Jimmy Kimmel

joke. But streetwear wasn't always on celebrities' radar, and vice versa. In fact, streetwear, in its early stages, did its best to work outside the mainstream spotlight. When I think back on those years and how trends ignited, I think it was more about brands working together to reject the status quo and impact the market. The greatest example of this is what happened with all-over print in the mid-2000s.

Allover print is exactly what it sounds like: a repeating screen-printed pattern that covers an entire T-shirt or hooded sweatshirt. Military camouflage is the original allover print. We begin with camo and end somewhere around Louis Vuitton's LV monogram. Somewhere between exists a recurring trend that permeates streetwear every five to ten years. As you read this, depending on the season and where we're at on the fashion spectrum, allover print sounds either fun and irreverent or downright hideous. It's a recurring trend that never ages well. But every few years, we catch a collective bout of amnesia and welcome it back with open arms. It's like swearing into the toilet, "Ugh, I'm never drinking again!" while rolling around the cold tile with a hangover and twelve hours later taking another tequila shot to the neck.

Fashion volleys between extremes. Responding to the urban industry's slate of sedated tones and uninspired graphic design in the mid-2000s, young independent streetwear brands cracked the color palette wide open. I think we were all bored of department store labels like Rocawear and Akademiks. The more sophisticated consumers wanted to stand out. They didn't just want to wear something that was exclusively found in Japan. They wanted their clothes to pop in a crowd. A Bathing Ape did that. The premium Japanese label wasn't afraid of dancing all over the Pantone book. While American street labels were conservatively paring their hues to dark grays, navies, and reds,

Bape was vomiting fluorescent Skittle rainbows over their customers. In fact, their oversized allover-print sweatshirts were often ridiculed and compared to pajamas—loud, Technicolor, and immature.

We wanted to make something like that but didn't have the means to produce overseas. We couldn't cut-and-sew allover-printed sweatshirts here in the States, and even if we could, we couldn't meet the minimum orders. So, we resorted to an old-school screen-printing technique called belt printing using antiquated machinery that most shops discarded at some point in the 1980s.

By the mid-2000s, there was one factory left in L.A. that had held on to its belt printer. Pac Splash knew that allover print would find its way back after a mad run in the 1980s.

"You T-shirt companies and your belt prints," grumbled the man in charge. "One day everyone wakes up and decides that they want allover prints again. What do you do, call each other?"

He leads us to the back of his warehouse and pulls back the covering on the Gutenberg press of screen printing.

"Sure, we'll dust off the machine, work it to the bone for a year, and then y'all will kill it outta nowhere, for no reason. Happens every decade."* He shakes his head.

The way belt printers work is by repeating a pattern over a garment's seams. A typical screen-printing machine snags a hemline or collar, and the paint pools around the bump, making for an unsightly error along the creases. But a belt printer steamrolls right over those stitches. It's not an entirely clean and exact process, but it's a convenient alternative to doing it the long way (printing the T-shirt panels first, then sewing the piece together).

The Venice-based, Rob Dyrdek–owned Rogue Status did it

---

* He was dead right.

first. You may remember their Gun Show pattern, with rows of firearms marching around the tees and hoodies. Other popular allover prints in streetwear at the time were Nom de Guerre's Arabic writing, Crooks & Castles' Chain Gang, and Mighty Healthy's MCM rip.

Our first contribution to the allover-print craze was the "Paisley," offered on a black zip-up hooded sweatshirt, incorporating repeating white (or tonal black) *buta* droplets, inspired by a classic bandanna print. To be honest, I don't even like the paisley pattern, but I did like how it looked on a sweatshirt template. This allover print was uniquely ours. Pac Splash printed five hundred of them, and we planned to sell them for $100 each, which we thought was fair considering the elaborate printing costs and *because we were cool, dude.*

There's a video I'd shot floating around on YouTube of 7909 Rosewood Avenue—not yet our first store, but our first office. It would become a makeshift clubhouse in the early afternoons, depending on how much we felt like doing our jobs, how much our friends felt like doing their jobs, and who had weed. In the video, there are a few of us hanging out front on the narrow sidewalk, including Nick Tershay of Diamond, Mega of Black Scale, and Aaron Pepper (RIP). The guys are hovering around a brown cardboard box that is overflowing with black hoodies. Sleeves are haphazardly hanging over the edge like tentacles as the guys dig in. Ben and I had just gotten back from Pac Splash with a fresh batch of Paisley hoodies, and everyone wanted first dibs. You can see Nick and Mega pull the zips on, throw their hoods up, and study how the pattern locks up along the sleeves' edges.

Seeing the sweatshirts on their backs, Ben and I couldn't wait to share them with the rest of the world. We didn't have the patience to go through the traditional wholesale channels, selling them to stores and shipping them out weeks later. So, I went on our website and announced the Paisley hoodie would go on sale later that night in our online shop, even though we'd never set up a proper e-commerce platform before. I uploaded the video to our blog, along with flats of the sweatshirt and photographs of the homies in the Paisley hoodie.* Then I jury-rigged the PayPal cart together with a spool of dental floss and passed out on the sofa around 3:00 a.m. The splash page for the-hundreds.com now advertised the new Paisley hoodie for sale. The last thing I remember was turning my phone off. I wanted to sleep just a tiny bit before Ben blew my phone up in the morning with something I'd mistyped out of exhaustion.

THUMP. I cracked an eyelid open. That sounded as if it came from . . . *thump thump thump* . . . my front door. What time was it? I looked at my phone. Dead battery. I looked for the clock. Eight thirty in the morning. It must be my landlord. I'm late on rent again. "Hold on, putting pants on."

"Bobby! It's Misa!" It's my girlfriend. She's usually on her way to work at this time in the morning. What's she doing at my apartment? I swing the door open and the world rushes in. The angry morning traffic, streaks of sunlight through the trees, and Misa in her work clothes with a flushed—yet excited—face.

"Is your phone off? We've been trying to call you all morning!"

"We?"

---

* Social media hadn't been invented yet, so I updated my blog several times a day as you would an Instagram. Except I was processing photos and embedding them into Dreamweaver HTML through an FTP. I was literally building and rebuilding our website every few hours to get fresh content out there. You kids have it so easy with your status updates and camera rolls.

"Me and Ben. He sent me here because we couldn't get through to you." She catches her breath, setting up the important news. "Pull the website down! You have to take it down, now!"

"What? Why?"

"You guys sold out of those Paisley hoodies, but you *over*sold. I guess you blew out of them in the first hour they went up, so for the past five hours, you guys have been selling tens of thousands of dollars of hoodies you don't have!"

Oh, my Gucci. As preposterous as this sounded, she was making perfect sense. One of the problems with substituting a legitimate shopping cart for a PayPal button was that there was no way to set an inventory or limit. Neither Ben nor I had foreseen this problem. We'd anticipated selling only a handful of hoodies overnight. We'd planned on absorbing the orders as they rolled in over the next few days, one by one. What we hadn't imagined—no way, no how—was that we would sell thousands of sweatshirts overnight. I hastily kissed my girlfriend, thanked her, and then whipped my laptop open. Within minutes, I had pulled all traces of the Paisley hoodie off our website. Then I booked it to the Rosewood office, where Ben was pacing back and forth on the street, waiting for me.

"Fuck!" he screamed. As is often the case with Ben, I couldn't tell if he was mad or happy or mad that he was happy. "What do we do?"

We let the dust settle on that golden Friday morning and started by refunding over half the money and fulfilling the rest of the orders. Then we celebrated our win by treating ourselves to lunch at an Italian restaurant on Melrose. It was 11:00 in the morning, and we were the only patrons. Ben, Scotty, and I rolled up in our loud streetwear clothes. These ratty kids had just made $100,000 overnight. It was like waking up to find your band had topped the *Billboard* charts. We sat around that table in reverie, slurping our Bolognese, celebrating our first hit single. If there were this many people out there who were down to buy something from us, what else could we sell them?

Bigger question: What do we do with all this cash? We weren't stressing the luxuries and toys (I was perfectly happy with my rusty RAV4). What we needed was a way to make this money make more money. What would help our brand, a community-oriented project, be the best version of itself?

We returned to the office, stood on the curb, and stared at our big open windows. Truth be told, Ben and I had forever talked about having a shop one day. But that future was now in sight. A retail store seemed adult and serious. Plus, it required a lot of money. I looked around and imagined kids shopping, learning, and making friends. Customers lining up for limited-edition product, locals skating up and down Rosewood Avenue. We already had a solid little crew forming around our clubhouse, but if we had a permanent home, The Hundreds could convert a generation of youth. Ben and I secretly wanted our first store to be in the corner spot of Fairfax and Rosewood's main intersection, but Sal Barbier had already planted his flag there with his SLB boutique. So, for the time being, we preferred to keep a low profile. We stayed in the cut. It was very streetwear of us.

"We're gonna turn this into a store now," Ben said, of 7909. "Our store."

Everyone already knew to find us there. It was time to make it official. Outside a couple plates of ravioli and some table wine, we didn't pocket a dime of that Paisley money. We drew up plans for our first store, instead. Now was the time for The Hundreds Los Angeles.

This was the end of the beginning.

21. WE DON'T BUILD STORES. WE BUILD STORIES.

ONE DAY, I'LL have to explain brick-and-mortar retail stores to my grandchildren. "You know that big apartment building on the corner? Where your friends X-343a and m29u live? That used to be a shopping mall," I'll tell them. "Each one of those apartments was once a store that sold stuff we needed."

"Like a hundred little Amazons?"

"Yes, dear, something like that."

"But Grandpa, didn't they just drop off everything you bought with drones?"

"Not quite, it was the other way around. Before Amazon

delivered our military rations to us, we had to get into our cars and drive ourselves to the stores."

"Grandpa! You drove your own cars?"

"Yes, as dangerous as that sounds, the government trusted us to control our own speeding death machines down the highways."

"Wow! How did people find the time to go to the store for eggs and shoes and things between fighting robots and fleeing the receding coastline?"

"Well, it's worse than you think. We had to drive all over town and go to different stores for different items. We bought our groceries from a supermarket. We bought our phones from an electronics store. And there were entire shops just for greeting cards!"

"Sigh. No wonder Emperor Trump came into power. America wasn't making very good decisions back then, Grandpa."

"No, I guess we deserved the fall of democracy."

"Grandpa?"

"Yes, dear?"

"What's a phone?"

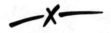

WE HAD four hundred square feet to play with. A white box the size of a large living room. This was to be our first store, and we needed to make a statement. Plus, we were still looked at as a small-time T-shirt project—a couple of kids with an elaborate extracurricular activity. A physical home base would tell the world we meant business.

Japan was driving the street fashion trends, especially with regard to store build-out. If you looked at what New York boutiques were doing, there was a minimalist influence that trickled down from Tokyo retail architecture. Blank walls, cold gray concrete, floating racks with spaced-out hangers. A single item of each style rested quietly, immaculately folded on a birchwood shelf, enveloped with incense smoke. I'm not sure if it was conscious, but because the inventory wasn't grab-and-go, you were at the staff's mercy for sizes and colors. The clerks dictated the shopping relationship. It was in their power to judge whether you were worthy of buying something in their shop. And thus, the snobby, cool guy stereotype of streetwear retail was born. Although, for better or worse, that cool guy attitude and snobbery contributed to streetwear's enduring mystique and allure.

Eventually, a new wave of sneaker and streetwear stores would open across the world, simulating the clean and subtle aesthetic. How convenient! Minimalist design was not only easy to duplicate but also gentle on the pocketbook. All that was required to complete the look were a set of IKEA LACK shelves bolted into the wall, glass countertops, and some Medicom Bearbrick toys.

If we wanted our shop design to stand apart and be noticed, we had to fall out of line. Instead of stark concrete, what about warm wood? We invested in dark custom cabinetry and flooring that synced up along the edges and projected a seamless design. As opposed to sterile white tones, we made our store black, which correlated with the color used most prominently throughout our brand.* No prefabricated IKEA furniture in the shop, not even in the bathroom. We didn't cut any corners. Fearful that our brand's longevity would last only as long as the fixtures, we paid top dollar for the finest-quality materials.

---

* Although we're known for pop accents, our base is black. It's a nod to the intersection of eighties California sports teams like the Raiders and Kings. It was also a common denominator among heavy metal, punk, and rap.

I admired the serene brook that flowed in the Undefeated store on La Brea and the skate bowl inside Supreme's new Fairfax location. These artistic touches were conversation pieces that had nothing to do with selling clothes and everything to do with relaying a message. The artist Tofer Chin installed *Corn Mouth*, a diorama of a journey from good to evil, along one of our walls. Although the art took up valuable retail space in an already cramped store, it gave the shopping experience life and was what people first remembered when they thought of The Hundreds Los Angeles.

Out front, I dug out two grave sites, one on each side of the door. I'd raided a local prop house that supplied the skeletons for the *Pirates of the Caribbean* films and planted two sets of skulls and bones into the ground. I also buried spray cans and my broken skateboard. The installation symbolized my and Ben's fossilized remains; the message was that our life experiences and souls were kneaded into this store. The artifacts were an homage to the California culture that raised us.

It worked to our advantage to be short on space. The staff couldn't get away with being assholes in an intimate environment. I know it's cooler to have dickheads crossing their arms behind the counter and making everyone feel like diarrhea, but the elitist vibe doesn't align with us as people or as a brand. We aim to hire chill, welcoming shop kids who greet the customers and make them feel at home. They also retrieve sizes and colors, even though much of the inventory is stacked up in the front for the customers to sort through. Our staff ends up doing their share of refolding and hanging, but it also means that the customers feel comfortable in our home and feel a stronger connection with the brand. Which ultimately means they stick around longer and have more opportunities to spend their dollars.

I LIKE to say that we don't make stores; we make stories.

As important as The Hundreds Los Angeles is for selling clothes and marketing awareness, its primary function is to provide a shelter for our community and lifestyle.

To fertilize this brand ethos of "People over Product," we teased the store opening months before with our first annual Labor Day Block Party. There's nothing Ben loves more than throwing a good event. He saw the opportunity to bring the burgeoning Fairfax streetwear neighborhood together by shutting down Rosewood Avenue, firing up a grill, and having friends DJ throughout the day. Streetwear is pegged for its product collaborations, sometimes to a wearisome degree. But we champion the human collabs as well: relationships and partnerships have made the culture strong. As new brands moved onto the block, one by one, Fairfax grew disjointed and awkward. The customer knew something was happening there, but without any camaraderie the neighborhood felt forced and unripe.

The Hundreds' Labor Day Block Party changed that. On the hottest and most humid day of the year, the indie brands, the upcoming cool kids, and the shop clerks came out to fraternize and support the scene. Designers flew in from San Francisco and New York, got hyphy and inebriated, and linked. Then they blogged about it. Within a week, all eyes were on Fairfax. The brands themselves were already generating noise. Now that they had joined forces and were working together, a network was mobilizing. For four years (until the City of Los Angeles shut it down permanently), we produced that Labor Day Block Party, and it only got rowdier and more influential. Fairfax—as we know it today—happened for a lot of reasons. But most of those reasons can be traced back to those hundred-degree afternoons on Rosewood. (Anyone who says otherwise either is lying or doesn't know their history.)

So, by the time The Hundreds Los Angeles opened in February 2007, this spirit of community insulated the walls. As impressive as the build-out was, our audience fast learned that the shop had less to do with the structure and all to do with the company it kept.

Our friend KB Lee and I collaborated on an exclusive New Era baseball cap for the store. KB was inspired by a Polo reference, incorporating a navy twill crown with a soft mustard-yellow leather brim. I reduced "Rosewood" down to "RSWD" to mimic Polo's four letters. The hat sold out in hours, but RSWD lasted forever. First, the shop kids adopted it as their clan; then our customers took up the flag. As The Hundreds cast its net wider in the mainstream, RSWD has come to stand for our core tribe. On any given afternoon, you'll find bands of kids parked on our bench and curb, barbecuing on the former store manager Five's grill, or huddled around the utility box facing the shop. Rolling blunts, playing a game of S-K-A-T-E, or talking barbershop BS.

The church isn't the building. It's the congregation. Generations of youth have passed through our door and camped out on our sidewalk, not just to buy product (they can do that online) but to live the experience. It's like The Hundreds is their favorite band and our stores are the concert venue. You can buy our apparel elsewhere and soak up the culture through social media, but to witness the real thing, you've got to see and hear it live, the way it was intended. Our clothes are essentially concert merch. You purchase the gear to prove to the world that you were there.*

---

* There is this sense of earning your stripes in following streetwear. There are specific barriers that make a product rare and exclusive. First is price. Obviously, the more expensive the clothes, the less people can afford them, the fewer kids at your school will be wearing the

At our first Black Friday sale in 2009, the first kids showed up two days before with sleeping bags and folding chairs. It rained that week, and at night temperatures dipped low, even for Southern California. On Thanksgiving, parents dropped off trays of turkey and gravy for their kids so they could partake of the holiday. By then, the line was inching around the corner. When we opened our doors in the early-morning hours, however, I noticed that the first few campers barely bought anything, if anything at all. I caught one of them on the way out. A heavyset brown kid with bad skin and foul sneakers.

I looked down at his empty hands. "Nothing?"

The kid shook his head.

"And your boy, he's only getting a couple T-shirts. You guys slept out here for two nights, just to buy two shirts? I don't get it. Why?"

He stank. This kid hadn't showered or brushed his teeth in two days, and it smelled like four. God knows where these dudes were relieving themselves.

"To say that I did it," he answered with a crusty yellow grin. "Nobody else can say shit."

A FEW months after our L.A. shop opened, a collective of San Francisco brands and stores invited us to participate in a local warehouse sale. We were riding off the high of our first store opening and were curious as to other potential markets for The Hundreds stores. Could the Bay Area be one of them? There

---

same thing. Then there is distance. When I got into the game, it was a geographical challenge. If someone wore a Bape polo or Supreme cap, you knew he had traveled to Tokyo or New York to get it (or his cousin had gone on vacation and hooked it up). E-commerce and eBay changed that. Nowadays, it's about how long you were willing to wait in line for something. To say you camped out for an item scores bragging rights, as ridiculous as that sounds.

were no analytics to gauge hot spots. E-commerce wasn't instrumental enough to measure where our customers were coming from. So, we traveled constantly, feeling out the vibe of new markets by hanging with the locals, research shopping, and getting the lay of the land.*

We crammed boxes of old product in the back of Ben's Explorer, burned the seven-hour drive from L.A. to S.F., and pulled up the next morning to throngs of hypebeasts camped outside an abandoned downtown building. It wasn't until we were inside the warehouse that we were told most of those kids were there for our booth. We unpacked the boxes halfway before the crowd did the rest for us, tearing into the cardboard in pandemonium. Ben and I literally had our backs up against the walls, the folding table in front of us barricading the kids who'd formed like a mosh pit. All we could do was laugh and hold on. We had run out of stock by mid-morning. I could feel the eyeballs crawling on us from jealous vendors and curious shopkeepers.

"These L.A. motherfuckers. Who do they think they are?! In our town?"

Until that point, Ben and I had had an idea of the size of our following in Northern California. We were always told we were an L.A. brand with a SoCal aesthetic and that our designs wouldn't resonate in the Bay Area. I never understood this logic and refused to subscribe to it. There was a lot more Giants orange than Dodger blue in the crowd, but it sure looked to me as if NorCal kids still appreciated dope T-shirts and baseball caps.

---

* You can pay for all the accurate data, but there's a social current that paints a truer depiction of the people, the consumer climate, and a brand's viability in a specific market. I don't know how to explain it, but that's the emotional X factor that keeps tastemakers and influencers ahead of the curve. One day, an algorithm will consider all environmental causes and trend fluctuations in reporting what's next, but there will still be those of us who connect off-line and make authentic movements happen outside a computer's scope of comprehension.

The naysayers, the gatekeepers, and the excuse makers would attempt to sell the same lie to us about New York, Europe, and international markets overall.

"You're an L.A. brand; it won't work here!"

Nonbelieving distributors told us to stop writing "Los Angeles" on our clothes, fearful our hometown association would hinder sales. Meanwhile, nobody handcuffed those limitations on New York or Tokyo brands. It was a ruse to throw us off the trail, a speed bump to derail us, but our success at that warehouse sale was the truth. Turns out people appreciate quality clothing regardless of where it comes from, whether it's West Bumblefuck or Maysville, Kentucky, or Los Angeles, California.

By the fall of 2007, less than a year after we had opened The Hundreds Los Angeles, we found a home in San Francisco. The building at 585 Post was a shuttering uniform shop on the sloping corner of Post and Taylor with cumbersome interior pillars, a parking garage belonging to a neighboring building, and a hostel upstairs. But when we looked at the space, we imagined another frontier. The shop had more than double the square footage of our first store, it was located on the border of the touristy Union Square shopping district, and right around the corner on Sutter the local brand Huf was holding it down as the city's skate/street centerpiece.

Ben and I hired our same architect friends (TylerSpencer) who built THLA, but with more cash in our pockets and higher expectations to fulfill, we cranked the volume to ten. The idea was to make a clothing store feel like an amusement park. We installed a replica of Peter Pan's Skull Rock on the back wall (because we likened ourselves to the Lost Boys in our brand narrative) and hung the clothing on curved fasteners that symbolized Captain Hook's "hand." Half of the store was encased in sleek Kubrickian cabinetry with blinking lights and levers ripped from 2001: A *Space Odyssey*. A monolithic mirror greeted you at the door, as it does the apes in that film. The rest of the store was assembled with black cavernous rock, molded from the same quarry where the California gold rush began. The next evolution of The Hundreds Los Angeles's expanding art installation: we wrapped those pesky pillars in the S.F. store with hundreds of skulls (these now represented not just Ben and me but our community) and lifestyle-related cultural artifacts like broken vintage skateboards and spray cans. The result was a dark, super-futuristic cave that merged yesterday and tomorrow— equal parts French catacombs, California culture, and sci-fi spaceship. The store cost us roughly half a million dollars to build. The literal bombproof sliding laboratory door alone cost us $15,000.

And it happened again. The kids started camping out days in advance. We opened our doors to a line that stretched down the block. I can't say I wasn't a little disappointed that none of the customers seemed to appreciate the intricacies of the build-out once they'd entered (they were more interested in scooping up the limited Hieroglyphics collaboration T-shirts). But word soon spread about The Hundreds San Francisco. Why would a fledgling streetwear brand go to such lengths to build a store like this? Why didn't they just work with IKEA fixtures and save that money? Was it really necessary to dim the lights and play roller-coaster sound effects whipping around the speakers to make it feel as if you were in line for Disneyland's Space Mountain? I know I'm biased, but ten years later, The Hundreds San Francisco remains the coolest shopping experience in the history of the world.

Twelve months later, we opened our third store, this time on the East Coast in New York's trendy SoHo neighborhood. Playing off this recurring theme of time, The Hundreds New York was designed by the acclaimed architecture firm Johnston Marklee and was imagined as a store designed for today, aged eighty years into the future. Stanley Kubrick's presence was again referenced in the build-out, with an overpowering monolith running along the ceiling. To preempt the N.Y. haters, we launched a stealth wheatpasting campaign in the months leading up to our grand opening. Our posters shouted, KEEP THE HUNDREDS OUT OF NEW YORK, and were plastered across downtown and the boroughs. We even made The Hundreds stickers that were intentionally designed to look as if they were torn or scraped off. When our friends wore the "Keep The Hundreds out of New York" T-shirts out in the streets, native New Yorkers would shout, "I don't know what The Hundreds is, but I don't want it here!" The message board trolls and bloggers had a field day with the movement against The Hundreds New York, jumping on the bitter bandwagon, ignorant to the secret that we were behind the campaign. By the time our store opened, we were orchestrating our own backlash, which made it easy for us to deflate once we carried out the big reveal.

For our fourth and final flagship, we set our sights back home. With Rosewood Avenue barely able to accommodate the inpouring of traffic and sales, we convinced ourselves that Los Angeles could afford two The Hundreds stores. The Hundreds Santa Monica debuted ironically on April Fools' Day, sandwiched between the Promenade tourist trap and Fred Segal. Our sales history came full circle by moving next door to the fashion boutique. Seven years after we'd sold our first T-shirts to Fred Segal's streetwear department, we erected a shop not more than twenty feet from our original home.

Design-wise, The Hundreds Santa Monica was devoid of the theme of time altogether. Stanley Kubrick's influence returned with a stark white space that felt eerily *Clockwork Orange* yet antithetical to our darker themes. I returned to the grave site conception from our first store on Rosewood Avenue and expanded the installation in Santa Monica to include even more relics born of subcultures we admired and in which we'd participated. Beyond skateboards and spray cans, there was a surfboard, the *Judgment Night* soundtrack on cassette, *Kids* on VHS, and a turntable. Here was a comprehensive study of our inspiration pool, frozen in time. Everything that fueled our imaginations and influenced our lifestyle and aesthetic.

We teased the space by slapping together a *Garfield* collaboration pop-up shop. Our opening party featured a group art show with Barry McGee, Dave Choe, and Slick, and a signing with *Garfield*'s creator, Jim Davis. The line was so long that it wrapped around the block twice. At one point, I'd gazed over the second-floor balcony at the sheer number of people inside and out. The photographer Mark the Cobrasnake was standing next to me, muttering to himself, "And I thought streetwear was dead."

It was 2011, and we had four stores that were pumping out the brand across both coasts. Not only was our own retail cracking, but it seemed wherever we planted a store, the surrounding wholesale accounts benefited from the energy as well. And as our stomachs grew, so did our eyes. The next logical step was going overseas. We could start slow and safe with our northern neighbors in Vancouver, but Ben and I really wanted to do the unthinkable and hit Tokyo or Seoul next. We outlined blueprints for a Paris pop-up and flew to London to check out vacant spaces on Carnaby Street. But less than a decade later, three of our original four stores—The Hundreds New York, The Hundreds Santa Monica, and The Hundreds San Francisco—would end with a whimper.

On paper, The Hundreds stores were a bright and shiny success. Real businesspeople—the kind who carry briefcases and use acronyms like "EBITDA"—were popping boners over our numbers. We were drawing heavy profits in lean locations with low overhead. Hundred-thousand-dollar months with only a few hundred feet of selling space, even though we were selling the same product on the internet and at five other shops nearby.

For most shopkeepers, running one store is a life's career. Here we were, steering four of them in different cities while introducing a footwear brand, a print magazine, a digital content platform, and—oh yeah—a clothing line. Our charts were stacking commas and zeros, and the lines kept growing outside our big releases. But while everything was baking a golden brown on top, the retail business was burned and charring on the bottom. We were outrunning ourselves, fueled on adrenaline and hype, neglecting any infrastructure or strategy. It's as if we were the fastest marathon runner in the forest. We had no idea where we were headed or how long it was going to last. We just kept sprinting and charging into the dark, unaware that the trail ended just beyond the tree line.

22. BLOW UP

Rather be forgotten than remembered for giving in
—Refused, "Summerholidays vs. Punkroutine"

SOMETHING WAS HAPPENING within The Hundreds, attracting a lot of attention and dollars, but silently eroding the foundation; it was almost untraceable and invisible at the start, a slow-moving infection.

Strange as it sounds, we didn't have a logo for the first three years of the brand. There were variations of "The Hundreds" written out in different fonts and hand styles, but we didn't lock in a visual identity. I just wasn't ready to commit; I needed time to get to know The Hundreds. You don't tattoo a toddler. I had to feel out the brand's character and personality before marking it forever.

Until then, we lined the business with T-shirts and cut our voice with graphics. Like a breakthrough pop artist blitzing the *Billboard* charts, our T-shirt designs were instantly recognizable, even though people didn't search for us by name. We were known for conceptual tees like "California Is for Haters" (a flip of "Virginia Is for Lovers") and "Mousey" (Mickey Mouse reimagined as a Nike Dunk–loving hypebeast)—conversation starters that were reminiscent of nineties skateboarding's subversive parodies.

Our first hit came in 2004 and had the phrase "Hip-Hop Is Dead" stenciled onto the front of a stark black T-shirt. I came up with the message late one night in the library as I was listening to Power 106 on my headphones. As a hardcore kid, I was familiar with the "Punk is dead" doctrine (inspired by a Crass song) after mainstream radio and Hot Topic fashion got ahold of melodic pop punk bands. By the early 2000s, the authentic rap music I espoused and loved also felt abandoned, bastardized by a cannibalistic record industry. I didn't understand this next generation of rap, nor was I meant to. The music was dumbed down, derivative, diluted. Hip-hop was a shadow of its former self.

Hip-hop was also quite literally dead. The nineties crystallized rap, but by decade's end we had lost our generals: Biggie, Pac, and Big L. I wanted to include their likenesses on the T-shirt as homage. There was no Google Images to source photos of these rappers, so I hunted for old *Vibe* and *Source* magazines in libraries and used bookstores. I cut their pictures out and scanned them into Photoshop. Then I billed them on the back of the shirt with hip-hop's other fallen luminaries: Big Pun, Jam Master Jay, and Eazy-E. "The Hundreds" was spelled out in a Compton-style Old English behind the figures. But that was inconsequential. Even though nobody had heard of the clothing company, they rode with the statement.

Or, they refuted it. The Roc-A-Fella camp requested the shirt, but Dame Dash supposedly hated it. Meanwhile, Bushwick Bill of the Geto Boys wore the tee on a publicity tour, our first celebrity placement. There were countless knockoffs and bootlegs that followed, and a lot of people made money off the controversial sentiment. Even Nas adopted "Hip-Hop Is Dead" as an album title years down the road. We had a winner and stores wanted it. Now we had a centerpiece to build a collection around. As our retail doors grew, so did our line. Within a couple seasons, our footprint doubled.

Every three months, we unloaded another ten T-shirts into the pipeline. "Honkys" (the Cleveland Indians' mascot turned into a redneck), "Cans" (Warhol's Campbell's soup cans appropriated into spray cans and paint buckets), and a collaboration with the Japanese artist Usugrow performed well for us, but after a couple years of printing the best graphic tees, I wanted our name to stand on its own as a brand. At this point, we were only as good as our last clever T-shirt, which was both unsustainable and exhausting. I had created hundreds of original designs, and T-shirts that simply read "The Hundreds" were our worst sellers. We were nothing more than a novelty T-shirt company, an edgier version of what you'd pick up as a stocking stuffer in an airport souvenir store.

I knew, however, that the value in our clothes wasn't the kooky parody or nervy design. It was the attitude and status that hummed in the background of our product. If you looked at the art that came forth from The Hundreds, there was a singular vision and tone that was uniquely ours, and people wanted more of it. We just had to package it against an insignia or mark that our following could cop as an identity. It was time to institute a logo for the brand.

The problem was that designing a logo was far from a priority for me. This was an era where fat DC lockups, Sean John emblems, and Juicy Couture ass slaps dominated the fashion landscape. I was tired of big, heavy logos overwhelming the clothes. Even the Polo horse mushroomed in size. Clothing was diminished to a billboard. It's a shame how much of men's streetwear sales aren't motivated by design and quality. (Then again, male shoppers are motivated by brand names. Fashion, for a lot of guys, boils down to status, belonging, and tribalism.)

I wasn't formally trained and I lacked experience, but I had my own rules when it came to constructing logos. An impactful icon—a graphic representation of the brand—should be able to be drawn by a kindergartner in a few steps. Like the McDonald's M or the Playboy bunny. I wanted a logo so succinct, so potent, that you could trace the outline without lifting the pen. After all, it's been said that "brevity is the soul of wit." I also believe that the less alphabet letters are incorporated into the icon, the more conspicuous it can be. I hate when brands use an initial or the entire word(s) in their logo. It's a cheat, the easy way out. Plus, a brand might be confused for another sharing the same letters. What about an image that's one of a kind? Whittle the shapes down to such a simple and uncomplicated vision that a few intersecting lines can capture the universe of a brand. For example, Target. Apple. It's easier said than done.

There needed to be a reason for the icon, a story. It couldn't be arbitrary. It had to embody our philosophy. I listened for the brand's heartbeat. The 1980s stepped forward, and animation. Hanna-Barbera, Disney, *Looney Tunes*. Wile E. Coyote chasing the Road Runner with anvils and portable black holes. But there was one weapon that symbolized an entire chapter of cartoon history: the bomb. A black steel sphere, the size and shape of a small bowling ball, tethered to a long, sizzling wick. Upon detonation, it explodes into a jagged shape.

I drew a detailed bomb at first, then started editing. I reminded myself that not only should a kid be able to draw this in seconds but also people have got to be able to tell what it is from a distance. I kept the circle intact. Anyone can draw a circle; that's easy. Then I worked on the flare in the shape of a seven-pointed star. We were left with the silhouette of a cartoon bomb that unmistakably represented The Hundreds and all its inspirations. We debuted the "Solid Bomb" logo as our first icon, slapping the decals on street signs and—to this day—stamping it on the back collar of our T-shirts.

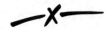

"YOU KNOW, for being such a cartoon guy, how come you've never drawn a cartoon version of our bomb?"

It was late into the morning, and we were working out of my studio apartment on Venice Boulevard. Ben took a break from hounding shops for past-due payments. We liked to get paid up front, but for the exclusive image doors we allowed "terms." Net thirty, at the most net sixty. This meant the owners had thirty or sixty days after delivery of our product to pay us. It was a good look to be in these more prestigious boutiques, so most brands swallowed the agreement. Of course, we also rarely got paid on time—if ever. We'd chalk up the loss to marketing expenses. It was a tiring and frustrating game, but we all played it.

"What do you mean a cartoon bomb? That's what Solid Bomb is," I said in my defense.

Ben hovered over my desk, watching me illustrate a new T-shirt graphic: a set of three skulls with candles melting on top of them. The drawing was a commentary on how we were working ourselves to death: "burning the candle at both ends." I put down my markers.

"No. I'm saying a cartoon bomb with a cartoon face. Like one of your characters." He pointed to the loose scraps of computer paper strewn around my bedroom. I had sketches of pigs in cop uniforms, dead cats with their eyes crossed out (I'm a dog person),* and three monkeys in the See No Evil, Hear No Evil, Speak No Evil poses (subtext: industry hate). I liked drawing caricatures of people most of all, their faces taking on my own features in exaggerated form. Big, sad eyes, drooping under the weight of heavy lids. Full mouths, rails of teeth, long grotesque limbs.

A cartoon bomb character. Ben was hitting outside the box. I didn't think it served us to have a cartoony logo—we'd be limiting ourselves to a younger audience—but The Hundreds could use a fun mascot. Michelin has the Michelin Man and Geico has the gecko, while both corporations retain their classic logos. The Phillies have a timeless P on their caps, but the colorful Phanatic revs the crowd. Post-Y2K, corporations eased off mascots in favor of sleeker branding, but I dug the wistful nostalgia around them. I always had a thing for Americana advertising characters.

Later that night, long after Ben left his desk and I'd reached the bottom of a syrupy Merlot, I cracked open my bedroom window and let the crickets' chirps filter in. Under a fluorescent desk light, I gathered my yellow pencils and sketchbook. Page after page, I drew disembodied facial expressions. Wide, toothy grins. Leery eyes and pursed lips. None of them seemed

---

* The rapper Iggy Azalea later bought this character from me as her first logo: "SUPERIOR PUSSY."

to apply. If our bomb were to have a personality, he wouldn't be smug or aggressive. How would he react to the dwindling spark above him, the imminent boom? He wouldn't want it at all, I decided, and drew his face in a state of shock.

I liked the idea that this moment was frozen in time. The bomb was just about to explode, but the blast would never be realized. It was a frank metaphor for our brand strategy. We wanted to stay underground for as long as possible, serving our loyal niche audience. The Hundreds would hover right under the surface of the mainstream but never give itself over completely. The character represented the discipline required in keeping our brand from blowing up.

Overstated, anxious eyes. A mouth held agape. Tilted forward and flinching at what's to come. I scanned the final rendering into my Dell laptop and vectorized the cartoon in Adobe Illustrator. The loose, wiggly pencil lines stood straight and bold now. He needed a name, but it was nearing 4:00 a.m. and I had class in five hours. I was eager to share our mascot with the world, so I uploaded him to my blog and asked our readers to come up with something. I guess this was our first contest. "NAME OUR MASCOT!" the flyer read. Ben and I would choose the winner in the next twenty-four hours. The winner would get a free T-shirt.

I woke up to over two hundred emails in my in-box. There were a few "Bo(m)bby Hundreds" votes in the pile and a "Kablooey Louie." And two separate fans submitted "Adam Bomb." It stuck. There was something funny about giving a catastrophic explosive a banal human name (like Brian, the dog on *Family Guy*). We called him Adam for short and treated him like a real person.*

---

* Over the years, we've worked closely with Disney on collaborative projects. It's amazing how it treats its characters—especially Mickey Mouse—as actual beings with behaviors and histories. "Donald would never say that! Minnie doesn't wear shoes like this!" Long

I built a Myspace page for Adam Bomb and listed in his bio "black," "round," and "has a short fuse."

The first time he appeared on clothing was the back of a Freshjive collaboration. He went unnoticed. The following season, our holiday collection of 2006, he got his own sweatshirt. Adam nestled between a lowercase *t* and *h* in block letters, but the product didn't sell. Our average customer was confused by the character. They expected social commentary, nostalgic references, or provocative designs from The Hundreds. Adam Bomb hadn't set in deep enough to prove himself. Plus, no one knew we were committing to Adam Bomb as our official mascot.

We tried a couple more times throughout the next year and struck out. But in November 2007, we converted Adam Bomb into an orange basketball,* and that fateful twist of the knob changed people's minds. The shirt, titled "Bridgeburners," was part of a sports parody collection with team names that complemented our MO like "Firestarters" and "Noisemakers." The "Bridgeburners" tee merged a basketball into Adam and not only blew the other designs out of the water but was the highest-selling piece of the season. We knew most purchasers were only buying "Bridgeburners" because it was the first The Hundreds shirt with a basketball on it (I could've drawn a basketball in crayon with my left hand, and it would've sold as much), but we rode the momentum anyway.

We went harder. Branding is about making your customers comfortable, secure with buying your product. It's about letting them know that you aren't going anywhere. That they are buying

---

after Walt's departure, after decades of worldwide proliferation, Disney remains a stalwart brand. That sacredness, that brand reinforcement, is a testament to how Disney persists and is so well-preserved.

* An old streetwear trick. If you ever have trouble selling something, slap a basketball on it and hold on to your butts.

something stable and unfading. They don't want to take a risk. Everyone wants to be unique, but no one wants to be the only one asking themselves, "Will I get teased for wearing this?" or "Will anyone know what this is?"

The only way to get your audience on board with your logo is by showing them how serious you are about it. Commitment! That means posting it and pasting it, expending the sweat to publicize it, and yes, investing dollars into it. Adam Bomb was featured everywhere—from T-shirts to backpacks, key chains to wheatpaste posters. He graced the backs of celebrities like The Game, Olivia Munn, Jaden Smith, and Wiz Khalifa. He dominated billboard campaigns in Los Angeles and San Francisco, without a mention of The Hundreds name. Just giant black walls with a forty-foot Adam Bomb painted on them. In 2012, Adam Bomb flashed on the highest marquee in Times Square, the advertising mecca. These are the lengths we went to to make our customers feel safe wearing that big, round bomb on their backs.

Adam Bomb—like Supreme's box logo or Bape's ape head—stands as one of the most recognizable icons in streetwear history, epitomizing the early-2000s chapter of naive and elemental brand establishment. The sneaker designer Jon Buscemi once commended us on it, saying, "You made your own Nike swoosh." We couldn't disagree. Adam Bomb was an unexpected power-up, like a *Super Mario* boost. We weren't invincible, but we had a clear advantage. While most of our competitors bounced between isolated designs, Adam Bomb was a panacea that compensated for weaker pieces and carried us over slower collections. Other brands—well, every brand—hunt for a bestselling logo like this, their golden ticket. Most fall short.

I knew so much of it was dumb luck. Adam Bomb was striking a nerve with the customer and the culture. At first, this was a rewarding and encouraging stroke of good fortune. Adam Bomb's animated nature lined up with the youthful emotion of street culture in the late 2000s. Kanye West had yet to turn irritable street goth, still bright-eyed and dazzling behind shutter shades and a College Dropout bear letterman jacket. Takashi Murakami was achieving peak gallery status with his Louis Vuitton flower prints and cheeky Dobby character. Pharrell's Stan Smith–inspired Ice Cream sneakers were draped in contrasting pastel prints of cartoon pagers and diamonds.

However, strokes of luck are often accompanied by unexpected consequences. Over the next five years, in spite of Adam Bomb's blessings, I slid from love to apathy to disgust with our character. I didn't anticipate how viscerally I'd turn against my own monster, but I started to curse my creation. As if Dr. Frankenstein were a T-shirt designer.

For starters, Adam Bomb—the silly, bug-eyed cartoon bomb—was supposed to be our mascot, not our logo. Remember, the Phillies embroidered their script P—not the Phanatic's furry face—on their official uniforms. Yet here was Adam, taking off in the marketplace by assuming our brand's total identity. Within two years, Adam Bomb eclipsed everything else we had accomplished in strategically building this brand: the apparel design, the exclusive interviews with iconic figures on our website, the marketing campaigns built around painstaking collaborations, and the experiences we infused into our stores. Initially confused by the mascot's takeover, our core customer stuck with us, supportive of our main endeavors. Then a new generation of fans glommed on to The Hundreds brand solely because of the bomb, wearing it head to toe like a uniform, ignorant to our surrounding brand narrative. A fan set up a "FuckYeahTheHundreds" Tumblr that was an infinite stream of teenagers distorted in fish-eye selfies, proudly flashing their Adam Bomb stamps. Tattoo photos flooded our in-boxes—Adam Bombs permanently inked on arms and necks. I didn't have the heart to tell the victims when the icon was inked inverted or backward.

Adam Bomb was a runaway train. Stores went from wondering, "What's with this bomb stuff?" to asking, "The Hundreds? You guys do Adam Bomb, right?" No matter how much we sweat over our cut-and-sew apparel, regardless of the thoughtfulness and consideration imbued in the T-shirts, the majority of customers were only scanning The Hundreds for that black, red, and yellow insignia. It got to the point where shops wouldn't buy pieces from us unless they had Adam Bomb on there somewhere. We were forced to stitch him onto cardigan sweaters and chino pants (garments on which Adam Bomb had no business finding residence) just to meet our production minimums and so the collection could see the light of day. The irony was that our design eye was getting more sophisticated and our taste levels more refined, and as our technique flourished, so did our design choices. Yet Adam Bomb contradicted this progression. No matter how smart our clothing was getting, that small patch on the crest or direct embroidery on the back compromised the piece's maturity.

I started to hate Adam Bomb. I hated the way people confused the metaphor. I hated how we'd score a sought-after collaboration with a cool brand, getting pumped on the innovative art both parties might produce together, only to have the other side submit their reworking of Adam Bomb as the proposal.

I hated how Adam Bomb's aesthetic failed to jibe with our punk rock, black-and-white photocopied designs and traditional men's clothing. I hated the inevitability that no matter what I did with my career, I'd be remembered as "the bomb guy. He drew bombs. One of the best to ever do it, really."

23. BOOM

What could a businessman ever want more
Than to have us sucking in his store
—Fugazi, "Merchandise"

BOBBY! CAN WE get a photo?"

This happens sometimes. No, I'm not a celebrity (contrary to what my mom might tell you), but like YouTube stars or social media personalities, I've got a niche fan base. They're the only ones who can decipher the difference between my face and the actor John Cho's. I'm recognized by fourteen-year-old Echo Park skate rats; or Filipino sneakerheads; or surly dudes hanging with other surly dudes, collared with neck tattoos, neglecting bored girlfriends. The way these guys do a double take when they catch me out of the corner of their eye, pause a beat, and inch the awkward approach flags (a) an oncoming sucker punch or (b) a selfie. Either way, I always brace myself.

"Hey, man! Love what you've done for the culture! Are you hiring?"

"My friends and I have a brand too. Can you take a half hour to look through my photos and tell me what you think?"

"I used to wear your shit all the time in high school. Then I grew up, wrapped it up in a garbage bag, and lit it on fire. Do you guys make neckties? Can I get one for free?"

But tonight, it's not some gold-grilled fuccboi inquiring about the next collab. It's my friends and family asking for pictures together. These are people I've known my entire life smiling at me, proud of me, as if I were a hero. Weird. Ben looks at me and grins. Together, we're standing in the courtyard at Disneyland, encircled by loved ones and loyalists who are snapping phone pics and posing with us as if we were Mickey and Minnie. It's 2013 and our company turns ten this year. To celebrate the anniversary, we wanted to go big. We'd thrown block parties and Gucci Mane concerts before—parties so big and memorable that riot police showed up—but our tenth birthday had to be exceptional.

"What about shutting down Disneyland for a night? Just for our community?" I wondered out loud.

It was the most outrageous, over-the-top party I could think of, outside flying everyone to Ibiza on private jets. Rap show? Art exhibition? Been there, done those. Stereotypical streetwear events bump for the night, then disappear deep down in the Instagram feed. But everyone remembers Disneyland: where *Inside Out*–style "core memories" are made. Only question was, could it be done?

"It's America," Ben said. "Money talks. Everything has a price."

Ten years after we'd stacked our shirts on Fred Segal's front table, we were making careless cash-rich decisions like these,* throwing money around like confetti. I still have vivid memories of The Hundreds' primal early days—the struggle, clawing in the dark recesses of my pantry for something to eat.† Now we were hobnobbing with celebrities at Mr. Chow and cracking $1,000 bottles of wine. Inside the office, Ben and I were doling out meaty paychecks to experienced employees, hiring assistants for assistants, and providing benefits. We even had a real-life human resources department.

Outside work, we were enjoying the fruits of our labor. We went from folding tables and rolling racks at Vegas trade shows to center tables and sparkling bottles in Vegas nightclubs. It was exhilarating and harrowing at the same time, like gambling at the high-stakes table with Monopoly money.

Look, it's nice to make cash. You can buy stuff you don't need like Supreme bricks and a 1981 DeLorean DMC-12 with less than five hundred miles on it. I bought the *Back to the Future* car before I even had a garage to park it in. So, I found a house that looked just like Marty McFly's (down to the swing garage and front doorstep). Ben went out and bought paintings that were taller than any wall in his house. Somehow, there was always a table open for any dinner reservation in Los Angeles. We ate

---

* Ben and I bought good, grown-up homes, and he eventually forced me to sell my RAV4. "It's not good for company morale for the boss to be driving the worst car in the parking lot," he said, shaking his head. I didn't see what was wrong with my SUV. It got me from point A to point B just fine, even if I was missing a taillight and the glove compartment's mouth dangled open as if it were aghast. I relented and leased a platinum BMW, with all the trimmings. ("What you think I rap for, to push a fuckin' Rav 4?" —Kanye West, "Run This Town")

† I once went two days without eating, before I settled on a can of Spam that had survived three moves. I dusted off the tin, but couldn't find an expiration date. I called the 800 number, and the lady asked me to read the last four digits off the stamped code. Turns out I had several years left. "Wanna hear a secret?" she said. "The truth is we don't know when it expires. For all we know, it lasts forever."

only the finest meals in whatever city we traveled to and be-friended award-winning chefs.* We got there flying business class and stayed in hotel rooms with corner views and Jacuzzi bathtubs. New cameras, DSLRs that shot 4K video, better lenses with lower f-stops, faster computers, an iPhone and a Samsung at the same time (I just couldn't decide). I was like a walking Best Buy vending machine. With so many chargers and cords on me, I looked like Doctor Octopus—TSA's worst nightmare.

There's also a quiet confidence and security that comes with a fatter Comme des Garçons wallet. Just the peace of mind, the not having to stress about rent, is priceless and made my manhood swell. We went from "nothing to lose" to "nothing to prove." I stopped carrying business cards because the logo on my chest spoke for me. The Hundreds was establishing a name and presence among industry and audience. We stood our ground and refused to be swept away. Even if people didn't like what we were making, they acknowledged the tenacity, the diligence. "I would never wear The Hundreds, but I respect the hustle" got a lot of up votes in the comments.

The best part, however, was the opportunities. Doors opened and relationships unlocked. As a creative person, my dreams filled bigger rooms, and I liked the freedom from budgets. Ben gave me a longer leash to pitch more prominent artists for spe-cial projects or licensed properties. The Hundreds ventured be-yond T-shirts and clothes into footwear, publishing, and music. I co-designed our first pair of The Hundreds eyewear—the Phoenix—with the designer Garrett Leight. A few seasons later, the luxury brand Celine seemed to have ripped off our chunky squared-off shades, but I took it as a compliment. High fashion

---

* Sampling frozen ants that Alex Atala (of São Paulo's D.O.M.) plucked from the Amazon rain forest (tasted like lemon!) or drinking sake at Hong Kong's Yardbird with Lindsay Jang and Matt Abergel.

was monitoring streetwear closely, and The Hundreds was on the runway's radar. *The New York Times* would later claim that Alexander Wang and Riccardo Tisci's direction with Givenchy borrowed from The Hundreds. "In the end does it matter? What counts is not whether major designers were pirating ideas so much as that they had taken note of something irresistible in the air."

Something irresistible. I liked that. We were in demand, but more than the money it felt nice to be wanted. I felt powerful and loved. People were listening. As a middle child, an Asian American artist, a skateboarder, and a hardcore punk, after thirty years I finally felt like I was being heard by a greater world that cared. My friend Tex used to say, "You're one of those people where everything always works out for them," and for the first time in my life I started to believe it. I would say it was all going according to plan, except I had never foreseen a future like this. Getting paid to sit around and draw pictures and hang out with my friends all day?

It was everything.

24. ABE

THE SUMMER AFTER the first year of law school is a critical one for students who are trying to pad their résumés with bullet points and work experience. You've got to get in where you fit in, whether that's a firm or a legal aid clinic. Many students apply to intern (or extern) at the local federal or state courthouses. Riding on my first-year high, I slid right into a choice externship with the Los Angeles Superior Court downtown. The judge was a bit of a good ol' boy and had a Chinese clerk named Robert Lee whom he nicknamed "the General" (you know, Robert E. Lee). I liked the General. We shared that Asian bond. He could tell I was a screwball.

Sometimes when things seemed especially crazy in the courtroom, I'd glance over and see the General roll his eyes and smile. Like most Americans, my only familiarity with a court of law came from evading jury duty or watching *Law & Order*. That summer, I learned that nobody really knows what's going on in the judicial system, the procedure is glued together with Elmer's, and you can wear the same suit every day and nobody else will care if they hate their jobs. That was my experience, anyway.

IT WAS going to be a hundred-degree day downtown, easily. I could tell by the way the heat baked into the car windshield in early morning traffic. My first morning of work, I showed up bleary-eyed with hair swirled in all different directions. I'd reached the door to my externship on time but hadn't factored in the half-hour line at the metal detectors. The Los Angeles Superior Court is a dizzying circus of deadbeat dads, parking violators, and TMZ paparazzi swarming around the weekly celebrity trial. Imagine showing up to your job and having to deal with Lindsay Lohan's entourage just to get past Michael Jackson's doctor and make it to your desk on time.

By the time I got to my assigned courtroom, the other interns were already hastily taking notes from a grizzled man in a loose sweatshirt. He was laying out the summer's syllabus and breaking us into the order of things. His name was Abe Edelman, the superior court's renowned research attorney. Behind a tired baseball cap and a wiry gray beard, his sunken eyes flashed in my direction and nodded toward the sign-in sheet. The wheezing apparatus attached to his stomach and the faint smell of stale urine rising underneath layers of clothing suggested something the other interns later confirmed on our break: at forty-something years old, Abe Edelman was slowly but surely dying of cancer.

Abe never talked much about it. But his condition was pretty obvious. While the other research attorneys scampered up and down the halls, barking into their phones in bespoke suits, Abe didn't move much in the course of a workday. You could typically find him propped up against one of the benches outside, exerting all his energy just to breathe, ruminating and staring vacantly at the cold marble wall in front of him. If you didn't know any better, you'd think Abe was a homeless vagrant, looking for an air-conditioned respite from the midday heat. He looked twice his age, and the pungent odor of his urostomy bag kept most people at bay.

I liked watching the nervous looks on people's faces as they sat across from Abe in the corridor, awaiting their trial. "Should I call security?" the Poolside Pattys wondered aloud. Then a ring of eager law students would congregate around this apparent grifter awaiting instruction, laughing at his stories, begging for more.

Abe was more myth than legend in the Los Angeles legal community. He'd graduated at the top of his class at UCLA Law decades earlier, but it was his unrivaled intellect and coarse personality that got people whispering. I remember meeting a veteran attorney during a big trial. We were chopping it up before the morning's announcements when he asked about school and my externship.

"Who's your research attorney?" he asked.

"Do you know Abe Edelman?"

"Edelman? That guy actually exists? Wow. I've heard some things."

At this point, I'm sure Abe's name was circulating in the

community for his illness more than his portfolio. Second to that, it was probably his genius that the attorney was alluding to. As interns, we spent a lot of our hours researching cases in the courthouse's law library, which was also Abe's sanctuary. Abe was never as comfortable and well situated anywhere as he was in the dulled acoustics of those heavy books and binders. The musty smell of old paper and binding glue invigorated him; those compendiums were the only friends of his I ever met. My first project for the judge was a memo in response to a complaint against the city for a busted water pipe. I spent the better parts of my evenings sifting through volumes of case precedent. To strengthen the judge's ruling, I needed to furnish as much antecedent support as I could dredge up, but it was like hunting Easter eggs in the Grand Canyon. Wasn't there a hashtag or a search bar to help me out?

Abe sauntered into the room one night, scanned my complaint, and walked over to the third aisle of books. He didn't say anything, just closed his eyes and walked along the rows, grazing his fingertips across the spines. One by one, pluck, pluck, pluck—until he paused, reached down, and pulled out a brown leather-bound book with a cryptic citation code embossed on the cover. He grabbed the block of a book in his creased and sallow hand and flipped through the pages. Like a street magician, he abruptly stopped, struck his index finger down on the page, and beneath his black fingernail—like a biblical annotation in size 6 font—was the smoking gun case I needed.

"How did you do that?"

"I memorized the library."

Abe wasn't kidding. He did this all summer long.

But beyond the debilitating cancer and the Mensa parlor tricks, I like to think it was Abe's dysfunctional charisma that stopped L.A.'s most powerful lawyers in their tracks. He had no filter and was possessed by his temper. Abe berated indiscriminately. It didn't matter if you were an intern or the judge, man or woman, the loose cannon decimated anyone who messed up: a clerical error, a faulty judgment, a corrupt power play. Everyone was inferior in Abe's eyes, and I could tell how much it frustrated him to deal with us Neanderthal regular folk every day. I don't know if people ignored—and absorbed—his boorishness out of sympathy, but in hindsight there was something very spectrum-y about Abe's savant nature and social incompetence. This just made me feel extra-superspecial sauce that he had taken me under his wing.

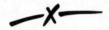

WANT TO hear Abe's quarter story? It'll give you a solid impression of him.

One day, Abe came to work and wondered aloud, "Hey, know what's weird? I've been noticing these quarters in my bathtub, but I have no idea how they get there." As the weeks went by, he'd spot more, sometimes pennies, a couple nickels. He'd shower, look down at his feet, and see another coin stuck in the drain. Because he was too lazy and baffled to clear them out, his tub eventually took on the speckled copper pattern of a public fountain.

"I figured it out!" he exclaimed in late July. It had been two months since he'd told me the bathtub riddle. "You'll never believe it." Let me preface this by saying that beneath the sweats, Abe was obese and misshapen like a dorm room beanbag. He lived on heavy fast food, minimal exercise, and bad television. I guess he'd determined that he was going to die anyway, so why not go out in a blaze of glory? He'd leave the office late and grab a fast-food bag on the way home or a Big Gulp soda from the corner convenience store. As soon as he set foot in the door of his apartment—without a girlfriend or wife to embarrass him or stop him—Abe would tear his pants off and unceremoniously toss them across the room into a heap of other torn-off pants. Whatever loose change was in his pockets would also go flying, mostly sprinkling onto the bedsheets. Then the shirt goes. The underwear. The shoes, socks—everything!

Abe would backstroke into bed butt-ass naked with his dinner, plow through waffle fries and ranch dressing, smashing a banana milkshake into his face. Mayonnaise, ketchup, In-N-Out spread splattered across Abe's nude body and bed like a Pollock painting. He'd wallow in the Taco Bell wrappers and straws, open condiment packets, hydrogenated oils, and trans fats throughout the night, rolling every inch of his flesh around the blankets. In the morning, he'd awaken with coins decorating his body like a Christmas tree. Too rusty to notice, Abe would make his way into the shower and turn on the warm water. By the time he had sobered up and accepted the new day, he'd look down to find another set of coins had encircled his toes like an upside-down halo. As I'm writing this, I realize Abe couldn't have been *that* smart, huh?

Whatever. That was Abe.

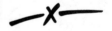

THE FINAL three weeks of my externship, Abe stopped showing up. His illness had ravaged his body and mind and forced him into an early retirement. I knew that must've been crushing. I'm sure he wasn't even supposed to be there at all that summer, but he truly loved his job and the students. I had gotten a good handle on things and finished off strong even without his guidance, applying the lessons Abe had taught me over the months.

On the last day of work, I was surprised to see him back in his corner of the bench. He was shockingly gray and emaciated; he could barely hold his focus while talking to us. One by one, Abe gave the externs their reviews. They hugged him, thanked him, and exited the building to soak up that last drop of summer before the new school year.

I went last. Abe was nearly out of breath and had to take a moment before starting.

"So, what'd you think? How'd I do?" he asked wryly.

"Oh, man, Abe," I replied, "I learned so much. Thank you."

"Bobby, in all my years of doing this, you were one of the best interns I've ever had. You're going to be a successful lawyer. You're going to have it all—the cars, the houses, the women . . ."

Plural. I liked this! I lit up. "Awesome! So, where do I sign up?" I never thought I was good at much, so if the smartest research attorney in the county believed I was qualified for a legal career, then I was on board. Had I finally found my calling?

"But you should never be a lawyer."

I hit the wall at a hundred miles per hour. Huh? "Wait. You just said—"

"I know what I just said," he cut in, a fiery look in his eyes. The lights turned on, the music stopped, the slideshow of dancing supermodels and Lamborghinis in my head shut off. I took a long look at Abe—his fingers gnarled like tree roots, the veins tangled under his skin like purple vines. His hands trembled from the medication; his wily spirit had been tamed. Hard to believe, but Abe looked defeated.

"You don't love this."

I got defensive. "Sure I do. I'm really good at it. You said it yourself, I—"

"Being skilled and passionate are two different things," Abe said. "Look. What do we talk about at lunch every day? Do we talk about memoranda and statutes?"

He was right. Most afternoons, against the sun's harsh reflection bouncing off the Disney Concert Hall, Abe and I would make the long trek to the food court in the downtown civic center. While he mauled a party tray of chicken tacos, I could barely focus on eating. I was too excited to show him what I had worked on in my black book. In the nights, I'd doodle sketches of T-shirt ideas in there. I mapped out the HTML framework for our website. I wrote down branding concepts and marketing plans and the stores Ben and I wanted to sell to. I'd share these with Abe, but he never said much, didn't pry or ask questions; he just listened as I waxed on about the importance of an open-ended cotton blank tee versus ring spun, or a rap group we wanted to collaborate with. The Hundreds didn't even have a T-shirt to show for itself yet, let alone a dot-com or an interested retailer, but in my mind I could envision the entire thing as it exists today. I just had to get it out.

"Your heart is with The Hundreds," Abe reminded me. "Do that. I have no regrets! I was the best at what I do, and I loved every second of it. And now look at me. How will you feel if you wake up one day and you're forty and you're dying of cancer? Will you be able to say you lived your life doing what you were meant to do?"

I didn't have to answer, and he didn't have to continue. That was the first time somebody I trusted and respected had given me permission to fulfill my dreams. I had forever written it off— the notion that I could make a living off my art and imagination. My parents, my teachers, nobody encouraged it. Most tried to talk me out of it. I had built this wall around myself, but Abe was showing me the way out. I guess I was giving myself permission too. It was a turning point in my life. I was growing up and taking control of my destiny.

The next time I saw Abe was a cold and soggy day in December, the afternoon after my winter midterm exams. I sat by his bedside at Kaiser Permanente. There was an older woman in the room with us; I didn't bother to ask if she was a friend or relative. Abe wasn't really there. I'm sure he was floating around somewhere in that strange and enchanted brain of his, but his body was thinner than the sheet that covered him. One of his legs was exposed, the translucent skin hanging off his bones. He was haunting and skeletal, and I don't like to remember him this way. I didn't even thank him out loud or say goodbye. I couldn't align this apparition with the brash and shameless man I had known to be Abe.

So, instead, I rewound to our last afternoon in the courthouse together. The world took on a different light then, and I haven't been able to shake it since. From that day forward, I avowed my commitment to The Hundreds but more emphatically to a life of pursuing passion. Ben and I had started this project for fun, as a creative outlet, but now I appreciated its significance and potential. There was no turning back, no other option. Abe was counting on me to have a life worth living, and I wasn't going to let him down.

Abe Edelman died a few days later, and that's when The Hundreds truly began. His spirit remains vigilantly alive and at war every day in this brand. But the greatest thing he ever did for me was put the wheel in my hands. Every year I inch closer to forty, this story flowers and ripens with colors I never noticed before.

I never got to say it, so I'll do it now.

Thanks, Abe. Goodbye.

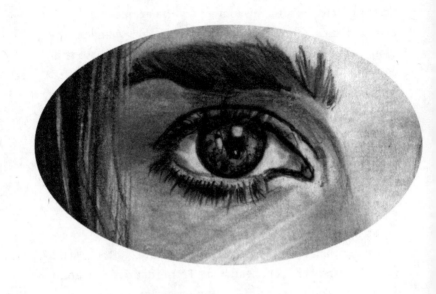

PASSION AND PATIENCE

PART THREE

25. BIG DEAL

Know something? The problem with money is I want more
Let's raise the price at the door. Starting tonight, 3,000 or four
—Minor Threat, "Cashing In"

WHEN THINGS ARE going well, you're not supposed to ask questions. But I'm a son of immigrants. I have whatever the opposite of entitlement is, where I think I deserve nothing and anything positive has come by way of dumb luck (I think it's called poor self-esteem).

I'm always bracing for impact. I remember being terrified, as a kid, of what might come careening around the corner after a birthday weekend. I would canvass the sky for that second shoe to drop. And I'd be so distracted by that imaginary shoe that I'd walk straight into a pole. There it is, I'd confirm to myself. I knew that pole was coming.*

I used to believe that life is a series of happy and depressive moments, strung together like Christmas lights. But I've come to believe that things happen and you frame them however you choose. What are success and failure other than two sides of the same coin? Trash and treasure. Trials and triumphs. Squint and it's hard to tell the difference, especially through the lens of time.

By all accounts, The Hundreds was on a killing spree by the early 2010s. We had taken all of the best boutique accounts by storm; we were being courted by the big-box retailers, who'd coaxed us with tens of millions of dollars. Our stores were firing on all cylinders. Love us or hate us, we were best in show, stealing the headlines, a regular topic of conversation. My blog was read by millions of people, and we were making as many dollars. By our seventh year in business, we were topping $17 million in sales, and climbing. Not bad for a couple of kids who started off with an idea, a few hundred bucks, and some crappy T-shirts.

Then the unsolicited emails with fancy signatures arrived: *"To Whom It May Concern, we represent Big Brother Capital, and we'd like to talk to the owners of The Hundreds about their future plans."*

Older industry friends started making the intros: "Are you guys looking for investment? I know someone who's interested in working with a brand like yours."

All of a sudden, there were "gray hairs" up in our business:

Silicon Valley tech investors seeking to diversify their portfolios.

---

* The way I've always understood it, nothing is guaranteed except disappointment because that's an outcome you can create. I think I'm part optimist, part pessimist. I just go with whatever works in my favor under the circumstances. Pessimists always win out, I've surmised. They're either wrong or pleasantly surprised. And I like those odds.

Venture capitalists looking for something a bit more traditional than apps and dot-coms.

Hedge fund managers who wanted something cool in their pocket to wow their teenage sons.

And old-school fashion garmentos who were hoping to climb out of a dying industry.

"Always take the meeting," our friend DJ Thee Mike B once told us.

At worst, you get a free Caesar salad and some experience. At best, you walk away from the table with a business deal. I felt weird leaving the designer's desk or getting off the Rosewood curb and spending my days and evenings with these opportunists. To fake-laugh through jokes, repeating our story from an emotional angle while Ben broke down the hard numbers investors really wanted to see. It was just about the most uncreative part of my job. But I always took the meeting.

These courtships always caught fire, like hot and heavy make-out sessions, like two teens tearing at each other's clothes, overwrought and eager to explore. Once we were disrobed, however, we were unimpressed with what we saw. Either that, or we'd stopped ourselves from waking up to a regretful morning.

First, there was Howard, the early Starbucks investor guy. Howard was old and kind, like a familiar neighbor, and we often met him at Nate'n Al's deli, where Larry King eats breakfast in the mornings. I think Howard was amused by us. We were feral and unformed, wild kids running around town selling T-shirts. He was accustomed to much larger food deals, fueling Starbucks' explosive growth, Krispy Kreme, and doing the same for the Pinkberry frozen yogurt chain. He introduced us to one of his partners, Young Lee, Pinkberry's cofounder, to answer any questions we had about their partnership. Young was a bold and honest Korean American entrepreneur with thick-framed designer glasses and a flair for expensive things. In their younger New York days, he'd worked retail with Undefeated's Eddie Cruz and Supreme's James Jebbia, so he "got" us and what we were trying to accomplish. He found the potential deal between Howard and The Hundreds interesting, and that meant a lot because Pinkberry was hotter than an Emily Ratajkowski pictorial at the time. They had sneaker-reseller-type lines into the night, except they were selling creamy dessert with cereal toppings.

Our numbers weren't hefty, but their momentum was staggering, and that intrigued both Howard and Will. Will—a mutual friend of ours whose son was a fan of our brand—had set up those initial meetings. He was captivated by the volume we were pushing out of our store. He'd sit outside our L.A. shop on Saturday afternoons and marvel at the perpetual demand. Ben and I didn't know any better—we had built it, they had come— but Howard and Will had been in retail for years and hadn't seen anything like it. That enthusiasm transferred. Ben and I licked our lips over the cash payout, but we also daydreamed about a Starbucks version of The Hundreds. We envisioned nationwide The Hundreds stores, kitted out like complete lifestyle emporiums, with multiple floors like Urban Outfitters or Muji and all goods designed and branded by The Hundreds. Of course, we'd have clothing, but we'd also publish our own books, produce our own recording artists, and even make bedding and housewares.

Over the months, however, Howard lost interest in The Hundreds, his shiny plaything. I don't remember why. Maybe he was never convinced at all. We were only six years in at that point. We were so amateur; none of the numbers made sense (even to us). The Hundreds was still just a reckless art project. A few years later, Young, the Pinkberry guy, beat up a homeless man with a tire iron* and got sentenced to seven years behind bars. Crisis averted.

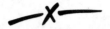

THERE WAS the hedge fund guy (to be honest, I still don't know what that means) who I'll call Roger. He was Republican and, by all indications, rich. A puffier John Edwards with the same penchant for extramarital affairs. The first time we met up, we found him in the bowels of the Cut's steak-house bar, sloshing around whiskey in a tumbler. He was reaching for the cocktail waitress, half to feel, half to hold on. By the time we led him to our table and ordered our main course, Roger was literally asleep in the chair. Ben and I rolled our eyes. This douchebag wanted to offer us millions to invest in The Hundreds, but who the hell wanted him as a partner? More than the money, if we were to join forces with anyone, we needed someone with experience. A friend first, but also a mentor who could connect us with resources and wisdom. This man couldn't handle his liquor. How could he handle The Hundreds?

There were two venture capitalists, I'll call them Cyrus and Gordon, who were collecting brands in the action sports industry but also toying with streetwear. It was trendy at the time for money guys to swallow up factions of up-and-coming brands simultaneously across different markets, and The Hundreds made a colorful pairing with a contemporary denim brand or action sports company. We were hot and we were hype. As owners, we came fully loaded with juris doctor brains, sans

---

* Something to do with a man who'd walked up to Young's car, rolled up his sleeve, and flashed a tattoo of stick-figure sex. Young drove away, then came back with a friend and broke the dude's arm. He later threatened one of the witnesses in the case with "I'm going to cut the throat of your mother, your wife, your daughter, and you."

addictions. There was this sexy tech element around my blog editorial and video content, and the brand wasn't tied to any one specific demographic. Streetwear was a panacea for a segregated market. White surf kids in Mission Viejo adopted streetwear, Filipinos in Daly City lined up for it, black kids in the South lived in it. "Skateboarding," "urban"—all of a sudden these demarcations didn't apply only to the young men's market.*

We went back and forth with Cyrus and Gordon for the better part of a year, but in the end we threw up our hands. This time, everything was in the right place except for the number. Ben and I were valuing our business at the $20 million mark, but these guys were lowballing us at around $15 million. Of course, they weren't factoring in our emotional attachments. We also knew the potential, because we had intentionally refrained from selling to bigger box stores in the mall at that point. Plus, we foresaw The Hundreds' next venture as a media-rich content platform. Our hopes were to make the blog an editorial showcase with contributors from around the world, like *VICE*, but more culture-specific. Eventually, we'd produce video content and become our own studio.

Gordon and Cyrus weren't interested in the content portion of our business, however. We were looking too far forward. Today, multi-hyphenate businesses are the rule, but back then the private equity world didn't know how to value brands that straddled multiple lanes—what to do with a clothing line that was also a media company? Their lack of vision and the valua-

---

* A brand like Diamond is a prime example of what the dollars look like beyond racial and cultural borders and customer silos. Nick Tershay's skate hardware brand was gunning for hundreds of millions, powered by high-profile apparel collaborations with Wiz Khalifa and Cassie. Diamond defied the skate industry's tired parameters and protocol, echoing Nick's interest in rock *and* rap, fast cars, and chunky watches. He created a lifestyle brand that made a lot more sense to the twenty-first-century teenager than a pigeonholed logo. Who was the next Diamond? Where was the next Supreme? Did the States have their own A Bathing Ape? The sharks circled. The Hundreds started to look a lot more appetizing.

tion gap separated us by oceans, and we reluctantly went our separate ways. They ended up scooping up a couple skate brands and dumping them shortly after, eviscerating companies like junk cars and selling them for parts and scrap metal. If we had gone with those guys, The Hundreds would have died a long time ago.

Then there was Tommy. No last name needed and truly one of my most favorite people in fashion. Although he had sold his own namesake brand, Tommy Hilfiger remained in charge of the label as principal designer. The Tommy Hilfiger brand was also poised for a comeback as the nineties reared its head twenty years later. I used to wear a lot of Tommy in high school. This had less to do with Aaliyah and all to do with the preppy sportswear look that was trendy in skate (a response to the sloppy, rave style of the early nineties).

Imagine my astonishment walking into Ben's office one day and seeing Tommy Hilfiger on his couch. Tommy wanted a tour of our building first. We traced our decorative history and introduced him to the team. He rifled through our prototypes in the showroom and made insightful commentary. He thought we could really use an icon, maybe a flag like his.* I had always admired Tommy's subtle design accents, like a lime-green bar tack or unexpected trim. I employed some of these touches in our earlier cut-and-sew collections. It was cool to have the man himself acknowledge them.

We met a lot with Tommy and culled as much sage advice from him while we could. I really liked him. Not only did he offer experience and resources, but also we gelled with the man. He was soft-spoken and deliberate. We trusted his vision for

---

* Obviously, I took that to heart. Years later, I designed the Wildfire flag logo that is our mainstay icon today. Thank you, Tommy.

our brand's growth, not far from what he was able to accomplish with his own. It made a lot of sense. He drew comparisons between him and Ralph Lauren, and us and Supreme. We even shared the same initials with Tommy Hilfiger. Of all the scouts, Tommy got the closest—to the point where we had the papers laid out in front of us.

There was one glaring complication, though, that quietly snuck up behind us and eventually smothered the deal. It was a small problem at first, like a nagging bellyache, and all parties did our best to ignore it. But as negotiations matured and our due diligence moved further into the year, we had to address the dilemma: Business was tanking. At first, the reports looked like miscalculations and computer glitches. Then all of the signals started working in concert, and we knew it wasn't a coincidence. The numbers didn't lie: The Hundreds' sales figures were inexplicably backsliding. International orders were plunging, and our online shop lurched. Troublesome vibes radiated from the business. Although our clothing was hotter than ever on the streets, inside the organization we were running a glorified trap house. The Hundreds had grown so fast that we'd never taken the time to pour the concrete, draw up a sound frame for our home, and implement strategy. We were patching holes with chewing gum, and the cards came tumbling down. One by one, and then all at once.

26. DON'T GET ME WRONG

Don't wait for the call
Strength above all
—Agnostic Front, "Strength"

CHING CHONG, CHINAMAN! Look at this nerdy bitch. Shouldn't you be doing my math homework?"

I hated Josh. Every day, my third-grade friends and I would line up at the tetherball court and wait our turn to play against the school bully. Josh was in the sixth grade but taller than my dad and with a pencil-thin mustache. He was a dead ringer for Shaggy from *Scooby-Doo*, but freckly and ginger. I don't know what was going on at home, but Josh was angry and messy. Sometimes, he'd show up to school with a bruised eye or a broken tooth. Unsurprisingly, Josh had no friends, and he seemed to really enjoy tormenting all the brown kids on the playground.

In back-to-back rounds, Josh wiped out Omar and Cruz, the Salvadoran twins whom he nicknamed "the Mexican jumping beans." And now I was up to the plate.

"I'm gonna kick your ass, you little oriental biscuit," he snarled. And then he followed through on his promise. Josh was so big and his arms so long that he spun the tetherball around the top of the pole in seconds. I could do nothing but stand there and watch as the ball wound up. Josh cackled like a banshee as I put my head down and returned to the back of the line. Why did Josh hate me so much? Was it just because I was an oriental biscuit? And what the hell is an oriental biscuit?

Bobby, meet racism.

It's like when you buy a car and then notice that car everywhere. Except this was prejudice, and once Josh drew a fat red box around our skin color difference, I couldn't help but see that line dividing rooms that had previously looked mixed and colorful like a rainbow.

I CALLED him Juggernaut. Raymond was a stocky half-white, half-Mexican kid who was friendly with all the blockhead jocks. He was the most athletic and coordinated in class, but he was also just a major asshole. Raymond punked all the weird kids during PE, like my skater friends, the goths, and the skinheads. He played dirty on the field and would steamroll anyone who got in his way like Refrigerator Perry. Thus, "Juggernaut."

One afternoon, as we were doing our stretches, he and his friends sat down next to me and taunted, "Hey, do you know any karate? I bet you know Mr. Miyagi." Raymond pulled his arms back and emulated the crane kick from *The Karate Kid*.

"Yup," I lied, just to shut his hole up. "I'm a black belt."

"Yeah, right. I'd love for you to try that shit on me," he said as he feigned a karate chop within an inch of my face. "Hi-yaaaa!"

Raymond's friends busted up and my throat closed. So did my fists.

"What's wrong? Gonna cry?" He stood up and bumped his chest to mine.

I looked him square in the eye, exhaled, and said, "Nah, man. It's all good. We're just playin'."

I turned around. All these guys giggling, getting over on me, the lone Korean kid on the blacktop. There were only a handful of Asian Americans in school, and we weren't seen for anything else but a punch line. In the wake of Pearl Harbor, and the Vietnam War, and as Japanese auto plants stole homeland jobs, American media in the 1980s and '90s depicted Asians as a defenseless political cartoon—exotic martial arts experts, clueless FOBs, or sexless geeks—framing us as the enemy and keeping us outside the American portrait. Raymond presumed the same— that I was an easy target, that I'd sit there and take it like the feeble "oriental" characters on TV.

It was Tuesday, so flag football day. I tied the belt of red vinyl strips around my waist into a knot. This was a total cheat move; we were supposed to attach the ends together with Velcro so they could be easily torn off if we got "tackled." But all the kids did it when the coach wasn't watching.

My quarterback had the football and was searching the field for an opening. Raymond was on the yellow team, and at the first snap he started charging me. I wasn't even near the ball, but he beelined it for my flags, and I stepped out of his way just in time.

I looked back. "What the hell, dude?"

He just grunted and moved back into position.

This time, the quarterback did huck the ball in my direction, but Raymond ran behind me and yanked me down by my flag before I could even jump up. Because the belt was twisted and locked into my hip, I crashed hard on my ass.

By now, the other kids noticed what was going on. Raymond was seeing red. He had it out for the Karate Kid. Whenever the ball was in play, both teams danced around it, and let him charge me like a deranged bull.

Then his team intercepted the ball and the momentum shifted.

"Hike!" the yellow team's QB leaned back and launched a Hail Mary far downfield. Raymond stood there, all alone, waiting with open arms. His mouth was bent into a crooked smile, his coal-black eyes clung onto the spiral as the ball arced and homed in on his chest with a soft thud. He tucked the football under his left arm, pivoted 180 degrees, and lunged down the sideline to the end zone.

Except I T-boned him.

When the quarterback released the ball, I was already rushing Raymond. While everybody else was skirmishing with each other, chasing their tails, I cut loose from the pack and high-tailed it for Juggernaut. He didn't see the angry Asian kid coming. Nobody did. They were all focused on the ball. Half a second after it landed in his arms, all 145 pounds of me met Raymond in his midsection.

Our bodies collided and tumbled in the dirt. I didn't give him time to catch his breath. I flipped over like a crab and pounced on top of him, my knuckles battering down like a hailstorm. One by one, my fists sank into his cheek, his chin, his nose. It was only a few seconds before the coaches pried me off, but I got hours inside there. My eyes opened wide to take it all in, watching Raymond's face contort and wince in full detail as I landed my blows like target practice. He never said a word to me after that, didn't come near me.

STEREOTYPES ABBREVIATE a human being into an abstraction—one that is, more often than not, completely wrong and ignorant. It's not just belittling; it's dehumanizing. And it goes back to what I said at the outset of this book: We are engineered to find one another, to love and support the other, and build community. But hate (like racism or misogyny or homophobia) drives people apart. If you think you know the entirety of someone by the color of their skin, their sexual orientation, their gender, or their class, then you cheat them of the opportunity to be heard.

Because of my ethnicity, my age, and my countercultural interests, people have assumed things about me throughout my life, instead of allowing me to tell them what I'm really about. It's frustrating to be misunderstood like this, and I've forged so much of my identity around proving them wrong. Like tackling Raymond. But it doesn't just start and end with surface stereotypes. I've also fought to be understood on deeper personal levels, especially when it comes to my creative endeavors like design and writing. The Hundreds was born of this desire to be acknowledged. I believe this was a universal struggle for all creators. We have a specific way of expressing ourselves and won't be at peace until the world gets it.*

When the money guys dismissed us because of a column of

---

* It gets worse when the majority of your audience misinterprets your offerings. I remember Fred Durst complaining about this with Limp Bizkit—how his fan base became the meathead bullies his music stood against. Creative people are forlorn types, but this is where things get profoundly lonely. To have all this love for all the wrong reasons.

lousy numbers, I felt unheard. And when the haters wrote us off as irrelevant and the critics declared The Hundreds a nonissue in new streetwear, I was bothered. Not because I was afraid that I was uncool or ashamed that my business was failing. I cared little about those things. But it irritated me because they were so myopic. By overemphasizing the numbers, they underestimated me and Ben and our community. Like Raymond, they stereotyped us and failed to appreciate the whole 145 pounds that was about to blindside them and take their heads off.

27. POINT PROVEN

THE BEST AND worst thing about entrepreneurship is that there are no rules. There's a history behind you to acknowledge, learn from, and build off, but you also don't want to follow the blueprint too closely; the past is in the past. Every generation progresses by questioning tradition, reinterpreting established practice, and adding its voice and style. It takes balls to forge new territory. It takes guts to say no to best practices. Whenever up-and-coming entrepreneurs ask me what it takes to gain the industry's recognition, I say, "You shouldn't care about earning their respect. You should be doing everything in your power to piss them off."

I also like to say, "If you play by their rules, they'll never let you win."

And trust me, the OGs and predecessors don't want to see you prevail. Your very presence eats up space, dollars, and spotlight, and no matter the size of the industry it's too small to accommodate anyone new.

In 2003, a few months into having established The Hundreds, we attended one of the first Agenda shows downtown, as guests. We didn't even have a business or product, let alone a viable concept or ideas. To get a feel for the clothing landscape and to soak up some knowledge, we visited Ben's childhood friend Richard, who was selling his brand (for the purposes of my story, let's call it Adjective Animal) at the trade show. Adjective Animal was on its way to becoming an established hip-hop-minded label with colorful graffiti-lettered T-shirt graphics and baggy cut-and-sew. As a punk kid, I was never into the rootsy hip-hop brands of the time, but I do remember admiring the full collection of apparel that Richard was exhibiting. We hadn't even printed a single T-shirt, yet this guy was somehow manufacturing pants and headwear. Making actual clothes in China and India just seemed so abstract and far off to me and Ben. We were still squeezing paint onto AAA T-shirts in Van Nuys.

"What are you guys doing here?" Richard marveled from behind his booth. Richard was tall and beaky and aloof. I never felt comfortable with this guy. He was dry on the tone and snarky on the delivery. He didn't even bother to get out of his chair. Instead, he interlocked his fingers behind his head, propped his feet up on the table, and said, "Aren't you guys lawyers or something?"

"What's up, Richard?" Ben asked, without addressing the jab. "We're thinking of starting up a T-shirt company. Wondering if you could tell us some things. You know, break off some advice."

Between Ben, Mak, and myself, the only people we knew in the fashion business were this asshole and my girlfriend's second cousin out in New York who designed wedding dresses. Without YouTube tutorials to refer to or DMs with our favorite designers to fish for advice from, our only hope was Richard.

"Yeah," he snorted. "Don't do it!"

Here we go.

"You guys are law students," he said, laying into us again. "Finish school, get your six-figure job, and be happy with that. People like us don't have any other option." He motioned around the room to the other starry-eyed dreamers, the designers and founders nervously toiling behind cluttered racks and folding tables. "Do you see how many new T-shirt companies start up every day? It's more than ever. Thousands! Yeah, go be lawyers."

Damn. The air was sucked out of the room. The background noise grew muffled, and all I could hear was my heart beating through my ears. What was I smoking, thinking I could make a living selling T-shirts? Richard was right. What made my designs any different from all these other artists and designers? They already had more experience, and some were clearly more talented and had better resources. Did I think I could just waltz into the marketplace and have strangers trip over themselves to buy my clothes? At no point did I stop to think about the alternative. Yet here was Richard painting me a picture: Of course you want to start a T-shirt company. *Everybody* wants to start a T-shirt company, moron. But it's challenging. It's emotionally taxing. It's financially draining. And nothing is guaranteed. Meanwhile, if I got through law school, there'd be a surefire pot of gold surrounded by girls in shimmery bikinis awaiting me, just as Abe promised. More money than any of these designers drawing pictures onto sweatshirts would see in a lifetime.

No. I shook it off. Richard was wrong. As we walked up and

down the halls, passing tables piled high with cheap stickers and pins, flipped through racks of splatter-paint T-shirts, and talked to designers about their concepts, I sensed a glaring absence on the floor: *me*. I didn't find my voice represented anywhere. My interests, my art, my style. Everyone was using this new buttery American Apparel T-shirt as their base, but I grew up on the rough and starchy AAA swap meet tees. There had to be other people like me who preferred a durable boxy shirt over a baby-soft fitted tee that hugged your pecs. There had to be an audience out there that preferred colorful, bold, parody T-shirt art over the digital graffiti aesthetic that was so popular in the early 2000s. What was everyone's obsession with embroidered crosses and pocket designs about, anyway? What happened to clean, forthright workwear?

We stood in silence as the elevator doors closed, our tails tucked between our legs. I don't know what Ben and Mak were thinking, but I was shell-shocked. With each descending floor, I thawed, the blood coursing through my veins, my head ringing like a Warner Bros. cartoon.

"Fuck him," I muttered to myself, but just loud enough for Ben and Mak to hear; they turned their heads toward me. I looked straight ahead. "We're gonna prove him wrong. We belong here. We don't have another option either."

By the time we got to the bottom floor, I was reinvigorated. Richard didn't know the future. Nobody did. That meant that we had just as much of a shot as any of these other hundreds of millions of T-shirt brands. And our greatest strength? Our perspective.

It's probably worth stating that Adjective Animal eventually blew up and soon after that blew out, and that The Hundreds eventually surpassed the brand. Ben and I ran into Richard at a local lunch spot not long ago, and he pulled us aside to apologize. "You were right all along," he confessed. But we weren't. To his credit, I didn't know the future either. Richard had based his judgment on what he'd learned of a dog-eat-dog industry. Odds were that The Hundreds would have crashed and burned out of the gate. It took a fair bit of luck to make it out alive. But we weren't just a clothing company like many of the upstarts at Agenda. We were assembling a community, and these types of fellowships are near impossible to break.*

The other thing we got right was to not let Richard's hot take sear into our heads. I've come across this time and again in this vitriolic, bitter, and hateful scene. Everyone has an opinion, whether it's supported by data or jealousy, but nobody knows what happens next. It's beyond our control. There are so many factors and outside influences that contribute to a brand's success or failure. The political climate, a new Facebook algorithm, technological shifts—they all play into fashion trends and market movements. These outsized factors always trickle down to even the smallest of labels, no matter how much they think is in their dominion. Everything exists within an ecosystem. Something that happened years ago, thousands of miles away, can affect a customer's decision to press "Purchase" today.

Ten years later, as our sales unexpectedly stalled, the bloodthirsty investors abruptly stopped knocking at the door and took their money elsewhere. They'd coldly abandoned us. To them, it was a simple equation. Statistically, declining brands— like ours at the time—are risky bets. They assumed they could predict the future of our business with Excel sheets. What they failed to quantify was our heart and avarice and how underdogs

---

* Social bonds and identities are not like businesses; they're not dependent on revenue. Once people feel as if they belong to a brand, they stick with the association forever, even if the business is defunct. This also explains the success of dead brands in vintage or why licensing companies resurrect labels time and again.

favor harsh climates. The basis of their evaluation was rooted in the past, but there has never been a brand like ours, with people like us, in a time like now.

You see it in the political climate. Strategists and forecasters are consistently proven wrong. I never thought I'd see the day when America elected a black president—not just once, but twice. Then, confounding every major poll and expert opinion, we elected a reality TV star. The Parkland survivors—a band of Florida teenagers—turned the nationwide sentiment on gun control, something lawmakers and other adults have historically failed to accomplish. Our naysayers completely missed the potency and combativeness of a core community. There is no exact science for this data; no one can measure the fight in an individual or the loyalty fomented by collectives. Just as no one could have predicted The Hundreds' success from our first garbage T-shirts.

My parents didn't get it. Nor did my law school professors. The print shop guys couldn't see it. The buyer at Fred Segal wasn't a believer. Accounts told us, "We've never heard of you guys; you'll never make it." Richard laughed us off. Tommy's people said no. And the streetwear market slowly turned its back on us. But they all just gave us a reason to carry on. Every morning, when I'd hop on social media and converse with our fans, I was reminded that my community understood me. The critics, the bloggers, and the buyers pitched their stereotypes and assumptions right down the middle, and I stepped forward to take a hurricane of a swing.

28. SOMETIMES IT TAKES SOME TIME

I know someday I'll get through to you
Until then I'll just keep screaming

—Uniform Choice, "In Time"

O**N THE HEELS** of the abbreviated Tommy negotiation, we were courted by Seth Gerszberg of Ecko, an urban label with a rhinoceros logo that was wildly successful when I was in college. By 2009, Ecko had achieved a $1.5 billion valuation, predating Supreme's record-breaking success by a decade. Seth is a bit of a rhino himself, stock and block, a mad scientist trapped in a football player's body. I loved my talks with Seth, and if he had pitched us the price that we were dreaming of, we could have taken over the world.

He and his designer/partner Marc Ecko initiated the conversation by gifting us with a Swarovski crystal hourglass. Seth was a big collector of timepieces—time was central in his life—and along with this $30,000 article came a congratulatory letter on all our success, noting The Hundreds as the most promising brand in our category. This was flattering and we were admirers of Ecko's work, so we replied with urgency. Ben and I flew out to New York to visit them in their offices.

Seth wanted to reimagine streetwear's mainstream strategy by curating a collective of auspicious players (there were only a few of us left by that time) and attacking the market with a united front. For four hours, we sat in Seth's office as he broke down the ebbs and flows of streetwear trends. He showed us charts of an apparel brand's growth and tenure and how that's accelerated over the generations. Labels used to climb for ten years and profit hundreds of millions of dollars at their peak. Today, they have a year or two to make their mark, for a fraction of the yield.

He broke the ice by recounting his outside opinion of The Hundreds when we first came on the scene in 2003. In the early 2000s, Ecko had been developing the perfect T-shirt, integrating the finest ring-spun cotton with a velvety hand-feel. Its pattern makers refined the T-shirt's cut to fit all the right corners on all the different bodies. The shrinkage was precise; the cost was manageable. But by the time Seth, Marc, and their company had gone out to introduce this innovation, all these novice T-shirt makers (like us) had appeared, running loose in the marketplace. Even though Ecko was sitting on the Tesla of T-shirts, the kids wanted the Ford Fiesta: rough, open-ended blank T-shirts made in Mexico. These shirts were cheap, matched the sneakerhead style, and the hot, young brands were reverting to this vintage look.*

---

* We were also reacting to the rise in American Apparel's popularity. White hipster T-shirt labels capitalized on Dov Charney's razor-thin, extra-medium soft tee, but there

The moral of Seth's story was that no matter what we do to stay relevant, when the campsite picks up and moves, you'll wake up outside the tent. In fashion, especially, it's unavoidable. In 2013, we were doing everything we could to connect with our customers. We opened flagship stores, released high-profile collaborations, and developed our own eyewear and footwear programs, but our fan base was slipping through our fingers. We couldn't do much but stand back and let them go.* Our sales lost footing, then plunged.

Like the "This is fine" meme of the cartoon dog sipping coffee in a burning house, for the next few years we struggled to maintain.† Men's fashion chose one of three doors, none of which welcomed The Hundreds: Americana or "trad," street goth, and core skateboarding. Our aesthetic landed in the center of the Venn diagram, but we weren't leading any one category. As the U.S. economy repaired itself, we upped our orders with overseas accounts. We swung wide into the media space, investing in video content and editorial. And here we were, resting in a new ninety-thousand-square-foot warehouse in Vernon, right outside downtown Los Angeles, having leased five times the space we needed at the time because our plan was to grow five times in size over the next five years.

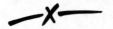

---

was nothing "street" about a threadbare thrift store shirt. The coarse and boxy Alstyle AAA T-shirt offered a sharp rebuttal.

* Cool is polarizing. By its very nature, Cool means Uncool to a smaller subset, and as Cool grows, it shifts the weight to the other side of the scale. With regard to streetwear, you're never as cool as you are on day one. Every day you lose a little bit of credibility to someone. As you gain popularity, you conversely lose traction. The yin and yang of notoriety.

† I must disclaim—in the interest of perspective and as an admission of privilege—The Hundreds was still a robust business at our lowest lows. At our worst, the brand was still operating as a $10 million company. While earnings dipped in the States and other key markets around the world, The Hundreds was stoking fires in new territories like Scandinavia, Southeast Asia, Dubai, and Russia.

IF I had to blame one thing, it's that we had developed too fast. In The Hundreds' formative years, the hype was so swift and blinding that we didn't have time to lay the right foundation for our brand. Ben and I never even had a business plan. We were signing Disney licensing contracts before we had a mission statement (I have yet to write one for The Hundreds). The blogs and media descended on us like locusts. Our entrepreneurial story was sensational and fun, and "I can't believe the margins these kids are making off T-shirts!" My blog was in widespread circulation in the design and business space, and our staff exploded. We couldn't even enjoy the ride; we just had to hold on.

Until that point, our business was a Winchester House of improvisations and wild guesses. No matter how we built it, they kept coming. The train sped up, more coal in the fire. Designs went from thoughtful to throwaway, without a difference in sales. Each exorbitant expenditure—like taking over Disneyland for a party—was classified as a "marketing" expense. We let the fires lead the way. So when the switch flipped and the train came to a screeching halt, we finally took a breather to assess the breakdowns.

In hindsight, our tumble was unavoidable. By the mid-2010s, many of us in the streetwear space were running into the same roadblocks: poor infrastructure prevented us from bridging the transition from garage brand to profitable business. We found ourselves facing production difficulties and straight-up fatigue. Nearly every brand in our category perished.

Most damning, however, was that we were losing relevancy. The kids who grew up with our generation's street brands aged out, and their little brothers were hungry for something fresh and different. A new breed of designers like PYREX, Black Scale, Hood By Air, and STAMPD deflated the whimsy of streetwear and painted street fashion in opaque black tones, incorporating sports jerseys and gothic art into a look that was popularized by A$AP Rocky, Rick Owens, and a crop of newly minted street corner fashionistas. Suddenly our denomination of streetwear (New Era fitteds, allover-print hoodies, and oversized graphic T-shirts) seemed obsolete.

High fashion capitalized on the look and moved in. Over the years, the term "streetwear" itself would be adopted, co-opted, and distorted by elite designers at Fashion Week and in the pages of *Vogue*. Streetwear and sneakers broke aboveground, and the sky was the limit. Fashion used to be partitioned between the Paris runway, the department stores, and the swap meet. Now the internet was stirring it all together with brands like Off-White, Alyx, Fear of God, A-COLD-WALL, and AMIRI taking center stage. Rappers turned designers sat front row. Nike and adidas battled it out like Godzilla and King Kong, devastating the street marketplace around them in the process. And outside, breaking down the walls, the direct-to-consumer upstarts challenged all the traditional rules. Babylon, Joefreshgoods, Chinatown Market, Carrots, and FTP capitalized on their zealous bases, drawing people to line up down the block and widening the generation gap.

With our genre of streetwear migrating to extravagant haute couture, The Hundreds was suddenly missing the mark. Internally, nothing had reprogrammed as far as culture and design process. I was still drawing inspiration from the same well, but we were a couple years into selling to the mall stores at this point. Although we had started slow with Zumiez and PacSun, neighboring indie accounts on Main Street complained and used this excuse of unfair competition as a crutch to taper off their buys. There was no distinction in the online chatter. For better or worse, The Hundreds had changed. There were more kids wearing our clothes now. And in the eyes of the "right kids," these were the "wrong kids"—the ones who weren't versed in the culture. The Hundreds had betrayed its community by attaining mass appeal, they cried. "The Hundreds sold out."

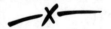

WE WEREN'T the new kids anymore with the next big thing. We were the awkward teenager now, trying to make sense of his bones, yet to grow into his body. It was time to act our age and nurture a healthy business. Ten years in, as the brand's energy decelerated in the news cycles, Ben said, "We have to look at this like we're starting over." And we did, but this time we did it the right way: our way.

In hard times, I like to call on my old friend Jim Thiebaud. Jim was a big skateboarder in the 1980s, but in my opinion his true success and impact came later as cofounder of Real Skateboards and vice president of Deluxe Distribution. If any industry has weathered the violent ups and downs of youth culture, it's skateboarding. There's this great line in the documentary *The Man Who Souled the World* where Steve Rocco, founder of World Industries, says, "Here's the thing about skaters, it's pretty simple. You set 'em loose. They do whatever they want. They will destroy everything around. And you can sit there and laugh at it, but the problem is, once they've done destroying everything, then they go for you. There's nothing left for 'em!" Skateboarders, more than anyone, are familiar with building your idols and breaking them down.

Jim has survived so many peaks and valleys that he's eerily Zen in the rainy days. Although streetwear has only surmounted a couple of these rotations, skateboarding off roads through a terrain of rise and demise in trends every several years. And every time Jim and Deluxe pull through to the other side, they're a little bit stronger, and wiser, and more prepared for the next round of challenges.

While everyone in our streetwear sector was scrambling, Jim gave us perspective. When the tides turn, the first order of business is to conserve as much fuel as possible. "Cut fast and cut deep" was one of Jim's first pieces of advice, in reference to any extraneous overhead that might be weighing us down. Whether that meant chopping staff or production or business-class flights, we ran toward all luxuries with a scythe. It was painful and embarrassing to edit our team down, but Ben and I forced ourselves to consider the greater good. Sacrifice one to save many, sure . . . but really it was sacrifice many to save ourselves. If we kept dicking around, the entire company could topple. We had to act fast.

As online sales escalated for The Hundreds (and global retail in general), we were forced to take a hard look at our own brick-and-mortar stores. What was their central purpose—was it sales or marketing? While we calculated, Ben put an immediate hold on any new The Hundreds storefronts. Although we were in the green in our L.A., San Francisco, and New York stores, and they were providing a sanctuary for our kids, they were also sapping us of overhead dollars: rising rent in gentrifying neighborhoods, staffing and maintenance, store-exclusive product, events, and so on. More critically, our stores drained us of emotional energy. A couple of the stores were plagued with personnel issues like employee theft (although we were angry about the money, the heartaches from disloyalty were an exhausting distraction from daily business). Then there were complications outside our control, like agitated neighbors ("Turn down the music!") and inclement weather (polar vortex problems).

Restaurants and nightclubs grow on the strength of their

newness. After a couple years, the novelty wears off, and they become a business like any other—relying on marketing and re-invention. We were spread so thin between all our endeavors (a quarterly print magazine, YouTube series, and international distribution) that we strained to circle back to our shops. Eventually, the retail energy subsided.

Ben also surmised that because he had locked in a once-in-a-lifetime lease on our SoHo location during the recession, we could make more money by just handing over the keys to a new tenant as rents doubled, then tripled in our district. I hated this solution at first, because our New York store granted us priceless exposure in the international shopping mecca. The banner of that store sailed over a historic neighborhood and was itself worth the marketing expense. But now was not the time to be stressing over brand awareness. When the shit hits the fan, advertising is the first thing to go. We had to salvage the business before we could afford to spread the good news with retail stores again. Ironically, we passed the store on to a new "high-end streetwear" brand that capitalized on all the trends that missed us: jogger pants, fashion fuccbois, and celebrity endorsements.*

After New York, Ben took the same course of action with The Hundreds Santa Monica. When we moved in, outside of tourism Santa Monica wasn't exactly a hotbed of commerce. By the mid-2010s, however, climate change had wrapped summer's warmth around Los Angeles for eight months of the year. The city cut the ribbon on a Metrolink train stop on our building's doorstep. The neighborhood was gentrifying around the rise of Silicon Beach, America's best new restaurants opened along

---

* This store met an early end just a couple years later, once this short-lived streetwear trend subsided. We empathized.

Abbot Kinney Boulevard, and property values in the area were exploding. In 2015, after half a decade in Santa Monica, Ben realized we could cut down on overhead while simultaneously making a fat profit from subletting the building, and we bade goodbye to our Broadway location. We happily subleased our space to a small-time women's clothing boutique with its own bright-eyed California dreams.

We continued to tinker and toy with the internal business, scraping up loose change from our seat cushions. Ben and our vice president, Joey Gonzalez, made more strategic buys, meaning they were making better-educated guesses as to which pieces to produce. My early design process, which I'd developed in Hong Kong, consisted in my producing whatever I wanted and Ben going out and selling it: reflective corduroy pants, gingham cargo shorts? Ben would sell it.

This system is effective for an avant-garde, boutique brand on a small-time scale, but for a larger brand selling to a wider audience, most customers can't swallow a turquoise T-shirt printed all over with cherries. Our designers still conceptualize garments that are art and passion led, but now we're realistic about their range with the consumer. Think of the flamboyant ensembles on the runway. Typical shoppers can't wear these items in their everyday lives, but they look to these examples— these *opinions*—to set the designer's tone and the brand's attitude. So, we produced the off-the-wall apparel in more sensible quantities, accentuating them as seasonal statements for editorial shoots and advertising. Conversely, we found a sweet spot with "dad" caps, color-blocked knits, and anorak jackets, so we included them as a baseline throughout regular deliveries. As a result, our brand was less schizophrenic in design offerings and felt tighter as a unified presentation. Smarter business doesn't always mean stronger branding, but in this case sales consideration refined our look and voice. Plus, our product sold through faster in our stores, leaving us with less fat stocked up in the warehouse.*

STREETWEAR IS special for a number of reasons, including its limited-edition distribution and hype economy, but its most distinguishing mark is collaborations. Of course, the idea of a co-brand or an artist project is nothing new. Brands have long cross-pollinated across disparate markets. Collaborations have worked for everyone from the Allied forces in World War II to Madonna and Britney Spears, with their MTV-broadcast kiss, and Doritos with their Tapatío-flavored chips. Streetwear, however, mastered the art of the collaboration by distilling it into noisy and punchy hits, like capturing lightning in a bottle and selling it in editions of one hundred. In recent years, this consistent pattern of collaborations has resulted in the "drop" calendar. Where fashion historically worked on a seasonal delivery schedule, the releases are now continuous and arbitrary. At The Hundreds, we now do a drop a week, with collaborations and special projects interrupting your Instagram feed twice a month.

Due to the frequency and success of collaborations, it's often the go-to conversation topic with our friends and fans. "What's your next collab?" and "How do collaborations work?" The latter is a question by which I'm often stumped. I don't know—how do you make new friends? You just do it. Yet I know what the kids are asking: "How do you negotiate the terms of a collaboration with a partner?" In that regard, the answer is quite simple: dif-

---

* Then we rented out that extra warehouse space to a rising star in the fashion industry, our friend's label Fashion Nova. Score.

ferent partnerships require different agreements. Licensing projects with movie studios takes lawyers and contracts. Meanwhile, if you work with your friends' T-shirt label, you can divvy everything up over handshakes and beers.

But how, and why, do collaborations work so well in streetwear? That goes back to our foundation as arbiters of culture. Collaborations make sense because they require different minds to come together and create something original. It's not just about Virgil Abloh and a Nike Air Presto. The shoe is an embodiment of progression, a new idea that didn't exist before. Collaborations literally make something out of nothing. The friendship between me and Ben was a collaboration that yielded The Hundreds. Our community itself is also a collaboration of people and stories. Accordingly, collaborations also speak to our championing of diversity by mixing independent groups and creating unexpected bonds.

When sales were slumping, we pared down our weaknesses and pinpointed our strengths. Collaborations are in our brand DNA and can be found in The Hundreds' first collection in fall 2003. Since then, we've offered our customers a series of collabs with artists, musicians, other labels, and entertainment properties. Some of our biggest projects have included adidas sneakers, Casio G-Shock watches, Kenny Scharf jackets, Lil B T-shirts, and Death Row Records hoodies. We've designed Eames chairs with Modernica and gloves with Mechanix. We've collaborated on snowboards, aprons, hot sauce, and a DeLorean. Some of my personal favorites include an apparel collection with the estate of Jackson Pollock, Stanley Kubrick, a Nerf Turbo football, music projects with Revelation and Epitaph Records, and a Roger Rabbit line with Disney that took over eleven years of negotiations.

We were offering collaborations like these a few times a year, but it wasn't nearly enough to satisfy an attention-deficit-disorder-addled marketplace. So, we focused our efforts on scouting and locking in collaborations scheduled to drop every other week. And it hasn't been easy for our team to ramp up the release calendar. First, we have to find partners that make sense for us to collaborate with, the ones that contribute to our character just as much as to the bottom line. Collaborations are like hooking up. A little of them ends up in you, and vice versa. There's also shared reputations to consider. So it's important to aim high while staying true to your brand.

While other brands may shoot for the easy and obvious, we try to pursue the narratives that align with our interests, even if they aren't attached to recognizable properties. Everything we do begins with a story. So, when Disney offered for us to interpret Mickey Mouse, we asked for the slightly more obscure Peter Pan's Lost Boys instead, because the Lost Boys offered a better analogue for us as a crew.

There were more hardships. Negotiations around collaborations can be backbreaking. Sometimes, we would go back and forth with a partner for years before the rug would be pulled out from under the project—failure to agree on a contract's terms, interference from a rival brand, or just plain cold feet. For every The Hundreds collaboration you see, there are another nine that never saw the light of day.* Any proper business would laugh at this return on investment. We knew, however, that the labor and emotion invested into all ten potential collaborations made the one success story worthwhile.

With so many drops, of course there was the fear of diminishing returns. Could an onslaught of releases exhaust our customers? In practice, the more special projects we offered, the

---

* Some examples of missed connections: The Hundreds X Coca-Cola, Deftones, Pixar, Teva, *Street Fighter II*, Stüssy, *Mad* magazine, Hayley Williams of Paramore, Mortimer Mouse, Theophilus London.

more invested our audience became in our storytelling. Collaborations with outside partners weren't opportunistic money grabs—they provided us with the space to reveal other facets of our character. The Hundreds became nuanced and complex instead of a one-dimensional clothing company.

Our fans not only kept coming back, but they multiplied. As we spoke to different subcultures, we attracted the curiosity of new communities. For Elvira fans, our Halloween collaboration with the cult horror personality was their first introduction to our brand. The next week, much of Andrew Lloyd Webber's niche theater fan base discovered The Hundreds for the first time through a co-branded project. More drops and releases also meant we were in the news more. We held the world's attention, and The Hundreds ingrained trust in our audience. Every week, they could anticipate something new and meaningful from us as people and as storytellers. If they wanted to keep listening, I wanted to keep talking.

ON THE personal front, my wife and I suffered through a scary season when our doctor suspected she was sick. She's fine and healthy now. But in those weeks, I spent a lot of time reflecting on mortality and purpose. I had been busily pruning and modifying the company and consumer-facing brand, but what of personal fulfillment?

"What makes me happiest?"

I wasn't motivated by money or respect. I was driven by the work itself, the process. That was the fun part. I also loved meeting new people and investing in existing relationships. My reward was the connection I was making with our fans and the connections our fans were making with each other.

Beyond work, it was surfing or reading that put the biggest smile on my face. These were simple and relatively free pastimes. It'd hit me as I sat in the ocean: Anything beyond this was ancillary, superfluous, another distraction, something new to stress about. Life and work are hard enough as it is, why clutter my vision with things I don't need? I sold my DeLorean. I dumped my sneaker collection. I freed myself from this fictional idea of worldly success.

I concluded that above all, what matters most is the opinion of my family—my wife and children. As long as they're stoked on me, everyone else can screw themselves. They aren't proudest of me when I lock in an epic collaboration, or meet a celebrity, or score big sales with a new product. They want me to be happy with my work. To bring that joy home is priceless and honorable. And nothing makes me love The Hundreds more than the fact that it allows me to do work of which I am proud.

I imported that philosophy to the office.

"From now on," I told my staff on my first day back, "let's try to work on projects that we will gladly boast about."

We knew what it felt like to do the right thing in the market's eyes and feel soulless. No amount of sales could fill that emptiness, but even worse our customers were so attuned to our heartbeat that they could sense if we were being off-brand. Product sell-through would suffer regardless.

"And sometimes we're gonna have to make things we aren't head over heels about, but let's infuse our flavor into it and make it ours. I want you to own your work here, be proud of what you do, and hold your head up high when you see your product out on the streets."

Our wholesale accounts begged us to make jogger pants and to revive Adam Bomb, surefire bets in a volatile marketplace.

We declined, frustrating them. We doubled down on our core themes of baggy chinos and L.A.-styled workwear, although all indicators pointed to East Coast nineties sportswear and luxe fashion. Stores dropped us, fuccbois dissed us, but we were curating our audience. Slowly but surely, we again carved out a niche for ourselves. The Hundreds wasn't the most hyped streetwear brand during these years, but we were uniquely us, and our pride radiated through our results. Our community held fast to us, as they would to an oak tree in a cyclone. And once the storm passed, our brand and its constituents were some of the last ones standing.

After four or five years of darkness, we were finally starting to see some light. The year-to-year reports were making an about-face. Not only had sales stopped diving, but in some categories we were doing the best we'd ever done. There wasn't one fix that explained this. What we were experiencing was the sum of all those tiny tweaks we'd diligently implemented over the years (tweaks we'd made without any guarantee of results).

"Maybe we should reuse glass cups, instead of buying five hundred red plastic Costco cups every week."

"Do we really need a full-time person just to cut party flyers? Can we find an intern for that?"

"Okay, fine, I won't fly first-class on Singapore Airlines . . . for now . . ."

Our staff had been broken down and rebuilt into a dream team that reflected and reciprocated our personal values: no more know-it-alls, arrogant assholes, and freeloaders. The designs were cohesive and consistently represented us. We'd cultivated a signature style, something that most designers never develop. We weren't in as many stockists as before, but we were in the right ones, stores that suited us and appreciated our brand, stores like P's & Q's in Philadelphia, Compound Gallery in Portland, and Wish in Atlanta. Our orders went as deep as our relationships with these accounts. Meanwhile, we quietly bowed out of our bigger stores like PacSun. There was no love lost. The truth was that we never performed that strongly in the malls. Our core customer refused to follow us there; meanwhile, our brand was too niche for the general mall shopper.

We were reminded that in our hearts we are a community-based brand. Maybe the Blog 2.0 with our army of freelance writers had put too much distance between me and our customer. But as soon as my voice came back into our social content and design narrative, the numbers spiked. In the wake of the 2016 presidential election, my opinions were finally striking a nerve with The Hundreds' fans. Our company's foundation was cemented in political discourse, social justice, and speaking out, but it often went ignored. In the Obama years, I'd blog about immigration reform rallies held in protest of the president's policies. But readers were more excited about streetwear gossip. The youth were unbothered during Barack's reign. But as Trump's regime began to threaten many of those values The Hundreds' customer holds dear—namely, diversity and equality—our designs and actions resonated with new noise.

In 2017, I took to my Instagram and challenged the purpose of ComplexCon, a popular expo for the street fashion community. The show sold out that year, earning tens of millions of dollars. But the daylong lineups, which sometimes erupted in physical violence, highlighted the disparity between commerce and culture. A couple months later, we provided an alternative experience for the kids by coproducing Into Action, a free, social-justice-themed art show and festival in downtown Los Angeles. Over nine days, we welcomed tens of thousands of visitors to absorb over 250 works of original art speaking to various causes. We didn't make the millions that Nike and adidas raked in at ComplexCon; in fact, I think we might have lost money, all things considered. But we had an impact on people's minds and hearts. The Hundreds brought people together for a positive cause, and they would never forget it. I would pay out of pocket to do that all over again.

29. DEAR MOM

WHEN I WAS ten, we moved to a larger house in the Canyon Crest neighborhood of Riverside. I had a new room all to myself, fresh Garfield bedsheets, and a big desk to draw and make art on. My brothers' bedrooms were stock and straightforward, but my mom wallpapered my room in a pattern of pastel pink and blue zigzag stripes. The repeating design was dizzying at first, but over time it jibed with the bustling noise in my head. I had trouble sleeping the first night, tossing and turning and calling for her to stay with me. She could tell I was nervous about the new house and room, so she sat on the corner of my bed and asked me to interpret the shapes on the walls. What did I see?

"They look like the letter M over and over again," I told her. "Um, are they lightning bolts?" I guessed. It was a fair crack, but she was unmoved by my response. Too on the nose.

The next night, she tucked me in and asked again, "What do you see?"

"Lightning bolts," I repeated.

"No, you can't use the same answer twice. Do you see anything else?"

I studied the sharp points and unpredictable lines colliding against each other on the paper. Like looking at a Magic Eye poster, my eyes soft-focused as the walls pinched and recast around us. Now I pulled seismograph sequences out of the pattern.

"Earthquake charts?"

She shrugged and said, "Okay. That's not bad."

The following night, I identified cascading waterfalls rolling over each other endlessly. The paper appeared to slide off the walls. I could almost hear the deafening roar of water barreling through the gully.

"Better."

Or were they the shoulders of towering mountain peaks, as if I were flying a helicopter into a snowy range?

"Teeth! No, fangs!" Gnashing simultaneously, a formation of wolves.

"Rocket ships, all launching at once."

OG fans of The Hundreds might have figured out by now that this wallpaper is where our signature JAGS pattern derived from. It's our trademark print, like a Louis Vuitton monogram or a Burberry plaid. I didn't even realize it until years after I'd created it. At the start of The Hundreds, I'd drawn up JAGS on Photoshop accidentally as I fiddled with the program for the first time. Ben didn't love it; he thought it looked messy. But JAGS resonated with me for some reason. It felt punk and disruptive. It wasn't until I was visiting my parents years later that my wife walked into my childhood bedroom and asked, "Is this where you got JAGS?" Throughout our history, we wrapped JAGS print around our shopping bags, jackets, hats, and BMX bikes. It had been a decade since I'd slept in that room, yet I was still writing my own narrative into those erratic lines.

My mom's wallpaper game became one of my favorite exercises. There are a million solutions for every problem; it just depends on how you look at it. So much of life, I learned, was about perspective—the way you frame and reframe a question to fit your answer.

The JAGS pattern is a reminder that I hold the pen and it's up to me to tell the story.

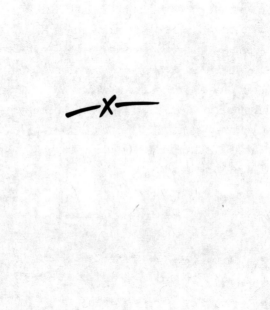

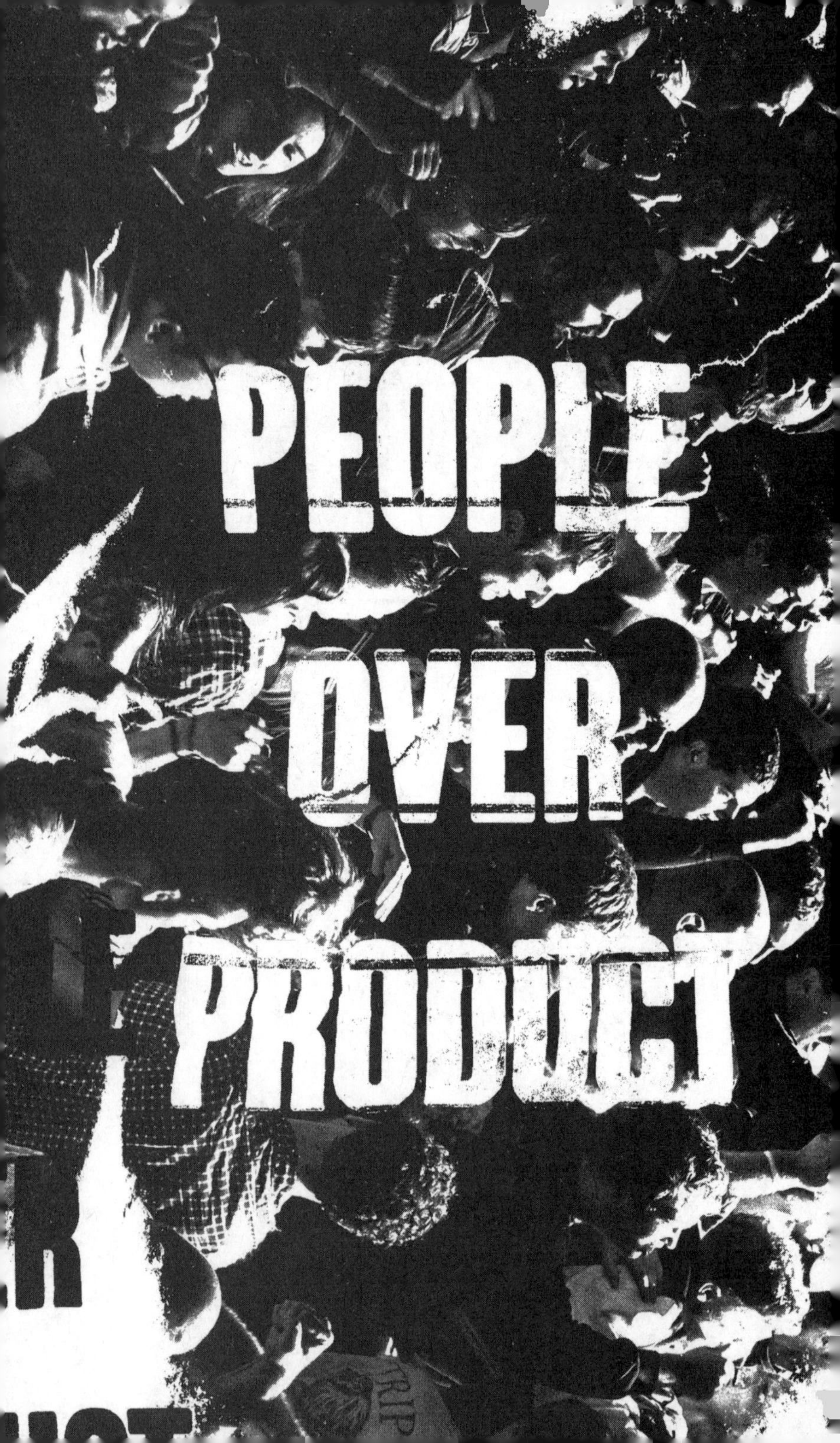
PEOPLE
OVER
PRODUCT

PART FOUR

30. BLOW OUT

SOMETIMES I TAKE in the work of esteemed artists like Shepard Fairey and Banksy and wonder if they ever get tired of stencils and painting political art (after all, this is what their admirers long for, to reclaim that mysterious first kiss, that initial high). The same way I imagine Radiohead hates playing "Creep" live or Cardi B has to pretend it's the first time she's performed "Bodak Yellow" at every concert. This is what the world wants of you. That's the double-edged sword of producing a hit. It makes your career but can break your creative spirit. It can imprison you in a parade of pandering to your audience. But what's most important—making them happy or making yourself happy? There's a fine line between a well-made home and a comfortable prison.

John Mayer once said to me, "You think I like playing 'Your Body Is a Wonderland' at every show? You think it doesn't scare me that maybe my best work is behind me?" As I grow older, inching closer to obscurity, and further removed from a "30 Under 30" list, it scares me too.

Is this it?

These are the things they neglect to mention: the dark underpinnings of success. As an entrepreneur or creator, you know the road is going to be rocky. You know hard work reaps rewards. But did you ever think you'd prefer to stay in that cool, secret unknown? What about being trapped by your own legacy? Painting yourself into a corner by virtue of your own achievements? Take consistent and powerful brands like Apple and Supreme. They've managed to remind their customer time and again of who they are, but has that allowed them room for change and evolution? Branding sells, but it can also suffocate artistry.

When it comes down to it, branding is much like human behavior. We have limited brain space to value the entirety of the world and its ingredients. This is part of why we stereotype people after all—selfishness and convenience. The same goes for companies: it's practical and economical to distill a brand into a single product. What's the first thing that comes to mind when I say "McDonald's"? Hamburgers. Red and yellow. Diabetes, perhaps. McDonald's is a $100 billion multinational quick-service food corporation with 130 menu items across seventy-eight countries, but all you can think of is a creepy clown in striped socks or sad burgers in yellow paper.

As for the brands of people, we regularly allow one trait or memory to define the whole of a person. Oprah is sage, while Trump is an utter moron. Brand perception may change, but we tend to collectively grant celebrities one defining characteristic at a time. Cosby is funny. Cosby is rapey.

No matter how complicated and sophisticated you believe your brand to be, you must accept the fact that (1) most of the world will never see your brand and (2) the majority of those who do glance at it will take away one microscopic detail that will color their impression of your brand forever.

I know this is a hard pill to swallow for a generation whose solar system spins around their multitude of accomplishments, but you really only have one shot to leave your mark on the timeline. This is why recording artists are defined by singles. Why the Verizon guy will always be known as the Verizon guy even when he's the Sprint guy. And as ingenious as Steve Jobs's varied contributions might have been, the iPhone will be canonized as his definitive blip on the radar—a device that experts agree will be obsolete in ten years.

I HAVE this recurring nightmare. In this dream, I'm Indiana Jones, deep in a dark cavern. I run as fast as I can in the blackness, my legs tangled in the ravines, my feet slow and sticky in the mud. A thundering noise rains down from above, and then a giant rolling ball descends on me. Except when I look over my shoulder, it isn't a boulder. It's Adam Bomb.

Our popular mascot turned logo, Adam Bomb, was a force of nature, unstoppable and ubiquitous. From Valencia to San Diego, you could play a road trip game of spotting Adam Bomb stickers on the freeway and wind up with an arm full of bruises. In the early 2010s, he covered the earth, from London to Tokyo to São Paulo. There he was on Lil Wayne's hat in Drake's "Motto" video or on the Warped Tour's main stage with A Day to Remember. He took up prime real estate in premier boutiques and chain stores alike, the central display of window dressings.

We knew, however, that we were running out of runway and that if we didn't curtail Adam soon, that bomb would blow up in our face. Fashion tires easily of such obvious trends. The more omnipresent Adam Bomb became, the more we fertilized our own backlash—not just from our core customer, but from the resistant shopper. Our mascot was so recognizable and obnoxiously out there that he polarized audiences like a pop star. Once a craze—whether it be Justin Bieber or tribal tattoos or the athleisure trend—dominates the market, resentment begins to simmer and eventually overflows.

We saw it, but we also felt it. I was long uninterested in, and fatigued by, Adam Bomb's overbearing presence. I was unable to reconcile his image with the updated, cleaner The Hundreds that our team was so diligently putting together. Our designers and salesmen were over it too. There are only so many ways to tweak and parody Adam Bomb into T-shirt graphics, only so many stores to which we might sell the same icon. For our customers, buying collections of Adam Bomb designs was like buying albums where every song sounds the same.

Behind the scenes, Adam's impression was so overwhelming and loaded that he locked us out of cool opportunities. Potential collaborators, store buyers, and industry peers couldn't see what else was behind the bomb, so they assumed that's all there was. The immediate money was nice. We were making bank; it was almost too easy. But it came at a cost to our brand cachet. Adam would have worked ideally for a short-lived hiccup of a brand. But Ben and I never wanted that. We wanted The Hundreds to be a time-tested company and had to start acting like it with time-tested designs.

The choice was clear. We had to revert Adam back to being our mascot. His demotion would open up the opportunity for a new stable logo, one that encompassed our true brand story. The only way out of The Hundreds' misperception, I figured, was brand renovation.

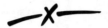

BACK WHEN we first sat down with our intellectual property lawyer about registering "The Hundreds" as an official trademark, he implored us to stick to one logo.

"I know how you artists get. As soon as you push one design out there, you're sick of it, and move on.* But you can't do that with your registered trademarks. Intellectual property is only as strong as how long you stick with it."

Every three to four years, I've willfully defied his orders by injecting another keystone logo into our brand communication. "Solid Bomb" turned into "Bar Logo," our name spelled out in the Raiders' font (Futura Bold). Then came "Adam Bomb," the next iteration of "Solid Bomb." By the early 2010s, menswear cleaned up and went bespoke and tailored. The Hundreds needed a logo that channeled this buttoned-up aesthetic. The "Slant" logo was informed by the Dodgers' (another L.A. hometown team) lettering. Having gone against my own unwritten law by relying on the "The Hundreds" name in our logo, I then conceptualized our flag, the "Wildfire." This latest logo, featuring our JAGS pattern, is a takedown of the Los Angeles flag and offers an analogy for a torn box.

---

* He was right. Artists and designers exist because the world isn't good enough. There's always an edge to round out, a wrinkle to flatten. If you give creative people a project, they will never be done with it. It'll never be perfect; they will find room for improvement, even if it's imaginary. And once a deadline cuts them off and forces a final result, they will be bored of it. Even if the world has yet to enjoy it, to the author the work is dead.

Each logo or icon has taken about a year to gain traction, two to become a favorite, depending on how extremely we pledge our allegiance to the design. Our "Slant" logo, for example, started to gain in the marketplace soon after we made a fifteen-foot, CNC-milled, light-up sign featuring the design for our Santa Monica store. The installation was such an audacious statement that our followers immediately trusted the cursive logo. To introduce "Wildfire," I wrote and directed a short film on our lifestyle, analogizing our community to an inferno, and concluded the movie with our red, black, and yellow* flag flying high.

The Hundreds' youngest fans were confused, as were our peers. To them, Adam Bomb symbolized the brand and was single-handedly driving the majority of our sales. Most competitors were desperate to match our success with their own icons and imitative mascots. Why would we scale back on Adam and forfeit our biggest advantage? Don't we adhere to the adage "The customer is always right"?

No. We do not. I know this goes against everything you might have learned on the internet, but the customer is not always right. Just as the child doesn't teach the parent and the dog doesn't walk the owner. I believe the customer wants the business to know its own identity, purpose, and direction. The relationship between brand and customer flourishes when the customer feels secure that the business is secure.

This is the problem with crowdsourcing validation: you give over control and ownership of your brand to the consumer. The entrepreneur's responsibility is believing you could do it better, smarter, and faster than whatever's already out there. The world just hasn't discovered you yet. You've worked your ass off to be

---

* A nod to Adam Bomb's colors.

heard; the onlookers are pulled toward your passion. The customers hand you their hard-earned cash because they believe in your vision and product. Now that you have their attention and devotion, why would you surrender the reins to them? How does this help them? How does it help you?

In 2010, Gap debuted a new logo to refresh its ailing brand (just as The Hundreds did with "Slant" and "Wildfire"). Where once stood an emblematic navy box with a timeless serif font, there was now a Helvetica "Gap" anchoring a floating gradient blue square asterisk. On first glance, the heritage clothing company appeared to have repackaged as a sleek tech start-up. The redesign was more Microsoft than Ralph Lauren, and the most vocal Gap customers (or at least the ones most active on social media) weren't having it. The backlash was immediate and merciless.

"This is the worst idea Gap has ever had. I will be sad to see this change take place," a customer wrote on Gap's page. "If this logo is brought into the clothing [store] I will no long[er] be shopping with the Gap. Really a bummer because 90% of my clothing has been purchased there in the last 15+ years."

Two thousand comments flooded Gap's Facebook. A Twitter profile to protest the new logo collected five thousand followers. Fourteen thousand parody logos were designed. The media also went to town. *Ad Age* wrote a piece titled "What the Gap Did Wrong," listing all the critical design errors apparent in the new logo. The BBC said the clothing company should have prepped the customers better, perhaps by improving the product first. This was the overarching commentary—that Gap didn't heed the customer. To put it bluntly, Gap didn't consider people's feelings.

Gap responded to the outcry right away.

We know this logo created a lot of buzz and we're thrilled to see passionate debates unfolding! So much so we're asking you to share your designs. We love our version, but we'd like to see other ideas. Stay tuned for details in the next few days on this crowd sourcing project.

Cringe.

I remember watching "Gapgate" unfold. It bummed me out. Gap shouldn't have ceded to vocal Facebook groups. It should have remained in control of its brand, even if it had to fake it. Gap should have dictated what Gap was, even if that meant being defined by amateur design. I understand that companies on Gap's level are beholden to shareholders and boards who only care about the bottom line, but we also look to the brands to know what's best for . . . the brand.

Of course the customer will be turned off by unilateral corporate decisions. But those disagreements are what make the relationship truthful. Would you rather have a friend who, by staying true to her convictions, manages to disappoint you from time to time? Or would you rather have a friend who lacks a sharp identity and molds her worldview around yours, echoing your likes and dislikes? The latter sounds most convenient, but in the long run what makes for a more trustworthy partner?

Slowly but surely, we held Adam Bomb back from our line. Our T-shirts went from twenty-eight Adam Bomb–inspired graphics to fourteen, then four. The changes ranged from nominal (swapping out the watermark on YouTube videos from Adam to Wildfire) to large scale (taking down our Adam Bomb billboard in New York's Times Square). When collaborators would request to work on Adam Bomb, we'd give them another logo set instead. When customers only filled up their shopping carts halfway because we had edited down the Adam Bomb goods, we swallowed the loss and crossed our fingers that they'd return down the road for the alternatives. Ben and I believed in our community. Even if they didn't grasp our Adam Bomb minimizing strategy, we were confident that they trusted us to set the long-term goals for the betterment of the brand.

From every vantage point, it looked like a dumb business move to curb our bestseller. But in clamping down on our greatest hit, we were able to showcase our broader range of work and diversify The Hundreds' successes. All our eggs weren't in Adam's basket anymore. Slant logo started outselling Adam Bomb. The kids outgrew the family-friendly cartoon and demanded something more mature and practical in a brand ID. Our pricier cut-and-sew apparel surpassed logo T-shirts.

Adam Bomb hasn't gone missing. Today, we still capitalize on our friendly mascot when the occasion calls for it. Instead of whoring him out, we design special collections where Adam Bomb is contained. The sales team restricts his pieces to specific accounts. We are now in control of Adam and can turn him off and on when we need him. He still makes us money, but by the time he started his descent on the trend boards, we positioned other points of the business to fill in the holes. I guess we diversified our assets after all.

It's so incredibly important to get out in front of your strengths and to govern how, when, and where to use them. I also realize that this is the theme of the *X-Men* series. You can be Cyclops with the visor, which allows you to harness your powers, or you can be Cyclops without the visor and have a laser cannon for a face and have nobody invite you to their staring contest.

31. END OF DAZE

I N THE CRISP and early days of 2018, we drew the curtains on my favorite of all four of our flagships, The Hundreds San Francisco, colloquially referred to as POST (because of its address on the corner of Post and Taylor). The register closed out its final sale on the store's ten-year anniversary. The night before, we celebrated deep into a damp San Francisco night. Our entire staff drove up from Los Angeles in a party bus to say goodbye in The Hundreds style: with hard drinks in red cups spilling onto wet floors, against loud Bay Area music. We weren't just bidding farewell to 585 Post Street; we were also signing off from the city.

San Francisco was a strange and different town by the time we left. The echoes of clattering skateboard wheels against the Embarcadero's floors had long ceased. In their place, electric skateboards for commuting developers. I used to travel from L.A. to the Haight just to see what was on Red Five's and True's racks. I could no longer hear the commotion for Earthquake Dunks outside Huf on Sutter. Silicon Valley plated the city in an aluminum veneer of yuppie riches, apps, and Michelin-star restaurants. The Bay had upgraded—it was the Bay version 2.0. The bugs that made San Francisco slightly dysfunctional—the Tenderloin crackheads, the crust punks with sidewalk dogs, the fixie girls with dreads—had all been purged. Facebook, Apple, and Google covered the city's tattoos with black turtlenecks and gray short-sleeve T-shirts. It's not that there wasn't any culture left; it just wasn't *our culture*. Ten years was a solid and respectable run for any store. Our San Francisco flagship lasted longer than all of the brands in the space and certainly longer than any streetwear shop downtown.

With all the money we were now saving—and making—we channeled our efforts into e-commerce and digital strategy. The Hundreds, we reminded ourselves, was inherently an internet brand. We came from the blog and found our groove with an internet readership, so our online shopping experience had to come correct. For the first time in over a decade, we signed a contract with a new web design company and revamped the e-commerce interface. We optimized the online shop for mobile phones and got smarter about how our editorial content converted readers to customers. We hired staff for a new digital department, collected emails of loyal customers, and strategized how best to reach our following on social media through transparent communication. When we combined the lessons of new-school e-commerce with the relationships and street knowledge we'd accumulated over the years, our revenue multiplied.

In the online marketplace, there are deep-pocketed digital brands with even deeper email subscription lists that have mastered targeted ads and user acquisition. Then there are organic upstarts that are soulful and scrappy but ignorant to the business trappings of digital commerce. We've done our best to cultivate both sides for The Hundreds, and I think that's a key to our success.

"IT'S TIME we tell the POST guys," Ben said from across his desk in our L.A. warehouse. He was looking up flights to San Francisco. I nodded silently. We both knew how hard this was going to be. Most of our Bay Area crew had been running The Hundreds San Francisco for at least five years. Bryan, our manager, had held it down for nearly seven years and was about to celebrate his thirtieth birthday. We had watched these kids grow up, but it was time for everyone to commence the next chapter in their lives.

The following Wednesday afternoon, we flew into SFO and took Bryan to lunch at Shalimar, a well-known Pakistani mainstay in downtown San Francisco, just a five-minute walk from our store. Ben's not the best at holding on to secrets, especially the painful ones.

"Bryan, we have to talk."

"Oh no," he said, removing his cap at the table. "Bad news?"

"Bad now. Good later."

And he let The Hundreds San Francisco go.

"Our lease is up at the end of the year, and we're not going to renew it."

He let Bryan and the rest of the gang go.

"We can't thank you enough for the hard work and dedication you've poured into the shop."

And then he let San Francisco go.

"It's time to close this chapter."

BRYAN TOOK a deep breath. He'd watched over the store reports every night for nearly a decade. He had seen the writing on the wall. Bryan admitted that he was already thinking of a new job, maybe in app development, something Silicon Valley based because he was born and bred in the city. We offered him a job with us in L.A., but he couldn't leave his girlfriend and family. The three of us walked back to the shop, gathered the rest of the POST crew, and this time it was even harder. Some guys stayed silent while others cracked jokes to cope with the unsettling news.

"I guess it's time we all grew up!" Budge said.

"One day, you will thank us for this," I said. "The truth is we should have closed this store three years ago, and if we had, you'd be three years into your next career by now."

Ben added, "You guys know we've been trying to find a better neighborhood, gotten near a few leases, debated on whether to move to Oakland since the kids have left the city. The main reason why we hung on was because you guys hung on. But now we all gotta let go."

The guys rolled one up and smoked outside the store. We reminisced about what once was in San Francisco streetwear. Benny Gold was still holding it down in the Mission, but Black Scale was long gone, as was Infinite. Huf got its start on Sutter but abandoned ship just a couple years into our move to S.F. The leader of the new school, John Elliott, moved to L.A. There were endless rumors of Supreme moving into San Francisco, but as the years sloughed off, that chatter diminished. My favorite sushi restaurant next door to our shop was now a hipster noodle house. A "For Lease" notice half covered the glowing pink sign over the seedy massage parlor on Taylor. If that didn't say it all: the oldest brothel on the block was about to become a yoga studio.

At that moment, a Jeep wagon pulled up to the curb. An older Persian man got out, looked at our store, then into the window next door to The Hundreds, took a step back, and stared at our neighbor's faded signage.

"Excuse me, where did the hookah café go?" he asked Ben.

"I'm sorry," Ben replied, "but they closed. The owner died of cancer a couple years ago."

"He died!" The man sat there with a curious look. He searched Ben's face for answers and found none. "He was my friend. He had a wife and a child. He owned this lounge."

"I know who you're talking about. I'm really sorry, but he died."

"Hmph!" The man absorbed the news, walked back to his car, and got in. He sat there for a moment staring through the windshield as the rain gathered on his hood. Then he turned his head to the side and merged back into the flow of traffic.

"Well, if that wasn't a sign."

KEEPING WITH POST crew tradition, we took the guys to dinner that night at the Greek restaurant Kokkari in the business district, a pillar of San Francisco dining. Most patrons wear suits and jackets, coming in from a long day in skyscraper offices, but we always show up in camo T-shirts and beanies. I think the staff kinda likes it: these stoned brown kids sweep through the menu, order tall drinks, and dust off a hefty bill.

While we were all mourning the death of The Hundreds San Francisco, we also wanted to make it a positive night to remember what we had contributed to the Bay.

"We can worry about the future tomorrow. Tonight, we eat and drink," I cheered in my merriest, medieval accent, right in time for the garlic shrimp and lamb. We updated each other on former employees and debated our favorite Bay Area–themed collaborations (The Hundreds has worked on projects with E-40, Grateful Dead, Mac Dre, and Too Short).

Speaking of which, unbeknownst to the guys, Ben and I were also celebrating another milestone. We were hours from releasing The Hundreds' long-awaited collaboration with the Warner Bros. cartoon *Animaniacs* in our online shop. This was a project that was near to our hearts, having first been broached early in our brand's history. We didn't have the wherewithal to pull it off as a smaller company, but now we were getting to realize another dream thanks to our growing legacy. The social media anticipation around this project had been building for weeks. Through his Shopify app, Ben could see that there were already hundreds of customers "lined up" on the website, refreshing the browser for the product to pop up.

After dinner, Ben and I retreated back to the Clift Hotel, our familiar haunt. We scurried to the bar, ordered up some smoky Scotch with fat ice cubes, and waited until the midnight drop. So much had changed since we first stayed there when The Hundreds San Francisco opened. We would party alongside early tech founders like Facebook's Sean Parker. Now there were just tired call girls fishing for olives in their martinis. As the clock struck twelve, our online shop got rebooted with the entire

Animaniacs collection. Two hundred customers jumped to four hundred, seven hundred. Ceilidh, our digital director, called us from L.A.

"We're making $1,000 a minute!" It was hard to hear her above the noise.

"Holy . . . What?"

"We haven't even posted that the product is available yet on our social. I'm just about to send out the newsletter, and we're getting this many sales!"

Ben and I took big gulps of our drinks and hunkered over our phones.

Three thousand dollars.

Refresh.

Fifty-five hundred dollars.

Certain styles were already selling out of popular sizes and colors. The complaints started foaming up on our social media feeds.

"This is bullshit! How are you guys already sold out of the green jacket?! You just put this collab up for sale!"

Thousands of customers from around the country drilled into our website, and it was the middle of the night. East Coast kids were setting their alarms for 3:00 a.m., waking up, only to find scraps left.

Seventy-eight hundred dollars.

Refresh.

We couldn't believe it. Ben and I knew our brand was enjoying a serious upswing in 2017, but the year was culminating in fireworks. Sales slackened into the after hours, so we hurried ourselves off to our rooms to steal a few hours of sleep. At 7:00 a.m., we were at $25,000. By noon, we had passed $100,000 in sales and had sold out of all our product.

The numbers didn't lie. Earnings-wise, this was our biggest

collaboration of the year and maybe our fastest-selling project ever. What was meant to be one of the most difficult days in our brand's history was cushioned by this unanticipated achievement.

Ben and I met downstairs for breakfast. "I don't know how we pulled it off, but I'm proud of us, Bob. We did it." We high-fived over sausage links and orange juice in the hotel lobby.

Ben wasn't just talking about the success of the *Animaniacs* collaboration. Nor was he simply congratulating us for having operated the San Francisco store for ten years. Ben was refer-ring to our perseverance over the years of drought. The break-through. And the sweet taste of scrambled eggs and victory.

"Not many people can go through what we just did. We made it out alive."

THE RETAIL roller coaster that was The Hundreds stores wasn't over just yet. As the dust settled on San Francisco, Ben and I had one last trick up our sleeve.

Back when we moved into L.A.'s Fairfax District in 2005, we were twenty-five-year-old kids with a few T-shirts and lots of big dreams. One of them was to someday open a store for our brand. We could keep the office where it was on the side street, but the emerald castle was the corner spot on Fairfax and Rose-wood. Pro skater Sal Barbier took the space first. When he was ready to move out, we begged him for the lease. He gave it in-stead to Orange County label RVCA, which held on to the prime real estate for the next several years.

It was hard to drive through that intersection every day and admit that the space wasn't ours. Like watching your soul mate marry someone else.

And then one day, she calls and says, "I'm available."

Before we could make the big move to the corner, we first had to button up our original store. It saddened us to close The Hundreds L.A. at 7909 Rosewood Avenue, but we were also overdue in sealing that chapter. That store was a four-hundred-square-foot black box theater where we groomed our brand in the shadows. We'd played the underground club for so long; we were now prepared for the main stage: 501 North Fairfax Avenue.

After our first day in the new space, the daily reports were off the charts. We chalked it up to grand-opening vibes, but then the numbers held steady and continued to escalate. Literally overnight, we were tripling sales out of The Hundreds Los Angeles. It showed us that we should have made that leap to the big top long ago.

The design concept for this new store was a concluding discussion of time and space. Elements of all four prior store designs were incorporated into the build, surrounding a mastodon skeleton emerging from a tar pit (inspired by the La Brea tar pits down Fairfax). The sculpture was a literal address to the elephant in the room: The Hundreds had thus far lived fifteen years, which was like fifteen million years in streetwear.

In the tar pit underneath the mastodon, you'll find fossils burbling up, like my installation outside our first store down Rosewood Avenue. This time, however, the artifacts aren't keepsakes of California, the 1980s, or any adopted culture as they were in past stores. After a decade and a half, we have built our own culture with The Hundreds—one that reflects us as well as those who support us. There's the $3 million Ben Baller chain from our April Fools' prank one year, our collaboration Garfield toy, and an RSWD cap buried in the black pool, among an assemblage of other familiar objects from our timeline. There's even an Adam Bomb in there.

32. THE REAR VIEW

I N A WAY, I never stopped driving after Ben and I had that blowout about selling The Hundreds to the malls. I kept on, past our shop on Rosewood. I left the noise and lines of Fairfax's busy streetwear neighborhood. I drove outside the big city, past New York, Tokyo, London, and Paris. I went higher, beyond the blogs and comment threads, far past the mainstream magazines and elite opinions. I reached the tallest vantage point, a bird's-eye view from the top of the highest mountain peak. There, I saw how big the world was and how much potential The Hundreds community held, and I had a change of heart.

It's been almost a decade since we turned that knob on

expansion, and I can replay the sequence of events with clear eyes. I don't have regrets, but I have review. If we didn't expand in the bigger chains, would The Hundreds be further ahead today? Perhaps we'd have preserved a particular image with a specific clientele, but could we have survived without the new fan base and revenue the exposure brought? With time, many of our peer brands that refrained from wider distribution eventually lost their edge. I'm sure some have maintained their cool somewhere and somehow, but the market and media spotlight moved on. Either those brands depleted their resources, or their following aged out and there was no one next in line to fill their seats.

The media loves direct-to-consumer brands like Glossier and Casper, because they cut out the retail middleman. Even in streetwear, young brands opt to sell directly to their kids through their online stores. They fail to appreciate, though, how a store's stocking of your brand acts as a cosign of your product to out-of-reach locales. The mom and pops, international distribution, and especially the chain stores gave us play in towns and neighborhoods we'd never see in our lifetime. They shared The Hundreds' gospel with legions of young kids who couldn't access street culture off-line. And on a practical front, selling to these stores injected us with consistent and hearty capital around which we were able to build a functioning business. This was the critical ingredient, without which we wouldn't be here today. Unlike most of our competitors, we've never had financial backers or partners in The Hundreds, so we siphoned cash from wholesale accounts to grow, create, and sustain. So, did the malls help or hurt? I really don't know and never will, but maybe that's not the right question to ask.

In building a brand, as in life, it rarely comes down to binary, right or wrong decisions. When I was younger and ignorant, the world was split into Pleasantville-like black-and-white. I was convinced, for example, that skateboarding shouldn't hold contests, be co-opted by celebrities, or be affiliated with corporate footwear companies. This was "selling out," the worst thing that could happen to a subculture. With more experience and knowledge, however, I walked around the problem and saw it from an elevated vantage point. The X Games, Pharrell, and Nike opened skateboarding up to an entire generation of young people, gave people jobs, and changed lives for the better.

When I was younger, I wanted The Hundreds to remain my private little secret forever. The closer I held the brand to my heart, the longer it would remain cool and limited by virtue of being unknown. Premium street brands have historically stayed relevant through this notion of finite inventory. They used to accomplish this by narrowing distribution—for example, by only selling direct through hard-to-find shops or by capping supply. The more physical hoops we put between the customer and our product, the higher the value. I traveled to London for maharishi, New York City for J. Money. The cost of the airline ticket was worked into the retail sticker, but that made the T-shirt extra-special. Streetwear, in the early 2000s, was like a scavenger hunt. In our foundational years, we stuck to this philosophy as well, situating our store on a side street in a quiet neighborhood.

But the internet changed that; now every "exclusive" brand sells globally through their online shop. Even if we didn't, there are gray marketers, auction sites, and reseller apps to be the messengers for us. This muddies the conversation about malls as "mainstream" distribution. Nothing is more ubiquitous than e-commerce. It's easier for your grandma to click on a luxe designer's dot-com from her sofa than shop the Urban Outfitters sale rack in a neighboring town.

Because e-commerce has razed geographical hurdles, the

modern means of keeping your brand out of reach from "uncool" customers is by pricing them out. This explains why streetwear's high fashion crossover has gotten so appealing. Four-hundred-dollar T-shirts. Three-thousand-dollar jeans. It's no longer about how hard you searched for something, how well you researched the culture's history, or how deep you dug into your networks for that hookup. It's now about *class difference*: whether you can afford to buy into streetwear. Do you want it for its exceptional design or because of how much it costs?

A couple years ago, there was this viral video series called *How Much Is Your Outfit?* that came out of Copenhagen. In one episode, the shot opens on a blond teenager wearing a satin zip-up jacket with a palm tree sunset design.

"Four thousand dollars," he states nonchalantly, pointing to his top. He lifts his feet up and says, "Four hundred dollars." His YSL jacket and Gucci shoes make his designer pants look like army twill at $120. The video then moves from this high schooler to the next person in the park. Two-thousand-dollar Vetements jacket. Vlone X Off-White. Fendi bag. This isn't a competition of athletic skills or talents, and it's not even a game of style. These teenagers are puffing and posturing by way of wealth inequality, comparing how much money they can spend on fashion. Halfway through, one kid jumps into the contest as the butt of the joke, chuckling as he lists his "paltry" Fred Perry shirt and Levi's jacket.

For the past several years, this has become the face and farce of streetwear. Price and monetary value have always played a role in streetwear's hype, but there was also once an emphasis on design and storytelling to balance it out. I'd be remiss to exclude Supreme's reselling prowess in propagating this virtual economy. They've done such a good job of making their pieces desirable and collectible that the majority of the people in the daily frenzied lineups outside their stores don't even wear the clothing. Instead, they flip it to the secondary market for a markup. Some of the reseller stores and apps like Round Two, Flight Club, and StockX have become significant names in streetwear, changing the course of our future. My little cousin made enough money reselling Supreme this summer to buy his first car. Meanwhile, he refuses to wear the brand itself.

I don't want anything to do with that. This is not why we founded The Hundreds, and it's also not why we got into streetwear. Our drops—although on a micro level compared with Supreme—also sell out immediately. But there's a marked difference. Some of it may pop up on reselling apps, but the majority of it ends up where we want it: on our customers' backs. My idea of streetwear is that it was born of the streets and is meant for the people. I want to reach as many of them as possible and connect them in the process. That means selling to accessible stores on their level, making quality, time-tested product that holds value, and keeping it at a place where they can get to it. Streetwear didn't excite me because of the hype. It drew me in because it inspired hope. It's about the chase, the hunt, and the journey. But with The Hundreds, it's a journey that anyone can afford to take.

Nowhere is this ideology more evident than at The Hundreds' warehouse sales. To relieve themselves of surplus inventory, clothing companies and shops hold sales throughout the year, back-door their leftovers to hidden territories, or dump product on discount sites. Some of the world's most exclusive and precious labels, especially in the streetwear ring, actually sell their overage to third-party retailers on the black market. The exchange is under the table and undisclosed to preserve the integrity of the luxury brand.

We take the opposite approach. Once every couple of years,

The Hundreds throws a widely publicized warehouse sale at our headquarters to clear out inventory. High-end brands with iron-clad reputations to uphold would shudder at that level of transparency. For one weekend, we mark down the prices on excess older product, fill up cardboard boxes on the warehouse floor, and open up our home to our community. Thirty-five-dollar T-shirts are twelve bucks, pants are forty, jackets are fifty. For many of our fans, this is the one chance they get to load up on clothing that is ordinarily above their budgets or otherwise out of reach. Some begin camping outside our door two days before the start of the sale. By early Saturday morning, there are thousands of fans in sleeping bags, prepared to wait another six to seven hours in line after doors open.

How could this possibly be worth it? The savings and the time spent don't add up. Yet all the kids (even those who cop just a few items) leave with smiles and with bags of clothes that will last until the next warehouse event. In fact, the majority of people who attend warehouse sales are dressed head to toe in clothes they bought at previous The Hundreds warehouse sales. And they always have a story to go along with their well-worn tee or scuffed-up sneakers.

"I met [The Hundreds employee] Daniel at a warehouse sale years ago. We became good friends, and now he's coming to my wedding!"

"My ex-girlfriend bought me this hoodie when I was in ninth grade. It's been ten years and I've only worn it twice since then, just for special occasions."

Streetwear lineups in general are kinda silly, and have become a dick-measuring contest for insecure brand owners. They're real-life manifestations of how cool and relevant your brand is at the moment. Every brand and designer thirsts for that glory. In 2005, Staple's "Pigeon" Nike Dunk caused a riot outside of Jeff Ng's Reed Space store. The *New York Post* ran a photo of the melee on its cover.

Whereas Altamont killed the hippie movement in '69, chaotic streetwear lineup stories have only added to the fanaticism around rare shoes and T-shirts. Supreme's demand has reached the point where cities and police departments have enforced a no-line system to maintain public safety. Some of the ugliest examples of modern streetwear-line chaos were seen at Complex-Con 2017 and the "Canary" Diamond Dunk release at Brooklyn Projects in late 2018.

I am trying, however, to shift the streetwear attitude of frantically buying something just to sell it. Our followers line up to be a part of the experience. They buy our clothes to wear them—a nearly rebellious idea in this new streetwear paradigm. There's less emphasis on reselling and rarely violence in our crowds. People make lifelong friends in our lines. Our warehouse sales are family reunions. I've watched some of these children grow into parents. I remember the stories of their high school hardships. I thank their moms for being patient. I sign their The Hundreds keepsakes right next to my signature from eight years before. Our warehouse sales are like conventions. People show up wearing their favorite pieces—kids who discovered and fell in love with The Hundreds this year in G-Shock watches and Chinatown Market collaboration hoodies; the OGs breaking out the classics like "Pins" hoodies and "Cans" T-shirts from circa 2007.

The point of these sales is to free up warehouse space and make money, but we could do it bigger, faster, and easier online. Instead, we hold these sales at The Hundreds' home base to bring our community together. Our designers, sales guys, marketers, accountants, even Ben and I work the floor. We ring customers up and stuff their bags. It's our chance to meet people;

for customers to ask us questions about the clothes they're buying. The sales also serve as a reminder that we're not just grinding away without purpose. We're in this building every day, drawing at our desks, crunching numbers, and answering emails. It's easy to forget *why* we do what we do, and *who* we do it for. I think every brand should have warehouse sales to restore a connection with their customers. But then I remember that most brands don't have a community and a culture like ours.

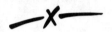

A FEW years ago, I was in Seoul, visiting the designer Chan Ho Shin of the Korean streetwear brands Liful and LMC. I was filming my streetwear documentary, *Built to Fail*, at the time, traveling the world to ask various industry pioneers and players to define what the culture meant to them. Chan Ho, our mutual friend KB Lee, and I sat in his rooftop office, above one of his flagship stores, sipping hot Korean tea and eating dried fruits. We veered into the familiar streetwear conversations about brands of the moment and marketplace shifts. Over a decade old, Liful is seen as more of a heritage player in the young Korean street scene, so I asked Chan Ho if he considers his label's growth and notoriety marks against his brand integrity.

"Can you stay authentic the bigger your brand gets?"

If you're reading this as a student of traditional business, you might be confused with this sentiment: that the longer a company has been around, the more likely that fact will work against it. For generations, American success stories were centered on businesses that were built to last: Ford, Apple, 3M. But in the social media era, especially with regard to streetwear brands, time is not necessarily on our side. By its nature, street fashion is predicated on urgency in artistry. It's designed and practiced by young creative dynamos who are as flighty and finicky as their pubescent customers. Trends move fast, T-shirt shelves need to be restocked, and kids can't be caught dead wearing the same logos in college that they donned when they were thirteen.

So, when I ask Chan Ho this, I expect the response I've gotten from streetwear personalities I've interviewed around the world: "The more you sell, the more soulless you become." "The more you grow, the less connected you are with your audience." "Stay poor, stay core." The popular belief is that as a clothing brand ages, it becomes less credible and loses authenticity.

Chan Ho doesn't miss a beat. "Not only do I think you can stay authentic; I believe you are even *more* so." He answers so immediately and confidently that it actually makes me feel kind of dumb for asking the question.

"Wait, how do you figure?" Of course I need him to elaborate.

"When I first started, I thought, 'I just want to make some stuff.' But then the brand took shape, and I wanted to make it dope. The company grew, I got more opportunities, so I had to work harder to make it look right. So, as my brand gets bigger, it requires more of my time, my money—"

"There's more of *yourself* in it."

"Right. As I grow, the company grows. And as the company grows, I grow. Doesn't that make the work more authentically me than ever?"

IN THE near future, there will come a point in time when The Hundreds will account for half of my life. Eventually, it will account for most of my life. My amusing side project—once daydream fodder, imagined to get me through class—will not only become inextricable from my identity but will also constitute the bulk of my identity. In a way, it's already happened. When we started this company, my T-shirt references were pulled from our backgrounds and past experiences. Today, our inspirations come from The Hundreds moments. We're beginning to appropriate and interpret our own culture. Like graphics professing "Maintain the Mystery" or homages to Ben's dog Wallace.

I used to ask our fans how they first heard of The Hundreds. They'd say they fell into the brand in middle school, following their older cousin's footsteps. Or that they'd read about it on Hypebeast because of some big collaboration. Nowadays, they reply, "Huh? I dunno. You guys have just always been around."

It's like asking people the first time they saw a pair of Converse All Stars or drank a Coca-Cola. Kids born after 2003 have never known a world without The Hundreds. In my rear view, I was starting to lose sight of that world as well.

33. HOMECOMING

WAS RECENTLY invited to speak at the University of Washington. There weren't too many formalities. Just a simple letter, a plane ticket, and a loose agenda for the evening. I'd give a twenty-minute summary onstage of how we built our brand; then the moderators and I would segue into a forty-five-minute Q&A session with the students.

I'd never given a lecture in Seattle. I knew we had customers in the area but didn't know the demo very well. We guesstimated that maybe fifty kids total would attend. Even when I'd done talks in our own backyard—USC, UCLA, even at The

Hundreds store—we'd ballpark somewhere around that fifty-person mark.

By the time the doors opened, there was a hefty crowd of UW students and Seattle locals pushing inside. Over three hundred students filled the seats in the room, and I walked out from behind the curtains to a full house. I guided the kids through a slideshow of The Hundreds' decade and a half of business, the ups and downs, and all the parties and collaborations in between. I read the room as I paced the stage. There were general streetwear kids out there as well as the fashion fuccbois and sneakerhead hypebeasts. It was also nice to see that the audience didn't just comprise dudes; half the auditorium was female. There were scholarly-looking students, athletes in team jerseys, and even some older folks, who I guessed were faculty or parents. But everyone was equally engaged. Even when I went over my twenty-minute mark, they didn't flinch.

As I took my seat for the question-and-answer portion of the night, I warmed myself up for the usual queries:

"What's up with the beef between you and so-and-so designer?" (Eyeball roll.)

"Longtime fan. What's your favorite collaboration?" (It's like asking me to pick my favorite child.)

"Do you have any advice for me?" (Yes. Ask more original questions.)

But those questions never came.

A blond girl with glasses raised her hand from the third row.

"Hi. Thank you for coming to UW. My question for you is, how do you feel about the lack of female representation in streetwear? The pervasive misogyny in your designs and rhetoric? And what are you doing to fix the inequality?"

Oh. I swallowed hard.

"I admit, we are part of the problem. I am guilty for objectifying women for T-shirt art and advertising materials, without consideration of their depth as people." I took a sip of water. "Also, early on in our company, we had zero females on staff. I can blame this on the fact that we are a men's brand and a lack of female applicants, but it doesn't excuse that the discrepancy is unrepresentative of the world around us and what we value as a complete team. We've spent years making a conscious change as to how we hire and who we elevate. We now have more women in leadership positions in our organization than men. Our editor in chief, head apparel designer, art director, digital director, and accounting department are all women."

The girl was somewhat satisfied with my response, as imperfect and inadequate as it was. She whispered, "Thank you," and sat back down.

The microphone floated to the top of the room, where a loud and sobering voice projected forward.

"You guys have made a lot of money producing . . . stuff. On top of that, you are inspiring others to create more. But have you ever asked if we really need more crap out there? There's so much waste already, yet you're pumping and dumping more and more clothes and designs into our world that we don't really need. Streetwear is the last sector to hit this topic, so I'm going to put it on you. What is The Hundreds doing about sustainability?"

&$@*!!!!!

"Who is that?" I held up my hand to shade the spotlight from my eyes. I surveyed the last row of the auditorium. The silhouette of a tiny Asian American girl stood up as the room turned around to find her. Then they turned back to see what I had to say.

"First of all, thank you. I've never been asked that before. And to be honest, I've never thought about that before." I paused and absorbed the issue. "I don't have a good answer for you, but I will tell you this. I won't forget your question, and now it will stay with me in how I direct the future of this company. You've changed the course of this brand. I don't know if I'm going to solve this problem tomorrow, but I promise you that I will work toward that change."

For over two more hours (until we were forced to leave the building), I fielded questions as thoughtful and challenging as these. Of course, there was the occasional ask about the next collaboration on the calendar and my thoughts on the designer of the moment. But something had changed. The kids used to care most about material and fleeting interests like T-shirts and sneakers. And, truthfully, I was always more than happy to talk about that with them, if that's what brought us together—the way our mutual love for Jordan IVs united Ben and me. Yet I often feared that I was distracting the youth from more pertinent matters, like their careers, finding purpose and happiness, and sociopolitical issues.

The journalist Rob Walker caught this dilemma way back when he profiled us in 2006. In his *New York Times Magazine* cover story, "The Brand Underground," he wrote,

> Even so, sometimes Bobby felt as if something were missing. When he talked about it, he seemed to be grappling with the kinds of things that had bothered me earlier when I had been trying to figure out whether there was more to the Hundreds lifestyle than buying certain products and brands. "I kind of feel like these kids—all they know is sneaker collecting and buying T-shirts, and they don't think about anything else. Every T-shirt brand is just something stupid—a rapper and some guns." Bobby said he wanted to steer the

Hundreds look in a more "socially conscious, activist-oriented" direction, maybe dealing with issues like the way efforts to defend freedom can curtail freedom. Now that the Hundreds has a voice and a following, he said, "I'd like to say something."

For the first time in my life, I was connecting with my community in a meaningful way that was on my terms. Everything was converging: being a minority, surviving as an underdog, thriving in a streetwear career, and having faith in the youth. In that University of Washington theater, we went from a standard guest speaker lecture to a town hall discussion on America's future: these kids, their hopes and dreams, their love for streetwear and cool brands, and their place in this world. Each one wanted to feel heard and un-alone, and just because I was the headliner didn't mean I wasn't searching for the same.

That night felt like one of the hardcore shows I attended as a teenager. I was now the singer, but we were all collectively chanting the same rebel yell. I passed the mic around through the crowd, and we pushed and pulled against each other in a churning pit of camaraderie, getting closer to the truth. This wasn't a bar basement or concert venue of filthy, angsty punks. It was a big university hall of college students in sweatpants. But we were still speaking our minds, sharing ideas, and taking our turns to spin the world. It was music to my ears.

34. LAUREN'S LESSON

YOU EITHER DIE a hero, or you live long enough to see your-self become the villain."

Remember this? *The Dark Knight*. Harvey Dent's warning foreshadowed an ending in which Batman, once heralded as a vigilante hero, would be cast as public enemy. It's not a terri-bly original comic book plot, but it is realistic. We (the nasty and vile collective "we") have the shameful habit of building idols to break them down. The entire tabloid industry is built on this system. America loves to paint its sweethearts as im-possibly sublime portraits, only to ravage them with controversy and imputations. Taylor Swift, Logan Paul, Tiger Woods, for example.

But Dent's statement is half-formed. I think it should continue. Something like this:

"You either die a hero, or you live long enough to see yourself become the villain. *And then you either die a villain, or you live long enough to see yourself become the hero again.*"

I mean, it happens for Batman, once he sets the record straight in the third chapter and reclaims his honor. It worked for George W. Bush, a war criminal turned convivial oil painter, warmly welcomed back as a relief to the Trump presidency. And we saw it validated with The Hundreds. We climbed out of our hole after years of crushing disappointments and runaway failure. By late 2016, our brand was on the upswing again.

Look, it wasn't all us. Our business was healthier, we were working smarter, but streetwear was also in vogue again thanks to Kanye West's aura. Taking cues from his Yeezy collection, rappers reworked their merch with streetwear scarcity. Kanye's biggest effect was opening the door to high fashion interference. Streetwear's postrecession slump laid waste to almost every brand from our generation, but from the ashes arose an onslaught of stronger and faster designers in the fashion space. Love it or hate it, the rising tide lifted all boats, high and low and the hundreds in between.

"You either die a hero, or you live long enough to see yourself become the villain."

Fashion has the shortest memory of all.

Just a couple years prior, circa 2011, "streetwear" as a fashion category was counted out. The market grew up and out of Nike SB Dunks and full-zip hoodies. Mustachioed men with SS haircuts shopped for looks to declare this coming of age: Red

Wing boots, cuffed selvage denim, craft beer. You know, serious man stuff.

First, they expunged the big logos. Then the market wanted no graphics on their T-shirts at all (this was a heavy blow against streetwear's profitability). Finally, no T-shirts. Real men, the customer was told, wore button-downs and were profiled on *The Sartorialist*. Funny thing is, the last time this happened was in the early 2000s, when Jay-Z expressed his desire to jettison baggy pants and Rocawear and dress like a businessman (or a business, man!). I remember the NikeTalk thread, pinned to the top of the forum, for all the guys who'd discarded their Prps jeans and Bape hoodies to "dress older." At the time, that meant Band of Outsiders, and tailored suits, and Italian leather. But I scoffed at that phraseology. Fashion nerds were always arriving at these arbitrary destinations, glazed with elitism. Of course, that "grown-up" trend also evaporated once our class of streetwear stepped onto the scene.

Not more than five years later, the Americana trend had faded. The headlines wandered over to the new kid on the block: luxe streetwear. Right back to baggy cargos, clunky basketball shoes, and funny hats. Again. And we were right here, waiting to catch that pendulum.

Nothing lasts forever. Not stores, not authentic cultures, not even the cities they call home. And certainly not streetwear. The clock is ticking. Then it's on to suiting or ballroom gowns or whatever, trad menswear again. The only thing that you can count on in this business is this endless loop of innovation and response. Fashion is a room of mirrors, an infinite reaction to itself, and so is business, really. My late therapist and mentor Dr. Lauren Ozen framed this for me best. She charted life along a series of struggles and prosperous moments: "THRIVE. SURVIVE. THRIVE. SURVIVE."

The hard part is you don't know when the next sentence be-gins. But the longer you stick around, the sharper you can cor-rect course when it does.

"And then you either die a villain, or you live long enough to see yourself become the hero again."

Rinse. And repeat.

EVERY MORNING, I wake at dawn. I make my sons breakfast and dress them for school as my wife gets ready for work. I frown at the news on my phone. I scoop out some avocado, dust my bite with some sea salt, and scan the surf report. An hour later, I'm sitting out in the cold green water of Venice Beach.

As with all sports and hobbies, surfing holds its share of life metaphors. This is a big piece of why surfers do it. Something about the elements (the movement of the air, the storm-turned water, the roiling sand underneath) colliding in a singular moment inspires and intrigues us.

I examine the lineup. There are the anxious teenagers,

feverishly hacking away at the foaming crest with their short boards. There are the silver veterans with leathery skin, anchored to the horizon on splintering long boards. The beginners crowd the whitewash inside with their Costco foam boards, yelping, gurgling, and celebrating small victories.

Even the amateur can tell you that surfing is a lot like real estate: Timing. And location, location, location. If you watch long enough, you'll see most surfers reading the waters and paddling their brains out to the swelling point right before it bursts. More accomplished surfers, however, appear always to be in the right place at the right time, as if they were willing the earth to roll the surf's peak in their direction.

Some days I try like hell. I don't know what's wrong, but I'll thrash after a wave, only to have it curl right through me and collapse like Jenga blocks. My heart racing, my arms rubbery, I'll look up just in time to watch a graceful long boarder take two freestyle strokes, lean into a slope with her weight, rise up, and tread the plank like a ballerina.

It's right around that moment that I'm thinking of when I allegorize surfing to work (between dolphins and sun rays, it's the rare window in my day to think about nothing at all—until, of course, my mind retreats back into work and legacy). There are career highs, when you're simply in the right place at the right time and you catch the universe's momentum. It's a fun ride. Then there are the slumps; no matter how hard you push, the earth spins out of your favor. A deep, heavy current tugs you downward.

The secret: knowing when and where to position yourself when the pendulum swings your way and the moment hits. You can't control the cosmos, but you can study and get in position for its curveballs. This is an education culled from time and experience and patience—those very things that neither money nor Instagram followers nor power can buy.

Time.

Things take time and time takes fortitude. Will immediate gratification and impatience be our downfall in the digital age? I will wait half a morning for the currents to align and the right wave to connect at my post. When it does, I have conserved all my energy for that juncture. I will own that flash.

I will wait half a lifetime to get this right, and when I do, I will ride that peeling line as the ocean surrenders to me.

THE BEGINNING

I WISH THERE were a way that I could answer all of your questions. To sit down with each of you starting a brand, embarking on a new chapter of your life and seeking advice. The closest thing I could think of was to write this comprehensive list of answers to my most frequently asked questions. I used to post this on my original blog, and lately I've been emailing this form to anyone who's interested in learning. I'm glad you asked and I hope it helps. Good luck and keep going . . .

Do you have any advice for my brand?

I can give you the boilerplate answers: Work hard. Have fun. But the truth is, I don't have advice for you and your brand specifically. I just told you how *we* did it—the saga of The Hundreds. But that's our way, in a different time and context, and it won't work the same for you.

Every brand is different, born of its own special set of circumstances. Every story is unique. Also, my philosophy on brand building is centered on responding to—or even *fighting against*—the brands that came before you. I know this is a confusing way to kick off this FAQ, but if you truly want to stand out, you should be reading my advice and then doing the exact opposite.

What does "The Hundreds" mean?

It does not stand for money. It's about community: strength in numbers. Our mantra is "People over Product."

How do I pick a name for my brand?

Oh, the fun part! (Hold on to days like these; they are the most exciting times!) Look, it's important to pick a good name, but don't overthink it. With time, your legacy will ultimately bestow the name with meaning. Before Steve Jobs, "apple" was a perfect name for a sweet, crunchy fruit and a strange label for a computing machine.

Choose a name that represents you and your perspective on the world. Every brand should have a purpose and a reason. I'm not interested in designers or labels that exist "just because." *Just because* you like streetwear. *Just because* you want to make money. *Just because* you want clout. So, first, why are you doing this?

You're doing this to be heard.

You should feel as if the marketplace is flooded with bad ideas. That everybody else is doing it wrong and you know best.

You should feel marginalized, disenfranchised, and counted out by existing brands. If no one is gonna represent you, then you'll do it yourself!

When we started, Ben and I knew that culture was vital to our project. The blog and web magazine were about bringing our community together and educating them. Same for our stores, events, and social media interaction. Some brands revolve around skateboarding or drugs or food. Others are politically driven. Some are about hometowns. Ours was about people, relationships, and movements (that's why we called it The Hundreds), and these were themes that I felt were missing from the brands of the time.

Once you settle on a few names, do some broad sweeps of the internet to see if they're already taken or could be confused with existing brands. Scrub through social networks; search the hashtags. You can also run the name through USPTO.gov to see if it has been registered as a trademark. Chances are it's already been taken, but that doesn't mean you shouldn't use it. It'll just be more of an uphill battle to clear that name the bigger you get. So, I suggest starting clean and making it easy on yourself. Don't pick obvious and commonplace words. You are unique. So is your brand. Your name should follow accordingly.

How do I start a streetwear brand?

First, you are starting a small business. The rules differ by state, but in general you have to register as a business structure (DBA, corporation, or LLC), open a bank account (to keep the company's money separate from your own), and then get a license to do business. These are easily googleable steps.

More important, you should do your research. I know Instagram tells you differently, but streetwear isn't just hoodies, sneaker reselling, and screen-printed graphics. Like rap, skateboarding, or anything worthwhile, you must know the history. This isn't just about paying your respects; it's for your benefit. History is there to teach us what did and didn't work in the past. It's a cheat sheet of shortcuts. Why repeat someone else's mistakes or even successes? You want your brand to be a distinct and extraordinary chapter in streetwear's history.

Do I need to worry about copyrights and trademarks?

Not necessarily now. I'd wait a bit to see if you catch some momentum. Trademarks (intellectual property, or IP) are costly, can involve lawyers, and take a lot of hours. I know you are ready to marry this brand and only see infinity in the future, but take some time to date and explore the relationship. After the initial rush wears off and you're in the weeds of your brand development, you may think of a better name. Your partners may drop out. You may lose interest. So, I don't want you to have sacrificed all this time and expense in registering trademarks for nothing. I think you'll know when the time is right to commit. (Of course, you wouldn't be foolish to consult an attorney about this.)

How much product should I give away to friends, or as a marketing expense?

There's no right answer here. There are old industry formulas that companies use to calculate an optimal return on investment (such as 10 percent of your marketing budget should go to giving out free clothes), but I go by gut more than math. It's nice to take care of the good homies and family who supported your endeavors, but it's also important for them to show their endorsement by chipping in some dollars, even if you offer the product to them at a discounted price.

As far as promo (sending out free clothes to notable personalities), Ben and I have never quite adopted that program. Some brands are built entirely on influencers, while others sponsor athletes and musicians. I agree it's important for your brand to have a "face" so that the customer sees a connection between your clothing and a community. However, I would prefer it to be more organic. So even if you're not friends with a celebrity, I believe it goes much further for your brand to show up on someone making noise in your own neighborhood than on a YouTube star with millions of subscribers.

How important is social media?

How important is electricity? Critical, yet at the same time, no big deal.

Social media is a tool, so treat it like a hammer or a car. It's not what makes or breaks your brand, but it can help you to get the job done. Instead of worrying about the tool, think of the person using it: the driver, the artisan, the storyteller. That's you. Focus on the message most of all, and then work on how you'll get it out there. There will always be another device to help you communicate, amplify your voice, and reach your audience. Newspapers, radio, commercials. Today it's social media. Tomorrow it's VR and AR phone games. The technology itself is interchangeable. The people behind it are irreplaceable.

There are also other means of marketing and raising brand awareness that don't involve social media. Parties and community-based events tie brands to social experiences. Stickers and wheatpaste campaigns can have better results than a Facebook ad. It can be more productive to impact a few people locally than to flash across someone's feed. For The Hundreds, collaborations are an effective way to cross-pollinate two niche fan bases that would otherwise have nothing to do with each other. For example, we know the MF Doom or Fatburger or Marvel fan is hard-core. So is The Hundreds fan. One plus one equals two, and after a successful collaboration, we now have double the rabid followers.

How do you do a collaboration?

The objective of any collaboration is not only to better tell your story but also to build onto your brand in a meaningful way. Collaborations should enhance your brand, tell another side that people don't know about. Make you multifaceted instead of one-dimensional.

It's a weird analogy, but collaborating is like hooking up with someone. You will rub off on each other, so choose partners in good standing and with strong names that can only benefit your brand. In other words, try to always date *up*. We have this unwritten rule that—especially when working with big partners—The Hundreds has to come away looking as if we gained the most from the arrangement. A collaboration is also a cosign, so it will affect your reputation. Be careful whom you vouch for.

The collaboration should also make sense. Even if it might look like an odd pairing at first, make sure that the project is supported by a compelling origins story. This will help layer the brand's narrative and plant deeper roots with your audience.

As far as contracts and agreements, they vary. There are handshake agreements over drinks and cocktail napkins where everyone splits the baby fifty-fifty. There are heavy-duty licensing contracts with entertainment studios where they take a 12 percent royalty. You can pay a partner a flat fee up front. Every collaboration is different and is strung together with its own deal points.

What's your favorite collaboration?

This is the most common question I get asked. Maybe because we've done so many impactful collaborations over our fifteen years: Casio G-Shock, *Looney Tunes*, Mister Cartoon, Revelation Records, adidas, CLOT, Kenny Scharf, Reebok, X-Large, and so on. This answer changes constantly, but today I'd say the two times we've worked with Garfield were my favorite co-branded projects to date. There was a lot of meaning and history to collaborating with Garfield, in that as a kid I learned how to draw by reading those comic strips. It was also a fun and easy experience to work with the cartoonist Jim Davis himself. It's always nice to collab with partners who "get it" and are willing to break some rules, try something new, and get creative. The worst projects are the ones where our partners see the deals as moneymaking plays and care little about innovation. The point of every collaboration should be to create something that's never existed before.

I can make T-shirts, but I want to make real clothing now.

First of all, why? Is it to make money? Because the hard truth is that many brands go out of business by venturing into cut-and-sew apparel. Designing clothing is a different ball game from illustrating T-shirt graphics. Production is on an entirely different level, and it consumes so much more capital. Meanwhile, there are plenty of T-shirt labels over the decades that have made hundreds of millions of dollars by selling one-color screen prints on stock T-shirts made in Mexico.

Is it to get respect? That's a terrible reason to get into clothing. If you don't care deeply and passionately about garment design, sewing, construction, and sourcing fabrics, then you will produce subpar clothing that will degrade your brand. The best clothing designers are nerds about the technicalities and process. Otherwise, you will burn out quickly.

If you are that person, however, then cut-and-sew may be your thing. You can make clothes locally and it's honorable, but it can be prohibitively expensive, time-consuming, and, surprisingly, of poor quality. If you are considering overseas production, you can walk the floors of a sourcing trade show to be connected with factories. If you don't have personal relationships with anyone in the industry, you can also scour the internet for leads: Reddit, Alibaba . . . Don't be afraid to knock on doors and ask for help. Don't stop until you get answers.

Should I quit my day job/school?

No. Ben and I stayed in law school for the first two years of our brand. Unless you're a rich kid, you should expect to go for broke, and you'll need to survive by making money elsewhere. It took us three years before we paid ourselves a dime. Everything we made until that point just got dumped right back into the company. Pace yourself. It's a marathon.

Is wholesale dead? Should I sell directly to my customers through my online shop?

This is very topical as more retailers slough off and the next crop of brands pledges allegiance to DTC (direct to consumer). And I totally get it. Why sell your brand to someone else's store, where you reap half the profits and lose control of your image? I'm gonna play devil's advocate here. The reason why wholesale is just as (if not more) important than selling DTC is that the store acts as your ambassador in its community. Sure, you can access every neighborhood in the world through the internet, but we all know that relationships are much deeper when established IRL. The stores have already built a rapport with the locals. They've been designated as tastemakers and curators to narrow down a thoughtful range of brands for their customers. So, by stocking your product, they are not only acting as a human face of your brand; they are cosigning you in front of their audience.

Plus—and there's no way to objectively quantify this—some of the biggest and most profitable internet brands tend to remain exactly that, obscured from the main-stage conversation. You may even prefer to stay underground and niche, but as your dreams get loftier, it helps to have a familiar name aboveground to broaden your opportunities.

I'm from a small town in the middle of nowhere. Can my brand make it?

Yes! In many ways, the internet has equalized the playing field for smaller markets, giving a voice to the little guys. We are also living in a global economy where culture doesn't just ripple out from L.A., New York, Tokyo, and London anymore. For example, over the last decade, South Korea has become a major player in world music and fashion. Even here in the United States, Seattle has become a tech capital, Houston is a rap hub, and Austin and Las Vegas are ushering in a new wave of talent and industry. Reframe every weakness as a strength. Being from a small town grants you the opportunity to be the big fish in a small pond. You can get an entire city behind you, whereas here in Los Angeles it's dog-eat-dog. And with so many new brands and designers popping up every day, it's difficult to stand apart in a big city.

Somebody stole my idea. What do I do?

I hate to break it to you (and your ego), but no idea is original. Occasionally, I'll get a small brand attacking me on the internet for stealing its T-shirt graphic idea, when in reality we designed it two years before and were also parodying the same cultural inspiration (a popular eighties movie or a vintage skate logo). As special as your mom tells you that you are, we are all ripping off the same references, drawing from the same pool of inspiration.

There are only so many Tumblrs, T-shirt books, and album covers.

And let's say someone did blatantly rip you off. They maliciously jacked your logo, or they saw a sweater you were working on and copied it, right down to the blind seams. Let me remind you that you are bigger than one idea. You are larger than ten ideas. Let them chase you and steal, because that means they're forever one step behind. You can always sue if you believe there are damages. You can handle it on a street level or shame the thieves over social media. But did you know that fashion designs are very difficult to protect legally? Shockingly, the reasoning behind it is to encourage the creative process. That's why fashion houses are always referencing past seasons and shopping for vintage treasures. They are constantly "being inspired by" or "paying homage to." This remixing, reinterpreting, and updating of existing ideas is what fashion is based on. Have enough confidence in yourself and creativity to keep moving forward and let the biters eat off your scraps.

What do you think about "XYZ" brand?

I don't.

It's only unfair when you compare. This is about you and your brand only. If someone is doing better than you, that's your fault. If a competitor is stealing the spotlight, take back the attention. Be better and smarter, and design something new. The longer you do this, you'll realize that 99.9 percent of competitors defeat themselves. Put your head down and keep on going.

How do you deal with the hate?

I just don't take myself too seriously. So, someone doesn't like me and I should be surprised? What—is everyone supposed to love me? Am I a toddler? A wise woman named Dita Von Teese once said, "You can be the ripest, juiciest peach in the world, and there's still going to be somebody who hates peaches."

I am comfortable with my value as a person and can separate it from my work. And to be honest, the critics *can* be right. Most of the time, they're bored or jealous or have some personal vendetta that I don't know about (I call these "invisible wars"). Once in a while, however, I can stand to be corrected or at least taught something new by a hateful stranger. Be humbled. Remember that it's just clothing and there are much more important things happening on this beautiful planet; then nothing can deter you. Same goes for all the praise and sycophancy. Take it with a grain of salt as well. You didn't do this for anyone's validation; you did it for yourself.

What do you think about the state of streetwear?

I think the media likes to cast streetwear in a singular light (high fashion, Supreme, resellers), but the truth is that streetwear is complex and nuanced. There are so many kinds now, so many degrees, and it's exciting to see how far it's come from a few T-shirt designers bucking mainstream fashion. Unfortunately, I don't think the media and industry limelight will stay on streetwear for much longer, but personally I believe that's good for its health. It'll be nice to scale back, collect ourselves, and watch the cream rise to the top. There's just so much fat out there that I think we've lost our way. Once the money's lessened, I hope we can place our emphasis back on the culture.

I've been doing this for a few years and haven't seen much progress. Should I quit?

It's fundamental to dream. Don't let anybody tell you that you're chasing the impossible. You don't have to listen to anyone, *but* you must be in tune with yourself. Be realistic: head in the clouds, feet on the ground. If you've invested years of your life into a brand and you aren't achieving the success you'd hoped for, there's no shame in letting it go. And take the lessons with you! I believe everyone should do a brand whether they think they can build a fashion empire or not. Because it's not about the destination. It's about starting the car and seeing where it takes you. I've met famous chefs, weed farmers, and wet-suit manufacturers who began their entrepreneurial journey by reading my blog and building a streetwear brand. They never became the next Virgil Abloh, but they did drive their car to the destination that was right for them. But you gotta get the car started. You can't steer it unless it's moving.

Can I collaborate with you?

No(t yet), but don't stop trying. If you really mean it, you'll get your work to a point where you'll be impossible to ignore. Create such a remarkable brand that I'd be an idiot to say no to you. But of course by then you won't need to work with my brand. The irony.

What's the best part of your job?

Meeting people. I'm endlessly fascinated by people, I think they are each their own book, and I want to read them all. I'd say traveling also, but really I just like traveling so I can meet new people with different vantage points. I prioritize my life according to the definition of a noun: a person, place, or thing. People first, places second, things last.

What's the worst part of your job?

I don't like being a boss. I'm not a good manager. I wish I could be friends with everyone on my staff, but I've been reminded time and time again that there is a distinct line there, and with good reason! I hate being double-crossed by staff that I trusted, stolen from, and shit-talked by disgruntled former employees. I've lost a lot of valuable friendships because things got weird with a work arrangement. I've seen the ugliest sides of good people because money and power confused the relationship. I've seen a lot of careers explode after working with The Hundreds, without an acknowledgment or return. But it comes with the territory. The employees' duty is to complain about the boss. They literally make entire TV shows around this premise (there's enough resentment to make two *Horrible Bosses* movies!). So, although it stings sometimes, I'll fill the role proudly. Because most staffers, present and former, are none of these things, my proudest accomplishments with The Hundreds aren't collaborations or clothing. They're lives changed and careers built.

What's it like seeing a random person in public wearing your brand?

It never gets old. It's funny because there are no bigger fans of The Hundreds than Ben and I. So, when I see someone wearing our clothes, I get excited for the brand, not for me personally. And I feel an immediate kinship with that person, because we have something in common. I hope everyone who supports The Hundreds knows what I mean. That's why we do this—to make the world feel a little bit smaller and more relatable.

In this political climate, how important is it to vocalize your personal beliefs?

The Hundreds started as a political statement, so it's impossible to divorce the two. The fact that Ben and I founded this brand is a display of activism. Over the last fifteen years, I've done everything in my power to clothe you while also informing you about important issues. If you just want neutral fashion by a neutral fashion designer, I can point you in a million directions. But if you're here, you probably came for an opinion. Whether you agree or not, I appreciate you taking the time to listen to a brand that stands for something. Now it's up to you to make your own choices. Let's keep the dialogue going.

How do you know whom to hire?

Hundreds of people have caught a check from The Hundreds, and Ben and I are pretty proud of that. So, when it comes to deciding who gets to hop on board, we can identify within the first five minutes of a job interview if the candidate is gonna work out. It's all about fit. We've had employees who did terribly with us but thrived with another brand or career path. Their personalities didn't jibe with their teams, their skills were subpar, but one man's trash is another man's treasure, and those traits were exactly what someone else was looking for. Therefore, it comes down to personality and cultural complement, even more than talents and assets. The staff that does best with The Hundreds are not unlike Ben and me in temperament and worldview. And if you're an asshole, you won't last long with us, but there's another company full of assholes that's waiting for you to come home.

What is your biggest regret with The Hundreds?

I don't have one. I believe success and failure are two sides of the same coin. They are relative, and context and time change how I perceive them. At first, selling to the malls was a big regret, but looking back on that choice now, I see that it provided us with the capital and brand awareness to get where we are today. Working with *Back to the Future* for its twenty-fifth anniversary was a win on paper, being that it's my favorite film franchise. But the negotiations with Michael J. Fox's team were so off-putting that the collaboration left me with a bad taste toward the movie and my favorite actor. So, I don't know what qualifies as a "regret." I made choices, I stuck with them, and for better or worse they made me who I am (and the brand what it is) today. I refuse to apologize for any of that.

I love my brand, but I have all these other ideas and opportunities coming my way. Should I take them?

Absolutely. But! *Not yet.* Young people today are multi-hyphenates, spreading themselves thin through an evolving and rotating set of impassioned pursuits. Our attention spans run low; we are more distracted than ever. Especially for creative personalities, it's a challenge to hunker down and focus on one project at a time. I think the true test of success will be in endurance and commitment. It's natural to entertain competing passions, but they will also divide your attention from the task at hand. Make sure you can delegate your duties to a staff member before you tackle another subject. It's possible to do two things at once (or three, or four), but it takes organization and management. Ben and I don't have just The Hundreds. We are partners in other prominent streetwear brands, a fish restaurant chain, commercial properties, a bar, and even this book. But we only dove into these extracurricular concepts once The Hundreds had built a solid and deep foundation and didn't require our personal attention around the clock.

How do you balance work and life?

I can't. Work is life, and vice versa. I don't clock out at 5:00 p.m.; I'm on call every waking moment. I'm lucky in that I'm surrounded by loved ones who have agreed to this contract and encourage me to devote myself to my work. I don't think it's possible to tend to career and home equally, so the only way to pilot through this ambitious lifestyle is by having understanding, supportive, and empathetic partners on both sides.

When did you know you had made it?

I don't know, because it's never happened. And I hope I never make it. Because that means it's over.

ACKNOWLEDGMENTS!

Thank you for reading my book.

Thank you, God, for your grace and mercy.

Thank you, Marc Gerald. You were the first person to truly believe that I could and should author a book. You gave me permission to give myself permission. That means a lot.

Thank you, Sean McDonald. You'll never totally appreciate how much you've changed my life. It was an honor to work with you and Farrar, Straus and Giroux. Talk about a collaboration!

Thank you, Ben Shenassafar, for letting me speak on behalf of both of us. Our stories are forever intertwined through The Hundreds. The best things we ever made together were our partnership and friendship.

Everybody asks how I accomplish so much with so few hours in the day. There is a simple explanation. My team is superior. Thank you, Patrick Hill, Joey Gonzalez, Ceilidh MacLeod, and Scotty iLL, for your work behind the scenes. You never get the glory and credit you deserve, but you deserve all the accolades.

And thank you to everyone at The Hundreds, past and present. I hope you look back on your life and remember your time with us as significant.

A big thank-you to Anna Shinoda, Holly Madison, and Iva Pawling for your guidance and encouragement along the book-writing process. If anyone hates this book, blame these people above.

Thank you, Alyasha Owerka-Moore, Ben Cheung, and Dominick DeLuca. Big brothers. Mentors. There is no word to express how important your support has been to Ben and me and The Hundreds' story.

I lost a number of beautiful friends in the two-year span of working on this book. Even if I didn't name them, please know that they contributed to this story. Rest in power: Jimmy Briggs, CJ Tambornino, Chris Garcia, Merf Osborne, Lauren Ozen, Chester Bennington, Stevie Ryan, and Nipsey Hussle.

Thank you to my parents; thank you to my brothers, Larry and Jimmy. I know I never say it enough, but I love you. Banzai!

To my true love and best friend, Misa, you never doubted me. You just wanted me to be happy, and you trusted everything would fall in place. I am living the life of my dreams because of you. I'm coming home.

Kalen and Barrett, I did this for you. I can't wait to read your stories one day.

Hey, Abe, I did it.